Knowing
Jazz

Knowing
Jazz

*Community, Pedagogy, and Canon in
the Information Age*

KEN PROUTY

UNIVERSITY PRESS OF MISSISSIPPI • JACKSON

American Made Music Series
Advisory Board

www.upress.state.ms.us

The University Press of Mississippi is a member of the Association of American University Presses.

First printing 2012
∞
Library of Congress Cataloging-in-Publication Data

Prouty, Ken.
  Knowing jazz : community, pedagogy, and canon in the information age / Ken Prouty.
      p. cm. — (American made music series)
  Includes bibliographical references and index.
  ISBN 978-1-61703-163-2 (cloth : alk. paper) — ISBN 978-1-61703-164-9 (ebook) 1. Jazz—History and criticism. 2. Jazz—Social aspects. 3. Jazz—Instruction and study. 4. Musical canon. I. Title.
  ML3506.P77 2012
  781.65—dc23   2011017742

British Library Cataloging-in-Publication Data available

Contents

Acknowledgments

This book is the culmination of many years of research, stemming from my days as a student in jazz and ethnomusicology. The roster of people who have in one way or another contributed to its eventual and long overdue completion are too numerous to list. All of the fellow musicians who participated in conversations with me on long road trips to dance halls or clubs, and on the set break at someone's wedding reception; fellow students in the break room or our regular meetings at a local pub; colleagues in both casual conversation and formal critique: you have all written yourselves into this book in some way, and I only wish I had the space to acknowledge you all personally.

There are a number of individuals whose work has gone above and beyond. First and foremost, my teachers through the years, beginning with Jack Clifford, Bruce Brown, and Stan Buchanan, who instilled in me a love for jazz before I even knew what it was. At the University of Maine–Augusta, Chuck Winfield, David Demsey, Gary Whittner, Tom Hoffmann, Mark Polischuk, Dan Murphy, and Isi Rudnick were all crucial to my development as both a musician and an emerging scholar. I would also like to thank the jazz studies faculty at the University of North Texas, who provided the behind-kicking that so many of us need at some point in our lives: Neil Slater, Jim Riggs, Mike Steinel, Dan Haerle, Paris Rutherford, and Fred Hamilton were as fine a group of musician teachers as you will find. I would like to single out David Joyner, now director of jazz studies at Pacific Lutheran University, for offering unfailing mentorship, for providing me with my first jazz history job, and for consistently disproving the old saying that "those who can do, those who can't teach." Lastly, I thank Stephen Friedson, who introduced me to the wide (and wild) world of ethnomusicology.

At the University of Pittsburgh, I was fortunate to have the guidance and mentorship of the outstanding faculty in the Department of Music, particularly David Brodbeck, Mary Lewis, Deane Root, Akin Euba, Don Franklin, John Chernoff, Bell Yung, Matthew Rosenblum, and Andrew Weintraub. I owe a debt beyond measure to Dr. Nathan Davis, my advisor, mentor, and friend, without whose constant support this book would not exist. I also wish to thank Prof. David Baker of Indiana University, whose advice and knowledge was indispensable, and whose work as a musician and educator continues to inspire to this day. In conducting my research on jazz education, I was selflessly assisted by many students and teachers in the Pittsburgh area, especially Paul Scea of West Virginia University, Kent Englehardt and Dave Morgan of Youngstown State University, and Mike Tomaro of Duquesne University.

During my time on the faculty at Indiana State University, I had the great fortune to work with John Spicknall, Tim Crain, Todd Sullivan, Randy Mitchell, Tom Sauer, Chris Olsen, and the late Francois Muyumba, all of whom took an interest in my work and provided opportunities for me to develop as a teacher and scholar. I am particularly grateful to Bob English in the Provost's Office and the administrator of the Lilly Promising Scholars Program, of which I was a recipient during the 2006–2007 academic year, and under which research on this project was conducted.

My colleagues at Michigan State University have been a constant source of support and encouragement, commenting on parts of the manuscript and shaping my ideas in ways both profound and subtle. I would particularly like to thank the faculty in the musicology area, Michael Largey, Carol Hess, Kevin Bartig, Marcie Ray, Joanna Bosse, and Dale Bonge, as well as in jazz studies, including Rodney Whitaker, Etienne Charles, Rick Roe, Diego Rivera, Randy Gellespie, Sunny Wilkinson, and Wess "Warmdaddy" Anderson. I also would like to acknowledge the support of Ron Newman, Mark Sullivan, Charles Ruggiero, Joe Luloff, and the rest of MSU's superb faculty, as well as our deans, Jim Forger, Curtis Olson, and David Rayl, and the many students in musicology and jazz studies who have taken an interest in my work, particularly Elden Kelly for his research assistance. Finally I would like to acknowledge David Stowe in American studies and Chris Scales in the Residential College for the Arts and Humanities for their support.

At conferences and meetings around the world, many individuals have been willing to share their thoughts on my work. I especially wish to thank Lewis Porter, Andrew Dubber, Tim Wall, Tony Whyton, Alan Stanbridge (whom I always seem to be meeting at whatever conference I attend), David Ake, Tammy Kernodle, Krin Gabbard, Ingrid Monson, John Murphy, though there are many others whom I have undoubtedly forgotten. I especially want to thank Scott DeVeaux, whose comments on my early manuscript were critical, in the best sense of the word, and whose work has provided a model for myself and many other jazz scholars. I would also like to thank the staff at the University Press of Mississippi, in particular Craig Gill, Anne Stascavage, and Will Rigby, for their invaluable assistance in bringing this book to completion.

Finally, I must thank my family; my wife Kate, whose willingness to serve as a sounding board for my ideas has helped me more than she knows; and my children, Allison and Simon, who always remind me to keep everything in perspective. It is to you that this book is dedicated.

Knowing
Jazz

Introduction

Studying Jazz Studies: Toward an Epistemology of Jazz, or:
How I Learned to Stop Worrying and Love the Canon (or at
least live with it . . .)

All of us who listen to, perform, or study jazz seem to know what this music is, and what it represents as both a musical and cultural system. Yet claims to an authoritative knowledge of jazz are deeply contested among and within various communities. In recent years, what we thought we knew about jazz has come under sustained critique, as even basic assumptions about jazz are now openly questioned. Musicians increasingly define themselves not within traditional paradigms, but in conscious opposition to them. Jazz scholarship in particular has witnessed the emergence of an increasingly iconoclastic stance, even as the institutionalization of jazz has gained momentum. Krin Gabbard notes the following in his 1995 edition *Jazz Among the Discourses*, often heralded as one of the opening gestures in what has come to be known as the "New Jazz Studies":

> Directly or indirectly, all the essays in this book and its companion volume *Representing Jazz* strongly argue that jazz has entered the mainstream of the American academy.[1] The institutionalization of jazz is consistent with the current demystifications of the distinctions between high and low culture, with the growing trend toward multiculturalism in university curricula, and with the postmodern cachet now enjoyed by marginal arts and artists. (Gabbard 1995, 1)

I would not quibble with any specific point here; these are all important developments in the academy. But there is something missing, namely, a sense of where jazz is actually located within the academy, as jazz studies had existed within the curricula of American universities for some time.[2] Jazz in the academy is nothing new, but what *is* new is the approach to jazz that Gabbard and the various contributors to his volumes embrace, an interdisciplinary method seeking to examine jazz through the lens of social and cultural criticism. Gabbard reduces the field of performance-based jazz studies to a single statement, noting that there are "a number of schools" that teach jazz performance (Gabbard 1995, 4), a remarkably uncritical comment for an edition that claims to treat jazz history critically. Generally the scholars involved in New Jazz Studies have continued to come largely from outside traditional jazz studies programs, and even outside academic musical study itself, and one senses a distance between this new project and jazz performance programs. Take the opening passage from the introduction to *Uptown Conversation: The New Jazz Studies*, a 2004 anthology of jazz scholarship:

> Our new century is witnessing the development of jazz studies as a new field in the liberal arts curriculum at the college and graduate school levels. For at least fifty years there have been maverick efforts as well as established classes tracing jazz's beginnings and development. . . . What is new here is the conviction that jazz is not just for players and aficionados who can count the horns and boxes of the music "from Bunk to Monk," as the saying goes. . . . (O'Meally et al. 2004, 1)

Two points are in order concerning this statement. First, the writers distance this new approach from the more than half century of performance-based jazz in academia, which is generally referred to institutionally as jazz studies; they are not outright dismissive, but one does sense a certain degree of "our approach is better." Second, this new "conviction that jazz is not just for players and aficionados" speaks to a new way of looking at the jazz community, one that departs from paradigms that focus squarely on those closest to the music's production. This is another way of calling for a more inclusive, broad-based understanding of just what the jazz community is.

The implicit dismissal of the "old" jazz studies stems in part from the fact that jazz studies programs within music schools and departments are almost always performance based, but the same could be said for the music school generally. But the interdisciplinary thrust of New Jazz Studies has no parallel in the study of Western art music; the "New Musicology" of the 1980s to the present arose from within musical academia, and its practitioners rarely come from outside musicology itself. Why should the same not be true for New Jazz Studies as well? Why have interdisciplinary scholars taken it upon themselves to advance a scholarly voice for jazz studies, separate from musicological discourses? Mark Tucker, in his 1998 review of the two editions edited by Gabbard, *Representing Jazz* and *Jazz Among the Discourses*, laments the lack of musicologist-authors, who comprise only two of the twenty-three contributors between the two texts (M. Tucker 1998, 133). Tucker notes the irony of the lack of representation of "New Musicology" in Gabbard's editions:

> If all this [research in the two texts] sounds like the "new musicology" applied to jazz, the remarkable fact is that virtually no musicologists or musically trained scholars contributed to Gabbard's enterprise. Given his claim that jazz has finally "entered the mainstreams of the American academy" (JAD, p. 1), one might assume members of the academic musical establishment to be leading the march. . . . Why so few musicologists? (M. Tucker 1998, 132–33)

The answer to this is simple, as Tucker himself acknowledges: unlike music in the Western canon, jazz scholarship has *always* been the province of interdisciplinary scholarship and research, with musicology-based research being a minority in the field until relatively recently. Many of the first jazz histories were written by non-musicians and non-musicologists, and jazz research was the activity of specialists in literature, history, sociology, psychology, anthropology, and other non-music fields. There were some who brought a musicological sensibility to the emerging field in the 1950s and 1960s (most notably Gunther Schuller), but musicological research on jazz was, at least until the 1980s, still a rarity. Tucker, for his part, perceived a sense of disdain for musicology-based research in Gabbard's comments, and it is not hard to see why. Gabbard suggests that jazz history is often taught by "musicologists more secure with Eurocentric forms or by a lone jazz musician retreating to the security of academia after some years of paying dues on the road" (Gabbard 1995, 4). There is an implicit stereotype here, in that these two classes of individuals do not really *know* enough about either jazz or history, respectively. Perhaps if more scholars like Gabbard had chosen to pursue careers in musicology instead of, say, film studies, this may not have been an issue. Much of jazz's intellectual discourse thus is coming from outside musical academia, and has increasingly attacked the very canons on which so much jazz pedagogy is based.

Critiques of canon are by no means a recent development in jazz discourse. Even in the early days of jazz criticism and scholarship, what are often thought of as basic assumptions about jazz were being questioned. In a September 1937 article in *Down Beat*, Paul Eduard Miller suggests that the importance of jazz soloists was overstated in the developing historical narrative of the music. Later in the article he makes the following remarkable claim: "The importance of [Louis] Armstrong, remarkable a jazz soloist as he is, has been overemphasized. A long-range view of the history of jazz indicates that while much credit has failed to go where it should, too much esteem has gone in other directions" (Miller 1937, 16). This passage easily could have been written last week, with its revisionist thrust and pointedly anti-canonical tone. I emphasize this passage to draw attention to the point that moves toward canon, and reactions against them, are part of the history of jazz itself. Arguments over who were the true innovators were likely taking place as soon as the first musicians claimed that they were playing jazz. Critique of canon is not a correction of jazz history; it is *part of* jazz history.

Two main lines of criticism of the idea of canon in jazz are manifest in the contemporary critical literature. In the first, canon is attacked for its exclusionary nature, that important figures are omitted from the narrative. The second main line of attack against the canon takes aim at the idea of canon itself, that the very act of canon is a distortion of important historical processes. In reality, these two approaches to critiquing the canon are not exclusive, and critical works often blend these two arguments into one sustained critique. In the exclusionary critique, the canon is problematic not because of what it includes, but what it excludes. Critiques of canon along these lines tend to call for greater representation either of specific musicians whose work has been ignored or of larger constituencies. One of the main critiques of the Ken Burns series, for example, was the belief that important musicians were left out. Many viewers and critics were mystified at the relatively marginal role in the series of figures such as Charles Mingus and Bill Evans, both of whom are today relatively canonical figures. As Terry Teachout notes in a three-part series on "Jazz Masterpieces" in *Commentary* from late 1999 and early 2000, these types of canons have led to an "incomplete" view of jazz:

> Not surprisingly, most attempts to draw up jazz canons have been marred by idiosyncrasy and poor scholarship. A case in point is *The Smithsonian Collection of Classic Jazz*, a 1973 anthology of 84 recordings selected by the late Martin Williams and issued by the Smithsonian Institution, in which a large number of key figures failed to make the cut, with others receiving token or otherwise misleading representation. (Teachout 1999a, 46)

Over the course of three essays he advances an alternative, in which the "gaps" in the canon are filled. There are several notable things about Teachout's canon, however, that mar his approach. First, there are no singers; he himself states that "I have omitted all vocalists" with the exception of Louis Armstrong, noting that they are "best understood and discussed as a variety of American popular singing" (Teachout 1999a, 47). Secondly, there are no women in the list, at least as leaders whose names are listed. Third, and most surprising given his criticism of the *SCCJ*, the most recent recording on the list is Weather Report's "Birdland" from 1977. Presumably *something* important had to have happened in jazz in the twenty-two years since. Should we really call what Teachout has done in his essays a critique of canon? Perhaps it is more accurately described as a different canon (although, given the prevalence of Armstrong, Ellington, and Parker, its core is not that different).

This strikes at the heart of a problem with New Jazz Studies as well. In many cases, those who criticize the canon are not really criticizing it as a concept; they simply want a different version of it. Again, consider, the controversy surrounding Ken Burns and his documentary. For all the charges of omission of various artists, few reviewers directly addressed the idea of canon, at least in the jazz press. As Francis Davis wrote in his review of the series for the *Atlantic*:

> Nearly every jazz critic I know has been angrily compiling his or her own list of current performers who were unfairly omitted from the series. Though my list of missing persons includes Albert Ayler, Keith Jarrett, and Sun Ra, it begins long before 1960. *Jazz* tells us nothing, or very little, about Mildred Bailey, Benny Carter, Woody Herman, Stan Kenton, Lennie Tristano, Erroll Garner, Art Pepper, any of Ellington's sidemen, or any of the arrangers—except Fletcher Henderson—who gave the big bands of the 1940s their trademark sounds. (Davis 2001)

Davis's review says very little about who *was* included, and this illustrates an important point about canon that makes it problematic for jazz musicians and writers. How do we critique the canon while still paying homage to musicians whose work has influenced us? It is relatively easy to call for a more inclusive understanding of jazz, which is surely a good thing; but that, by its nature, is not non-canonical. It simply includes more people in it, making it larger.

Another notable aspect of the reaction to the Burns series was that few reviewers seemed to take notice of the almost complete lack of women in the narrative, a point that in the New Jazz Studies has itself attracted substantial notice. Increasingly, the role of women in jazz has begun to receive attention, spotlighting another way in which the canon has distorted our view of jazz, making it into a male-dominated story. The efforts of scholars such as Sherrie Tucker, whose work on women in jazz has initiated a vital discussion of gender and feminist perspectives, are critical to the ways in which New Jazz Studies are applying methods of social theory to jazz. The extent to which they are critiques of canon is less clear. While Tucker, in particular, sees her work as providing an "intervention" into the canon (S. Tucker 2004, 13), nowhere does she suggest the major jazz figures ought to be de-emphasized. Again, I would suggest that this represents not so much an attempt to do away with canon, but to enrich it, an endeavor which is hard to oppose on its own merits. What is lacking in so much of the anti-canonical literature is a sense of what should replace it; it is not the canon that is the problem, but the fact that artist X is not included.

If the New Jazz Studies paradigm sees as its project an intense critical focus on canon and the application of new scholarly perspectives to the study of the genre, other "questioning" moves in jazz are emerging from the ground up. Jazz communities have for many years revolved around an implicit hierarchy of roles: artists, journalists, industry figures, scholars, each have had a role to play in the community. Audiences and fans, however, have largely been ignored in such discourses, apart from the very few reception studies on jazz that have appeared in the literature. Jazz audiences have been conceptualized simply as something that is there, either as consumers of the music and associated literature, or as unnamed actors in the social play that intersects with jazz at various points. Arguments that jazz has been a working-class music, or that certain forms of jazz resonate with social and cultural movements are, of course, very common, but give little attention to individual agency or perspective within the jazz audience. Yet jazz fans have always been active, forming listening clubs and fan groups to support and discuss the work of their favorite artists. These types of discourses have been largely submerged, however, and jazz fans remain mostly invisible in jazz discourses. Recently, this dynamic has begun to shift, with the emergence of internet platforms in which fans can engage in lively, public debates among themselves, and even with artists and critics.

This has implications for canon as well. Canon is not, in such an environment, simply an extension of a scholarly construct designed to give educators a ready method for talking about the music's history. It is something against which specific individuals measure their own involvement with the music, and as the voice of jazz fans gains increased resonance in jazz discourses, so too must the perspectives of fans be seen as part of its canonical formation. Canon, and the debates that surround it, has long affected the ways fans experience the music; increasingly, the opposite may also be true.

But every person, and every jazz community, understands canon differently; these differences are critical to understanding how different communities come to know jazz. In her essay "Conversing with Ourselves: Canon, Freedom, Jazz," Catherine Gunther Kodat discusses the work of Scott DeVeaux on reconceptualizing bebop's role as a statement of protest against commercial music:

the theory that bebop represents some sort of non- or a-commercial modernism . . . becomes a bit harder to sustain. . . . In other words, to canonize bebop in this way is to canonize correlatively the music's *reconciliation* with capitalist culture industry, its ability, as Adorno put it in "On Jazz," to "simultaneously develop and enchain productive power," rather than its ability to resist, or critique, culture industry imperatives. (Kodat 2003, 11–12)

Kodat is correct in her interpretation of DeVeaux that bebop was not intended as some anti-commercial statement. But I suggest that Kodat's linking of canonicity to issues such as commercialism overlooks a crucial point: she forgets that bebop was (and is) *music* first.[3] In terms of a musical canon, was bebop's place really defined by any perceived anti-commercial stance? Was it really defined as a deeply held expression of black consciousness? Or, is bebop's place in the canon constructed in relationship to the things that were *played* by Gillespie, Parker, Monk, Powell, and others, by the music itself? That, for many (if not most) jazz players and fans, is where bebop's canonical place lies—with its influence on the *sound*, the primary way most jazz fans come to know the music.

This brings me to a core argument: canon, the ultimate expression of knowledge about jazz, means different things to different people. For some, especially in New Jazz Studies, canon is about contested claims to ownership, social and cultural currents, relationships to adjunct histories, and alternative ways of looking at the world. These are all extremely important ideas, laudable goals as academic pursuits, offering much to our understanding of jazz history. But they offer little for the jazz history teacher whose job is to support a jazz performance curriculum. As much as such teachers may include such perspectives, they must also deal with a different historical canon, a sonic canon, in which issues of gender, race, economics, and similar ideas are secondary to the music itself. These two approaches are by no means mutually exclusive, and the best teachers and scholars are those who understand and adapt to both. But they are different ways of *knowing* jazz, reflective of different communities and needs. What's more, they are likely not the only canons, nor the only communities. European musicians will understand their own relationships to the music differently, as will beginners, or fans downloading music from iTunes. We all construct our knowledge of jazz and our place within a jazz community relative to where we are, and we all learn about the music in different ways.

In the chapters that follow, I hope to illuminate some issues that arise from discussions of community and canon. What underpins all these case studies is a belief that knowledge about jazz is negotiated and constructed within and between specific communities, all of whom are functions of a process of mediation, filtered through information technology. Through technology, be it mass-market publishing, recordings, or increasingly, digital networks, our most basic assumptions about jazz, our knowledge of the music, is formed and maintained. This is where we learn about the music, whether in formal pedagogical contexts, or in the more autodidactic pedagogy of the listeners, whose knowledge of jazz is created by themselves and for themselves, and influenced by their peers as fellow actors in communities of jazz. Both community and canon are products of the information age; without it, they could not exist. To know jazz, to relate oneself to canon, and to identify with jazz community are conscious acts that require a degree of self-identification. This is a critical point: different constituencies in the jazz community create and maintain knowledge of the music and its culture in ways that are most relevant to their own needs.

The first chapter, "The Problem with Community," examines jazz community as a concept that is frequently invoked in discourses on jazz, yet simultaneously misunderstood and applied uncritically. Positioning common representations of jazz community as inadequate to describe the complex processes of interaction and behavior among jazz musicians and others who share an interest in the music, I suggest a number of alternative models for understanding community in jazz, drawing from prevailing studies on community formation, including Anderson's work on "imagined community," McMillan and Chavis's studies of the "sense of community," and Howard Becker's "art worlds." I conclude by arguing that jazz community is best understood as a "community of practice," with a continuum of recording and listening as the center of this experience. In constructing this argument, I suggest that listening is best understood as a *practice*, in which the listener serves an essential role in the creative process. This perspective places audiences at the core of a creative process; as recorded media are produced with the intention of being listened to, the act of listening completes the process of creating the work, and thus represents a community of practice between artist and listener.

Chapter 2, "Jazz Education and the Tightrope of Tradition," examines how conflicting historical and cultural forces play out within the halls of musical academia. In so doing, I explore how the community of jazz education negotiates its existence within the context of larger jazz and academic communities. In the first of three case studies, I critique narratives of the history of jazz education itself, deconstructing established views of the field's development, in order to understand the role of non-academic practices in the shaping of the field. The second study examines formal pedagogy and curriculum in jazz education, specifically as related to the teaching of improvisation. Jazz improvisation as taught in the academy draws upon both established norms of academic musical study *and* an emphasis on individuality, creativity, and a certain iconoclastic approach. Specific methods that have been developed by jazz educators have attempted to negotiate these competing demands, but the practice of these methods has represented a delicate balancing act between disparate pedagogical and performative traditions. In the final case study, I consider the implications for these ideas within the culture of the musical academy. Specifically, I suggest that the adoption of academic norms in the development of jazz education has had profound implications for power relationships between musicians, and in this context specifically, between teachers and students. Rather than fostering a democratic musical ideal, hierarchies are often reinforced through the choices made by educators to construct institutionally acceptable methods.

The third chapter, "Doing and Teaching," extends these discussions to the field of jazz writing and scholarship, examining efforts to categorize and encapsulate knowledge of jazz's historical record. I propose that jazz writing can be seen as an effort to create community in jazz, and that texts, like recordings, can be viewed as a *practice*, one that is completed when a text is read. As Clifford Geertz asserts that a culture can be read "like a text," I argue that the reverse is also possible, that a text (or texts) can be interpreted as a culture. To this end, I examine the development of jazz historiography, starting with Marshall Stearns's *The Story of Jazz*, assessing the construction of canon, and how knowledge of jazz is presented in relation to it. The chapter concludes with an examination of the place of jazz history in the academic musical context, and the issues that "non-performers" face as a distinct community within performance programs.

The explosion of the internet over the last two decades represents a pivotal event for the development of community networks in many areas of social life. Jazz has proven to be no exception to this idea, and the fourth chapter, "The Virtual Jazz World," examines the types of jazz communities that have come into existence during the last several years. I contend that such virtual communities provide crucial links for jazz fans scattered across geographic areas to interact and exchange ideas about the music. Individuals who may have depended on critical and trade publications to read about developments in the genre can now have nearly immediate, unrestricted access. More importantly, the interactive nature of Web 2.0 has led directly to the development of a new, grassroots discourse in jazz, one that bypasses traditional media, journalism, and scholarship. Focusing on case studies involving Wikipedia and jazz message boards, I examine how communities of jazz fans engage in often contentious dialogue about what jazz is; such studies provide an opportunity to examine how constructions of knowledge intersect with users' conceptualization of their own place in community.

The final chapter, "The Global Jazz Community," examines how jazz communities and canons have become intertwined with discourses on globalization, itself increasingly tied to technological mediation. I suggest that the "flattening" effects of globalization and information technology have problematized traditional national hierarchies in jazz discourse. Claims to knowledge and ownership of jazz are often embedded within these discourses, and my case studies all deal with these issues. For example, the rise and collapse of the International Association for Jazz Education, a group that had long seen itself as a leader of the "global jazz community," stands as a metaphor for claims to identity in a global context. While the organization saw itself as international, in fact it reflected a very American perspective. This discussion leads to an examination of the conflation of the American neo-classicist school and its American exceptionalist view of jazz. Such perspectives have come under sustained, aggressive critique in recent years, due in part, I suggest, to broader challenges to American cultural hegemony in the first decade of the twenty-first century. I close the final chapter with a discussion of the 2009 documentary *Icons Among Us: Jazz in the Present Tense*, a film which attempts to portray a contemporary world of jazz in which American perspectives are but one voice, though this philosophy proves problematic in the film itself, underscoring the difficulties of negotiating knowledge and community on the global stage.

The broad themes of community, pedagogy, and canon are all present within these contexts to varying degrees. What links them all is their emergence as a function of a mediated experience in jazz, that is to say, that actors in these communities come to jazz through some form of information technology. As recordings, texts, and websites can only partially reflect the real-world processes of jazz, those on the receiving end of such mediation must by necessity engage with those mediated statements, bringing their own knowledge and perspectives to bear. Thus, two listeners may hear the same recording, and come away with different interpretations; two readers may have the same work of criticism, but interpret it in different ways; two editors of a Wikipedia article may have vastly different views of the role of race in jazz. Jazz communities will be inhabited by all of these types of individuals, and many others as well, making sweeping generalizations about how they are defined by a common core of knowledge about jazz difficult, if not impossible. It is no accident that the growth of jazz has gone hand in hand with the advent of commercial recording and inexpensive mass market (and now electronic) publications, and these relationships are deeply embedded within the formation of jazz communities, regardless of place or time.

CHAPTER 1

The Problem with Community

A Case Study in Contrasts

There are many constituencies within the jazz community, separated by race, age, mode of performance, level of professional involvement, geography, and other factors. I would like to offer two stories that underscore the ways that individuals position themselves within jazz communities, and how they are seen as part of those communities by others. The first offers us an aging African American saxophonist who, having experienced little acceptance for his music in his home country, relocated to Paris, where he finds his music appreciated more than in his native land. His gravelly voice and tendency toward self-destruction in his personal life reinforce commonly held stereotypes about jazz musicians, as do his deeply soulful performances, often in small, smoky, dimly lit nightclubs. Eventually, he returns to the United States to find that little has changed with respect to the treatment of African Americans, or the public's general disregard for his music. A short time later, he dies, a master artist relatively unknown in his own land.

The second scenario involves a fourteen-year-old trombonist growing up in a rural area of an even more rural state, playing in his junior high jazz band. With a repertoire ranging from stock arrangements by Nestico to arrangements of Lionel Richie tunes, his interest in jazz is sparked when he hears a Miles Davis record in his band director's office. He continues with jazz band in high school, traveling to rehearsals and concerts over snow-covered roads, gaining experience and winning some accolades along the way. Eventually he begins to listen to more jazz, learning the basics of improvisation via method books and Aebersold play-along records.[1] He too develops some bad habits, notably an affinity for coffee at an uncharacteristically young age (no doubt a result of too many morning rehearsals before physics class). He considers himself to be part of a community based first and foremost on his fellow students, whose bond is shaped by long hours of rehearsal and travel on under-heated school buses to festivals and contests. Occasionally, his world broadens to include like-minded students from other schools, whose experiences in the music are similar to his own. He too, is relatively unknown outside his immediate musical world.

These individuals seem far removed from one another, in terms of geography, generation, race, and in almost every other way. The single thread that links them is their involvement in jazz, and even here the experiences are radically different, one facing the end of a career defined by struggle, the other just beginning his involvement in jazz performance. Should these individuals be considered part of the same community? Is a shared interest in jazz enough to link them in this way, given the distinction between their personal and historical narratives? Despite what seems an impossibly wide historical divide, these two accounts are actually drawn from the same time period, the mid-1980s. The first account is fictional, the central character of Dale Turner from the 1986 film *Round Midnight*, based loosely on the lives of Lester Young, Bud Powell, and Dexter Gordon, who portrayed Turner in the film. The second account is very real, and is, in fact, my own, drawing on my experiences as a young musician in rural Maine, where I attended public schools until 1989. I remember seeing the film *Round Midnight* while in high school, and feeling a sense of exotic fascination with the story (reinforcing many of my own stereotypes about jazz), and with a musician who played masterfully this music I was coming to know; there was also a sense of distance, another world that was far removed from my own. Though it is horribly clichéd as a worldview of a working-class white household to say this, there really were only a few black students at my high school, and to see a figure such as Dale (or Dexter) and connect to him, at even the most superficial level, was a formative moment in my understanding of the music, and of my place in a wider jazz community.

The term *community* itself is often misunderstood and misapplied when referring to the identities or activities of groups, especially large groups dispersed over distances while sharing some interest or other identifiable activity. Burt Feintuch likens community to other terms such as *authenticity* and *tradition* that have become largely disconnected from their original meaning, applied at will in uncritical ways. Feintuch takes exception to the ways in which communities are conceptualized in academic discourses, pointing to his own experiences in folklore studies:

A few years ago, in a panel devoted to discussions of North American fiddle music at the American Folklore Society conference, I heard the word "community" used in ways that made me shake my head, especially when the conversation was about revivalist music sessions....I understand community as more than what happens in one, occasional sphere of interaction. To be in community is to participate in a web of connectedness to others that continues beyond special events. (Feintuch 2001, 149)

The scenario Feintuch describes could easily be applied to myriad ways in which jazz writers employ the term *jazz community*, carrying none of the "vital elements" of community as he describes. Yet community, both as a term and as an organizing concept, has meaning and power, allowing us to determine who is included, and equally important, who is not. As Feintuch argues, "We all seem to want what we do to stand for community" (150). By invoking a concept such as community in a broad, uncritical way, we often include ourselves within it. This idea of community is appealing to disparate individuals whose interests intersect, as Raymond Williams suggests: "Community can be the warmly persuasive word to describe an existing set of relationships, or the warmly persuasive word to describe an alternative set of relationships. What is most important, perhaps, is that unlike all other terms of social organization (state, nation, society, etc.) it seems never to be used unfavourably, and never to be given any positive opposing or distinguishing term" (R. Williams 1976, 66). This suggests a pressing issue with the use of *community* in jazz narratives: that it is not explained or qualified in any meaningful way. Let me present some examples to illustrate that the use of terms such as *jazz community* offers us little upon which to hang our epistemological hat in determining exactly what the community is.

In most occurrences of the term, the jazz community is seen to be possessed of a singular consciousness, without specifically defining exactly who the individuals are that comprise it. This tendency can be observed in the following passages, taken from works by Paul Austerlitz, Eric Nisenson, and Scott DeVeaux (emphasis added):

- At the same time, musicians cultivated an extraordinary openness; developing during the Harlem Renaissance and civil rights movements, the consciousness of the *jazz community* has articulated an aesthetic of inclusivity and an ethos of ecumenicity. (Austerlitz 2005, xiii)
- As usual, many in the *jazz community* simply could not accept change—to them it was deterioration. (Nisenson 1997, 99)
- More helpful observations derive from his experience as a performer, although there are relatively few of these, undoubtedly reflecting a scrupulous refusal to privilege his own thoughts over those of others in the *jazz community*. (DeVeaux 1998, 399)

In none of these examples is any attempt made to identify specific charac-teristics of the community, or to articulate individual identities within it or relationships between members. Such usage of the term is extremely common, and it is not my intent to criticize these specific authors, for the practice is so widespread that it has become a common trope (of which I myself have been guilty on occasion).

In other instances, the term is used in ways that draw upon specific iden-tities; jazz community is intertwined with race, gender, and other assumed identities and behaviors. Riggins Earl and Marvin Holladay conflate the jazz community with certain attitudes and behaviors that are directly related to a heightened racial consciousness (emphasis added):

- In the *jazz community* the term "brother" became an individual and corpo-rate creative response to suffering that gave blacks and whites the sense of being "soul brothers." It gave them a sense of affirming and being affirmed by each other's dialogical selves. (Earl 2001, 163)
- Interracial dating and marriage was an accepted part of the *jazz community* for those with courage enough to apply it to their own lives. (in Fitzgerald 2003, 23)

Similarly, Burton Peretti, George McKay, and Charley Gerard position the jazz community as sites where racial politics are played out (emphasis added):

- [Did] the *jazz community* become a great experiment in racial equality, or did it become as hypocritical and segregated as other institutions remained through the Second World War? (Peretti 1994, 177)
- Even in Britain the reaction of the *jazz community* to white racism directed at black migrants in the 1950s stood as a rejection of white intolerance. . . . (McKay 2005, 126)
- [Some white musicians] are respected members of the *jazz community* for being allowed into the realm of a group of [black] musicians who, because of their cultural background, are considered to be arbiters of the idiom, the figures who defined where it came from and where it is going. . . . Jim Hall gained the recognition of the *jazz community* after playing with Sonny Rollins. . . . (Gerard 1998, 106)

Still others note the male-centric nature of the jazz community, as well as the sometimes difficult existence for women and gays within it, as Eric Porter, Sherrie Tucker, and Barry Truax note (emphasis added):

- Even the more innocuous, heterosocial world of dating contributed to the development of the masculinist ethos of the *jazz community*. . . . [this] was also influenced by gendered ideas about creativity and genius that were entrenched in Western music cultures. (E. Porter 2002, 29)
- For many jazzwomen, *"jazz community"* has meant jamming in the margins of the margins (to elaborate on Krin Gabbard's expression), sometimes in women-in-jazz communities (ranging from "all-girl" bands to women's jazz festivals) with varying degrees of reluctance and enthusiasm. (S. Tucker 2004, 250)
- [The] traditionally male-dominated *jazz community* . . . also has been largely homophobic. Exceptions can occur, such as the case with Billy Strayhorn, whose homosexuality was tolerated through his professional role as Duke Ellington's pianist and arranger. (Truax 2003, 118)

I could go on at length with similar anecdotes drawn from dozens of written scholarly works, to say nothing of critical writings and more informal statements. Indeed, it is unusual to find sources on jazz that do *not* use this term, and in similarly uncritical ways. Suffice it to say that jazz community is a concept that is at once fundamentally important to the contemporary discourse of jazz at almost every level, yet simultaneously imprecise in its usage.

Situating the community within jazz's longstanding and contentious discourses of race and identity is also a difficult task.[2] Nevertheless, the jazz community is commonly represented as a site of racial cooperation, understanding, and social progress, particularly for those which seek to situate jazz as an expression of a particularly American, democratic ideal, a metaphor for what America could and should be. Some writers have positioned the jazz community as expressing some intrinsically "black" character, reflecting certain attitudes that are seen to arise from black vernacular experience. Robert Gold states that the "rapidly changing parlance [and] vocational idioms . . . were proud symbols of the jazz community's identity and separateness" (Gold 2001, 324), and arose from what were perceived to be historically African American verbal practices. For others, jazz communities were progressive sites that served explicitly as a social and cultural vanguard, demonstrating integration and racial reconciliation in advance of American society at large. Commenting on the work of pioneering jazz historian Marshall Stearns, Iain Anderson suggests that the jazz community was seen to provide "a model of harmonious integration" (Anderson 2007, 40). James Lincoln Collier makes a similar point in describing jazz as "the American theme song," citing Bruce Boyd Raeburn's argument that "The willingness to let talent or innovation serve as the standard (as opposed to 'race' or 'class') was a major breakthrough and helped to cement relations within the broader jazz community"[3] (Collier 1993, 223). This perspective itself has not been without its critics, who question such a halcyon view of the jazz community as representing some sort of racialized utopia. Burton Peretti suggests in his widely read text *The Creation of Jazz* that the perception that jazz communities "worked constantly towards cultural integration and biracial understanding" has been "argued incorrectly" (Peretti 1994, 209). Similarly, Sherrie Tucker points to the problematic nature of looking at jazz community through a prism of "nostalgia" in which the jazz community is a "color-blind liberal community where race never mattered and everyone got along" (S. Tucker 2004, 248). For Tucker, this idealized view of the jazz community was predicated on a "lopsided integration" in which whites could inhabit the social sphere of blacks, but not the other way around (248). Integration meant different things to different people, and the jazz community was a site where these different perspectives came into conflict.[4]

Still others argue that racial identity and discord in jazz communities have negatively impacted whites. Terry Teachout suggests that "reverse racism has become, if not universal, then potentially legitimate in jazz and indeed, how it has insinuated itself throughout the jazz community" (Teachout 1995, 53). In his 1998 book *Jazz in Black and White*, Charley Gerard extends this argument further, positioning the jazz community not as a bastion of racial progress and reconciliation, but as a site where claims to ownership of the jazz tradition are frequently linked to racial identity, often (in his view) to the detriment of white musicians. Gerard's study is important for shining an uncomfortable but needed spotlight on this sensitive topic, as he explores the genesis of race-related practices and attitudes. More germane to our discussion, his fourth chapter is devoted to "race and jazz communities," but here I find his casual conflation of jazz, race, and "heroin addict communities" in the chapter to be troubling, especially considering the prominence this topic is given, and I think this point is worth considering in some depth. Of course, the devastating effects of heroin use among jazz musicians through the 1950s are well documented, but I suggest Gerard misses some critical points.

First, black musicians were not the only ones to use heroin—white musicians Art Pepper, Bill Evans, Chet Baker, Stan Getz, and Gerry Mulligan, to name a few, were all known users. To be fair, Gerard does not explicitly make the claim that heroin was the exclusive province of black artists,[5] but this discussion's dominant place in a chapter on "race and jazz communities" is problematic, relying heavily on anecdotal arguments such as "heroin use was something that everyone in the black community was familiar with" (Gerard 1998, 87), without offering any specific evidence to demonstrate either why this was the case, or what it had to do with jazz (or what the "black community" itself was).

Second, much of his assessment of the heroin problem is drawn from sociological studies in the 1950s whose motives and methods were suspect. Charles Winick's study on drug use among jazz musicians in the United States, which Gerard cites, suffers from a number of flaws. Its assessment of the size and character of the community of jazz musicians in New York in the 1950s is by his own admission speculative, generated "on the basis of informal estimates by students of the industry" (Winick 1959, 240). On the following page, Winick notes the following: "The lack of reliable data on the age, race, or length of professional musical activity of the musicians in the New York area makes it impossible to tell how representative this sample is of working musicians in terms of customary classificatory criteria" (Winick 1959, 241). In other words, the sample cannot really be trusted. The sample he does use would seem to further undercut Gerard's linking of heroin communities and race, as white musicians comprised 69 percent of the sample group; clearly this is not a "black community."[6] But the most fundamental problem with the reliance on such a study is that it does not make any type of comparison of drug use among jazz musicians with that of other communities. The intense focus on drug use among jazz musicians magnified its association with jazz communities. Central questions remain unanswered: Did this drug use have something to do with jazz? With race? With the intersection of jazz and race? Or did it have to do more with the fact that New York, where the study was completed, was home to "43 percent of the nation's known addicts" (Winick 1959, 240), and thus *any* New York–based community might potentially have a higher rate of drug use. Clearly not all of these users were jazz musicians, but jazz musicians were frequently singled out as a convenient source for the examination of many different types of pathologies (as I discuss elsewhere in this chapter). Just as police understood that they could usually bust users at jazz clubs, researchers understood that jazz musicians provided a ready-made subject pool.

I do not wish to digress too far into a discussion of U.S. legal policies concerning substance abuse past or present, nor do I wish to downplay the use or impact of drugs among jazz musicians in the 1950s; clearly, this was a serious problem that cannot and should not be swept under the carpet.[7] But Gerard's argument is unconvincing in singling out heroin use as a significant unifying factor for members of a jazz community, and that this has some particular relationship with the topic of racial identity in jazz. Gerard's text is certainly not the only one that makes such arguments about community; it is but one example of the types of essentializing constructions of communities that pervade jazz writing, and that distract us from the more important issue of determining the relationships and dynamic processes involved with community formation with musical production at its core. To single out "heroin addict communities" as a site to examine race in jazz communities does not hold up under close scrutiny; it is simply assumed that this means something—just what is never made clear—about discourses of race in jazz. There is no explicit reason given for why the "heroin addict community" should be thought of as a "jazz" community, other than for the fact that some jazz musicians took heroin, or why these addict communities represent anything meaningful about the intersection of race and community.

It is one thing to illustrate this problematic nature of writing about community in jazz, and quite another to propose an alternative way to understand it. If these examples cannot adequately describe what the jazz community is, then what *is* it? What *does* define community in jazz? No one would question that there is, at some level, a certain type of community relationship among jazz musicians and others involved with the music's creation, dissemination, and reception. Groups of performers are themselves a community on the bandstand, in the recording studio, or rehearsal room. Geographic location is frequently a site of community formation, be it Minton's in Harlem in the 1940s, the Hill District of Pittsburgh, Cass Tech in Detroit, or Crispus Attucks High School in Indianapolis; each of these were sites from which numerous notable jazz musicians would emerge. But these are all examples of specific, bounded community groups, and from these we cannot extrapolate identities and practices for jazz musicians in other settings and contexts. Broader definitions of jazz community must be based on some other model that transcends these particularities. To that end, let us examine some specific ways for examining jazz community that might lead us to a greater understanding of just what community is.

Research on Jazz Community

The term *jazz community* seems to have emerged in print around fifty years ago, although I would speculate that it existed in informal discourses well before that. The earliest clear, documented reference to the jazz community as a focus of study I was able to uncover was a 1947 master's thesis by Richard Kamprath at Columbia entitled "The Jazz Community."[8] Subsequent references can be found in an article by Norman Margolis in the psychoanalytic journal *American Imago*, in which the author compares behaviors in the jazz community to adolescence, writing that "[the] equation of adolescence to the psychology of jazz gains support when one examines the jazz community. It is typically adolescent in many ways" (Margolis 1954, 281). Among these "typically adolescent" features are "clothing fads," language and mannerisms of speech, and a tendency toward "on-the-fringe-of-society" type behaviors, such as heavy drinking and drug use (282). Margolis continues his analysis by arguing: "In that the character of the jazz community is typically adolescent and has always remained so, the hypothesis is presented that the ambivalent psychology characteristic of adolescence is the psychological source of jazz" (289–90).

Almost certainly referencing Margolis, Marshall Stearns, whose courses in jazz history in the early 1950s were, in a very real sense, the pioneering efforts in historical jazz scholarship (which is discussed in depth in chapter 3), makes the claim in his influential text *The Story of Jazz* that the "jazz community reflects other adolescent qualities" such as "faddish clothes" and "unusual personal appearance" (a category in which he places goatees). Though not a psychiatrist, Stearns nevertheless repeats Margolis's assertions as virtual fact, as scientific proof of the nature of the community. Given the prevailing public sentiments on jazz at the time,[9] it is little wonder that scientific perspectives such as that of Margolis found their ways even into texts that were not only sympathetic to jazz, but celebratory of it.

The first focused attempt to assess what constituted the jazz community was published in 1960 by Alan Merriam and Raymond Mack in the journal *Social Forces*. Titled simply "The Jazz Community," Merriam (later recognized as one of the pioneering figures in ethnomusicology) and Mack (a sociologist at Northwestern) systematically described the character and behavioral attributes of those whom they identify as part of this group. Merriam and Mack's essay is often cited in references and bibliographies in jazz scholarship, and is recognized as an important contribution to the subject. It is also, according to some, the publication in which the term originated, as argued by Taylor Atkins in his book *Blue Nippon*. As Atkins writes, Merriam and Mack coined the term to "include audiences as well as performers in jazz sociology, to demystify jazz sub-cultures, and to critique the famed alienation and hostility of musicians towards outsiders" (Atkins 2001, 6). That Merriam and Mack "coined" the term is not accurate, though it is likely that they brought the term into prominence. While the Margolis article does appear in the references of their essay, there is no clear indication that Merriam and Mack borrowed this terminology from him, or from another source.

Merriam and Mack offer us not only a way of understanding jazz community as a group whose identity is fundamentally defined by performance, but also a sense of how the community coexists with mainstream society. The essay presents a "factual description" of an organized "community of interest" that exhibits "specific behavioral patterns" (Merriam and Mack 1960, 211). For example, while Merriam and Mack speak of a participation "to some extent in the occupational role and ideology of the jazz musician" (211) as an important marker of community membership, such participation can take a number of forms. Obviously, being a jazz musician would qualify one for membership in the community. But even this is problematic, for the "to some extent" qualification is ambiguous. The extent to which someone is seen as participating in occupational ideology is not always agreed upon, an issue which will be examined later in this chapter. Merriam and Mack further explain that membership of the community includes not only musicians but also "their public." Again, they do not explicitly state what this public consists of. Does it include fans? critics? producers? In attempting to define the jazz community in objective, sociologically informed terms, Merriam and Mack ultimately leave more questions unanswered than they are able to settle.

Further, they argue, members of the community share, aside from the "extreme identification with and participation in the occupational ideology of the jazz musician," a set of "expected behaviors . . . norms regarding proper and improper language, good and bad music, stylish and unstylish clothing, acceptable and unacceptable audience behavior, and so on" (211). As one might surmise from these passages, the main identifying criteria for inclusion within the community are exhibited behaviors, rather than a general sense of shared belief. The community's "isolation of the group from society at large" serves an identifying function, of shared rejection by outsiders who view their music and related activities as at best odd, and possibly pathological, a sense of which permeates Merriam and Mack's approach to their study. The community is viewed as a subculture, even a deviant one, which is understood in terms of its behaviors vis-à-vis established cultural norms.

It is easy in retrospect to criticize these types of studies for making assumptions about the jazz community that are, to put it mildly, disputed; but we should remember that they were working within the paradigm of their discipline at the time. A good deal of sociological research and writing from the early 1960s focused on the ideas of deviance as defining features of different social groups, that subcultures were seen largely as those that exhibited behaviors outside the "norms" of conduct.[10] It should also be noted that Merriam and Mack were not the only scholars to look at the jazz community from a behavioral perspective. Sociologist Robert Stebbins published his own "Theory of the Jazz Community" in 1968, based on his 1964 doctoral dissertation for the University of Minnesota. Like Merriam and Mack (though he makes scant reference to them in his piece), Stebbins also defines the jazz community as a function of occupation, and in even more explicit terms. For Stebbins, the jazz community is defined by the act of performance, not as music, but as a job.

Among the many noteworthy aspects of Stebbins's approach to the topic is his use of hierarchies to construct a social order, invoking Howard Becker's work on dance band musicians[11] in outlining the different levels of prestige accorded activities that inform identity within the group. An explicit link is made between performance and identity within the jazz community, as the community "is seen today at its most solitary and esoteric formation in those forms cast up by the modern jazz musician" (Stebbins 1968, 319). In categorizing various institutions within the community, Stebbins highlights five "core institutions," listed in decreasing order of status, including "jazz jobs," "jam sessions," "after-hours social life," "the musicians' union," and "cliques" (which he refers to as a "secondary" social institution). What all these activities have in common is interaction among musicians, within a professional context; these are the sites in which the community is maintained. What Stebbins classifies as "peripheral" institutions are those including family life, commercial music jobs, activities and spaces that tangentially impact jazz performance.[12] Stebbins's emphasis on the actual work of musicians as the defining feature of community identity is similar to the emphasis on "occupational ideology" advanced by Merriam and Mack. Stebbins does not, however, emphasize the "public" as a component of the community as Merriam and Mack do. Pathology also plays a role in Stebbins's study, as evidenced in his decidedly unscientific conclusion that the number of "legitimately married" jazz musicians within the community "are probably a minority," that marriage for jazz musicians represents a "liability," and that "most families attempt to discourage their offspring from entering it [jazz] as a career" (Stebbins 1968, 326). In the final analysis, argues Stebbins, the jazz community is a "unique form of status community," in which various professional activities, professional relationships, and family ties influence how members of the community interact.[13]

These early sociological studies probably tell us more about the perceptions of jazz in American culture than about jazz community itself. Merriam and Mack's study, with its focus on a pathological approach that examines the jazz community in relation to its isolation from mainstream society, presents us with a skewed picture of the community, especially in light of today's reception of jazz as "America's classical music." Peter Martin, writing in the British jazz journal *The Source*, chastises Merriam and Mack for taking a generally negative approach to jazz musicians, emphasizing dysfunction and deviance: "There is almost a 'film noir' atmosphere in Merriam and Mack's description of the jazz community, with its 'anti-social' members living on the dark underside of conventional society. Without a doubt, some members may have inhabited these shadows, but does it follow that the 'community' as a whole may be characterized in this way?" (P. Martin 2005, 6).

Martin's criticism is certainly on point, and he proposes an alternative framework for understanding community in jazz that I will return to later. Leaving aside the pathological perspective, the emphasis on performance-as-occupation is itself problematic. What defines a professional jazz performer is not always clear, nor is it clear that professional identity is itself a primary determining factor in establishing membership in the community. In the most literal sense, professional musicians are those who derive a substantial portion of their income from jazz performance—who do not depend on "day jobs." As Stebbins noted, "jazz jobs" occupied the highest levels of prestige in considering musicians' performance activities. But the number of musicians who can lay claim to such a jazz-exclusive professional existence today is relatively small. Apart from those at the highest echelons of jazz performance, almost all self-identified jazz performers derive some of their income from playing music other than jazz. Nevertheless, many such musicians still see themselves as jazz performers.

Let me relate some of my own experience on this front. While pursuing my doctoral degree at the University of Pittsburgh, I performed frequently with a number of groups, including a salsa band, a "neo-swing group," and a band that regularly played weddings and social functions. The money was generally good (except for the salsa band, where it had to be split about ten ways), and helped support my family while I was in school. In each band, though none of us were full-time jazz players, most of us considered ourselves to be jazz musicians. Some of my bandmates, in fact, went on to tour with professional jazz groups (two with Maynard Ferguson, one with the Glenn Miller Orchestra, a bassist who occasionally played with Stanley Turrentine, a superb pianist named Frank Cunimondo, who himself put out several jazz records in the 1970s and 1980s and is highly regarded in the region). Though much of our professional performance experience was not in jazz, we tended to self-identify as jazz performers.

Additionally, many of us played regularly in a pickup big band, the Balcony Big Band, named for a former Pittsburgh jazz club.[14] In our own version of the Village Vanguard Orchestra, the group played every Monday night in a Holiday Inn adjacent to main university campus. Though the level of the band was exceptionally good, drawing the best jazz players from the area, we would regularly make about $20. We certainly would have liked to made more, but we recognized that these performances were less about money and more about the experience of playing together with other committed jazz musicians. Among the regular performers were several college students from schools in the area, as well as an outstanding pianist and trombonist whose "day job" was as an eye surgeon. Kevin, the eye surgeon in question, had no financial need to work as musician, yet he was widely regarded as one of the best jazz players in the area. One wonders if Kevin would be a "professional" in the sense that Merriam/Mack or Stebbins propose.

While we might think of "amateur" musicians as languishing in obscurity, stuck in their everyday lives while dreaming of a playing career,[15] we should not ignore the subset of amateur jazz musicians that I would classify as "famous amateurs," those whose "day jobs" have given them both a degree of visibility and exposure, and an ability to turn their interest in jazz into something more than a fantasy. Individuals such as Woody Allen, Clint Eastwood, and Bill Cosby, due in no small part to their immense success in film and television, have been adept at using their primary careers as avenues to explore their passion for jazz. The financial security provided by producing, directing, and acting in some of the most acclaimed and profitable screen works of the late twentieth century provides an opportunity to explore jazz in ways that, say, a used car salesman or schoolteacher would not have access to. Allen, for example, has been active as a clarinetist with his New Orleans Band, performing frequently in his native New York as well as appearing at venues and festivals around the world. George Weinstein described Allen's playing this way, in a review from 1998: "Allen plays clarinet like an *inspired amateur* [emphasis added]; he's limited technically, subject to faulty intonation and a reliance upon stock phrases. But he has enormous energy and charm. The six other band members are highly skilled technicians—yet Allen's clarinet playing draws out, in the best sense, their nonprofessional (quirkily imperfect) selves" (Weinstein 2008, B7).[16]

Allen's interest in jazz has also manifested itself in his films, most notably *Sweet and Lowdown*, a "mocku-drama" which told the story of 1930s musician Emmett Ray (Sean Penn), the world's finest jazz guitarist, or actually, the second best, after "this Gypsy" in Europe. Allen's film is notable for its mixing of narrative fiction with faux interviews with "real" figures, including Nat Hentoff and Allen himself.

Clint Eastwood's interest in jazz has also found its way into a number of his films. In his 1971 directorial debut *Play Misty For Me*, Eastwood portrays Dave Garver, a northern California jazz DJ who is stalked by a woman obsessed not only with him, but with the Erroll Garner ballad referenced in the title. Eastwood includes in the film some footage from the Monterey Jazz Festival, and features a great deal of jazz in the soundtrack, at a time when it had fallen out of favor among popular audiences. Also notable were two Eastwood productions, *Bird* and *Straight No Chaser*, that have become part of the canon of jazz films. Eastwood has also used his films as a vehicle for his interest as a pianist, most notably in the crime thriller *In the Line of Fire*, in which Eastwood, portraying an aging Secret Service agent on presidential protection detail, spends much of his free time tickling the ivories in a local bar.

Bill Cosby, like Eastwood, has been an outspoken advocate for jazz and jazz education, frequently using his television programs as vehicles for jazz.[17] In the popular 1980s sitcom *The Cosby Show*, central character Cliff Huxtable's love for jazz was frequently used as a plot device, and numerous jazz recordings and artists could be heard or seen on the show. The theme song itself was rerecorded in different versions, such as a multi-tracked version recorded by Bobby McFerrin in 1987–88, and a Latin jazz arrangement for the 1989–90 season. In a notable episode, Cliff's birthday is celebrated at a dinner featuring Lena Horne; in another, Cliff's parents are treated to a performance by the Count Basie Orchestra.[18] Cosby has also been known to perform as a drummer, occasionally performing as a featured guest with a number of established jazz musicians. As Cosby himself stated in remembrance of his longtime friend Max Roach, "Why I became a comedian is because of Max Roach, I wanted to be a drummer," understanding that to be a professional musician of the caliber of Roach required a level of ability that Cosby did not have. In the realm of politics, former president Bill Clinton's saxophone skills were well known throughout his tenure in the White House; what is less known was his reportedly deep interest in the music of Thelonious Monk.[19] And, in a story that is strangely appropriate to the early twenty-first century, former Federal Reserve chairman Alan Greenspan attributes his decision to take up a career as an economist with a realization that he was not cut out for the life of a jazz musician, as he explains to Jim Lehrer in a 2008 interview:

> I actually enjoyed the clarinet the best, but I was a fairly good amateur, but a moderate professional. But what really did me in is I had, as an amateur, had to play next to Stan Getz. I was 16; he was 15. I decided, "Do I really want to be in this business . . ." And he was one of the really historic famous sax players. And the best economic decision I ever made in my life was to decide to leave the music business and go into economics.[20]

Narratives such as these work against the arguments advanced by Merriam/Mack and Stebbins. Few of these individuals would be considered professional performers despite their work as performers. Yet, many of them enjoy a high profile in national and international jazz discourses, arguably more recognized as members of the jazz community than many musicians, especially those whose reputations do not generally extend beyond the regional level. Does Woody Allen's status as an "inspired amateur" reflect Merriam and Mack's identification with jazz performers' "occupational ideology"? Does my ophthalmologist colleague's "day job" relegate him to secondary status in Stebbins's view of the jazz community, despite his high level of performance ability?

Aside from these studies, there has been little effort devoted to articulating a clear theoretical basis for understanding community in jazz. Though the term *jazz community* appears in the literature with frequency, its use and application reflect little of the specific perspectives outlined in the studies discussed. Given the problematic nature of many of their conclusions, I would suggest that this is in itself not a bad thing. The term, if not the assumptions it carried, has been appropriated and decontextualized. But this leads to another problem: what *is* the proper context for using the term? Is it appropriate for those engaged in the discourse of jazz to use the term in such a way? Or more to the point, does it really tell us anything meaningful? To address this problem, I would like to look at several specific models for understanding community in general, to demonstrate how they might be applied to the structures of community in jazz, as well as ways in which each falls short.

Community Models: The Imagined Community

A particular feature of broadly defined jazz communities is that the members of the community often have little actual interaction. The further away we move from local music scenes, the more this is the case. Relationships between members are largely constructed through media, whether recordings, trade magazines such as *Jazz Times* or *Down Beat*, films, and increasingly, virtual networks. Since jazz's emergence into popular and artistic culture, published, written discourses have served to facilitate jazz musicians' and fans' sense of identity within a larger community. One of the most influential studies of community to appear in the last several decades was written by Benedict Anderson, whose 1983 book *Imagined Communities* has become a standard, oft-cited model for conceptualizing of communities across distances. Intended to refer to members of nation-states in the formation of nationalist community sentiment, he refers to such communities as "imagined because the members of even the smallest nation will never know most of their fellow-members, meet them, or even hear of them, yet in the minds of each lives the image of their communion" (Anderson 1983, 6). Anderson further argues that the construction of such communities is enabled by mass media, specifically in his example, print, and later broadcasting. Although intended to refer to political constructs, Anderson's model of imagined community can explain a great deal about jazz—fans, critics, musicians, and others who share an interest in the music feel connected to one another through a shared interest, and through the mass dissemination of recordings, publication, and increasingly, virtual media.

Perhaps most notable in Anderson's work is his frequent employment of the concept of "print-capitalism" as a primary means of constructing community on the national level. According to Anderson, the advent of printing provided the means for geographically dispersed members of a nation to understand themselves as part of a national culture. Through print-capitalism, a growing sense of connection between members of the nation-state is fostered, leading members to construct for themselves a sense of national identity, to *imagine* their own place as members of an entity larger than themselves. The print-capitalism of jazz might include major trade magazines, reviews of recordings and performances, columns in newspapers, biographical and historical texts, recording liner notes, and similar types of media. Even the most casual jazz fans have, at one point or another, read something about the music, and the role of print-capitalism in the creation of a widely accepted and disseminated jazz canon is clearly an expression of this idea. The identity of a "jazz nation," if I may be forgiven for employing this term, strongly resembles the types of nationalist ideas advanced by Anderson, with certain core narratives and individuals shared by many of its members.

Through his focus on the role of print-capitalism in the formation of this imagined community, Anderson makes an implicit distinction between literate and oral cultures. This distinction was forcefully critiqued in an article by Peter Wogan in *Anthropological Theory*, who suggests that Anderson's focus on the cognitive effects of print-capitalism ignores important aspects of identity and community formation. Wogan notes, "it is clear that Anderson links print with cognition, since print accounts for the major cognitive transformations that engender imagined, national communities" (Wogan 2001, 404), and that Anderson's theories are "based on a systematic opposition between print and orality, which can be represented in the following series of binary oppositions," which include a sharp distinction between cognitive and emotional responses to information (411). As print-capitalism is primarily cognitive in how it generates community, oral traditions are, it follows, based more on an emotional response. This link between the printed word and cognition is reflective of the work of Walter Ong (who, it should be noted, is not mentioned in Anderson's text at all, and by Wogan only in passing). Ong's theories of the cognitive nature of orality and literacy, namely that the former precludes abstracted theoretical thought, while the latter represents a "restructuring" of consciousness, have been both influential and controversial.

But binary distinctions between orality and literacy, whether expressed as part of a legitimizing discourse on the nature of jazz, or implicitly suggested by Anderson as a feature of community in modern societies, are at best artificial, and at worst dangerously naïve.[21] Moreover, print-based intellectual, cognitive knowledge is only one means by which jazz audiences come to *know* the music. While print-capitalism certainly has played an important role in connecting members of jazz communities, the primary form of connection among and between members of jazz communities is an emotional one. The aesthetic experience of the music draws members in more than do the cognitive processes of print-capitalism. Yet these emotional bonds are also largely the product of a process of mass-mediation, of recordings. Perhaps the jazz community as "imagined" can be thought of not as a function of print-capitalism, but of "record-capitalism." As Stanley Crouch notes, jazz recordings often served as a way for listeners to "imagine" their own place within the jazz world: "In my mother's house, I found myself listening to those *In A Mellotone* Ellington pieces over and over and over, imagining the world for which they were originally made. . . . In my room, I imagined the dance halls across America that my mother spoke of with such joy and reverence" (Crouch 2007, 2–3). For Crouch, the recording served as a link to another part of the jazz community, to which his connection was imagined (in his own words) through the media of recordings. Clearly, then, recordings serve some of the "nationalizing" function of Anderson's print-capitalism, and shares this function with other forms of mass media. Pekka Gronow makes such relationships explicit, writing that: "Common sense tells us that sound recording—that is, records and cassettes—is a mass medium just like newspapers, films or television. In industrialized countries, listening to records is as much a part of everyday life as reading the newspaper or listening to the radio" (Gronow 2004, 108).

At some level, the mediating effect of mass recordings constructs a sense of shared identity, of community, similar to that of print media. But I would suggest that not all media are created equal, or more to the point, not all media have the same effect on the recipient. As a medium of sound, recordings exist in a sphere that is neither oral nor written, implicating both cognition and emotion. Along with Crouch's account of recordings as constructing an imagined community in which he could place himself, there is also a strong undercurrent of emotional connection through sound. The effect of the recording is not simply one of connecting a listener to the community in their own mind, but is more visceral, and Anderson's model of imagined community only goes so far to this end. I will return to this point later in the chapter.

Community Models: The Art World

Almost any jazz performance requires a collaborative effort between different entities: producers, managers, recording engineers, publicists, and so forth, not to mention the musicians themselves. While performers are often positioned as the primary forces behind the creation of music, an inclusive definition of the jazz community might include many different individuals, not simply fulltime professional performers. In publicity materials for its annual conference, the now-defunct International Association for Jazz Education (IAJE) suggested that its meeting, billed as the "largest gathering of the global jazz community," might attract:

- Arrangers
- Artist managers
- Arts administrators
- Band directors
- Booking agents
- Choral music directors
- Composers
- Elementary educators
- Enthusiasts
- Festival producers
- Foundations
- Historians
- Instrument manufacturers
- Journalists
- Librarians
- Musicians
- Music merchants
- Music supervisors
- Presenters
- Publicists
- Publishers
- Radio announcers

- Radio program directors
- Record label managers
- School administrators
- String directors
- Students
- Technologists
- Travel agents
- And anyone involved in the teaching, performance, presentation, business, and/or appreciation of jazz music.

While the inclusion of travel agents as members of the jazz community might seem odd at first glance, musicians do travel, and in the current climate of heightened security and scrutiny of large carry-on bags in air travel, travel agents who are sensitive to the needs of musicians are highly valued. But the extent to which such individuals are either involved with jazz activities or how they self-identify as members of a jazz community varies.

Certainly some non-performers are considered part of the community, and in fact, jazz discourses seem to "bestow" membership on a select few. As is the case with all musical forms in which there is some commercial involvement, jazz has been subject to the forces of both the market and individuals whose jobs influence the place of jazz within such markets. At the local level, many musicians are responsible for conducting their own business affairs, booking performances, handling tasks such as collection of fees and accounting, and conducting other business matters. Musicians at higher levels (of both ability and visibility) often engage specialists to manage these things, and in many cases, such individuals have played important roles in directing the development of the music itself. For instance, individuals involved with the production and distribution of jazz recordings have exerted enormous influence on the music.

The role of producers, and of recording in general, in what is a seen as a fundamentally improvised art form, is difficult to pin down. Michael Jarrett notes that producers "stood between . . . artist and public" and thus "profoundly affected what came to count as jazz or improvised music" (Jarrett 2004, 322). Jarrett also suggests, however, that in an improvised music such as jazz, the role of the producer is suspect, as musicians provide the main impetus: "John Coltrane simply didn't need Bob Thiele, Miles Davis didn't need George Avakian, and Charles Mingus didn't need Nat Hentoff—at least not in the way that the Ronettes needed Phil Spector or the Beatles needed George Martin. Jazz producers generally concede that their power resides in invisibility; their art, in concealing itself" (Jarrett 2004, 323).

Nevertheless, some record producers see themselves as instrumental in developing the sound of musicians in the 1960s and 1970s. Teo Macero, for example, was especially important to guiding Miles Davis's recordings for Columbia in the late 1960s. His work, for example, on Davis's seminal fusion album *Bitches Brew* went well beyond simply guiding the direction of the sessions, and into that of a creative collaborator. As George Cole notes:

> Macero had no doubts about the role he played on *Bitches Brew*. "I'm a composer. I'm a co-composer rather than a producer. He'd just finish a piece and I was let loose. I'd ask Miles 'Can you do it again? And he'd say no.'" . . . Macero believes that his role was similar to that of George Martin with the Beatles. "I was like George Martin. I had a similar role with Miles. . . . They should get down on their knees and thank George Martin. They don't give producers the credit." (Cole 2007, 22)

Davis himself seems a bit more reluctant to attribute to Macero such a role: "We started early in the day in Columbia's studio on 52nd Street and recorded all day for three days in August. I had told Teo Macero, who was producing the record, to just let the tapes run and get everything we played, told him to get *everything* and not to be coming in interrupting, asking questions. 'Just stay in the booth and worry about getting down the sound,' is what I told him" (Davis and Troupe 1989, 299). While the events of the session are described in roughly the same way, Davis leaves no room for interpretation as to who was in charge of the session. Perhaps Macero's comments about the Beatles thanking George Martin were meant to be applied to himself as well. All this illustrates the fungible identities of producers as related to artists. In some contexts, producers exert nearly complete control over the artist, while in other cases, as Davis seemed to indicate, they are there simply to get things down on tape. Even technical personnel are sometimes regarded as important members of the community. On the point of how engineers and other such industry figures might see themselves in relation to the larger jazz community, Ben Sidran suggests that famed recording engineer Rudy Van Gelder "is not unaware of his position in the jazz pantheon" (Sidran 1995, 310). If this sounds boastful, it only echoes what numerous other musicians and writers have said about him.[22]

We might expand this assessment to include not only those involved with jazz's production and recording, but also individuals involved with the creation of its discourses and historical narratives. Jazz community must be understood as a function of not only performance-occupation, but of others involved with its creation and dissemination. A useful model for understanding this type of

jazz community can be found most readily in the work of influential sociologist Howard Becker, who as a student moonlighted as a professional jazz
pianist. It was this experience that led Becker to engage in what might rightly
be regarded as the first significant sociological studies of jazz community,
though they were not termed as such. Becker's book *Art Worlds* proposes an
artistic community that includes many of these different constituencies. As
he writes, reflecting on his own experiences as a musician: "Maybe the years I
spent playing the piano in taverns in Chicago and elsewhere led me to believe
that the people who did the mundane work were as important to an understanding of art as the better known players who produced the recognized
classics of jazz . . . the craftsmen who help make art works are as important as
the people who conceive them" (Becker 1982, ix). He continues: "All artistic
work, like all human activity, involves the joint activity of a number, often a
large number, of people. Through their cooperation, the art work we eventually see or hear comes to be and continues to be" (Becker 1982, 1). For Becker,
the art world involves a cooperative effort between artists and others whose
work (a term Becker uses repeatedly and with emphasis) is essential to the creation and distribution of the art. Thus, the jazz community, to apply Becker's
theory, *must* include the Teo Maceros and Rudy Van Gelders of the world,
and given their role interpreting work for audiences, the Leonard Feathers
and Nat Hentoffs as well.

Peter Martin's critique of Merriam and Mack borrows heavily (and intentionally) from Becker's work. Martin suggests, in fact, that the jazz community could be best understood as an "art world":

> The concept of the art world is particularly appropriate in that it delib-
> erately includes not only players, but audience members, promoters,
> journalists, educators, agents, record producers, and so on—in short
> everyone whose activity collectively contributes to the creation of the
> jazz world, in terms of both real situations and the symbolic representa-
> tions which sustain our sense of that world as a community to which we
> belong. (P. Martin 2005, 10)

The key passage here is that the community includes "everyone whose activity
collectively contributes to the creation of the jazz world." What it means, precisely, to "contribute" is not clear in all cases. Certainly, performers contribute
through performance, club owners contribute by keeping and maintaining
venues, records stores make recordings available. But what of the audience?
What role do they play in the creation of the jazz world? Martin notes, in
addressing Scott DeVeaux's much discussed 1995 analysis of the jazz audience

for the National Endowment for the Arts, "Two other points from DeVeaux's analysis may be noted here—firstly the relatively large proportion of the jazz audience who themselves play or have played instruments at some level, and secondly the clear separation between the general audience for the music and the much smaller group who are active participants in the jazz scene" (P. Martin 2005, 8). I find Martin's treatment of the audience in this passage to be dismissive, particularly in his distinction between the "general audience" and those who are "active participants in the jazz scene." Nowhere in Martin's essay does he state what it means to be an "active participant," though one might extrapolate from the passage above that he would include the audience members who were, at some level, players.

Both Martin's model, and that of Howard Becker from which it is drawn, suffer from the same critical flaw. Neither study makes a significant claim for members of the audience as a part of the art world, or by extension, as a part of the jazz community. For Becker, the audience is often portrayed not as a participant in the community or the process of creating an art work, but almost as an obstacle that must be overcome on some level. Martin's non-assessment of the role of the audience as an active part of the community reflects a similar avoidance of in-depth discussions of the audience. While Becker does make some arguments concerning degrees of knowledge among more "serious" members of the audience who possess a greater understanding of technical aspects of the art form (Becker 1982, 54), he seldom treats the audience as much more than a receiver of the art work; serious audiences are those that are able to do this more effectively, but they are still not equal stakeholders in the art world, and their unique identities are largely absent. Audiences inhabit the end of a continuum of production-distribution-consumption, and the dynamics of relationships *between* members of the audience are conspicuously absent. The production of the art work still seems to be one that is at the heart of a *hierarchy* within the community. In this scenario, audiences are not participatory members of the community, but are cast in economic terms, how their involvement affects musicians' financial stability. Their status as participants in the community is dependent upon their patronage of performance, or in Martin's case, their involvement with it.

Community Models: Sense of Community

In the classic sociological view of jazz community, Merriam/Mack and Stebbins privilege performance-occupation as the defining feature of the group. For Anderson, membership within community is constructed through mediation; Becker (and Martin) suggests that community is a collaborative process that is centered on the creation and dissemination of art works. What all these perspectives lack is a sense of the internalization of community identification. How do individuals who feel that they are part of a jazz community come to such a conclusion? What path leads them to a self-identification with others who share similar ideas? Internalized processes such as these are inherently psychological, and it is to psychology that I turn for yet another model for understanding community, a "sense of community," a term popularized in the 1980s by psychologists David McMillan and David Chavis, whose studies on the psychological formations of community are still considered to be important models.[23] McMillan and Chavis argued that identification with community is largely a psychological process that defines our connections to others with whom we identify. Specifically, they cite four main factors in fostering a sense of community: membership, influence, integration and fulfillment of needs, and shared emotional connection. In invoking a term like "jazz community," users of the term rarely contextualize its use with these types of conversations. While the full scope of McMillan and Chavis's theory is beyond this study, their discussion of membership within communities can provide us with some important insights into how individuals place themselves within the community. As McMillan and Chavis argue, "Membership [in the community] is a feeling that one has invested oneself to become a member and therefore has a right to belong" (McMillan and Chavis 1986, 9).

What is notable here is the emphasis on individual agency and perspective. A "feeling that one has invested oneself" implies that community membership is largely a process of self-selection and self-identification. Following this idea, anyone can, given the proper "feeling" and level of "investment," be a member of the community. At the same time, they argue that communities must have boundaries, that "there are people who belong and people who do not" (McMillan and Chavis 1986, 4). Many of the elements of early research on the jazz community that might seem pathological or at odds with prevailing social norms can be interpreted as boundaries, in some form; "language, dress and ritual" are key elements of such boundaries (4). These might manifest themselves as the type of "anti-social" behavior that Merriam and Mack note. Similarly, a sense of isolation from society of which they write could be seen as the institution of a boundary, though the question of who erects this boundary, the community or the "outside," remains open. Nevertheless, at some level, such "deviant" behavior has at least some basis in practice.[24] Dizzy Gillespie, in his autobiography *To Be or Not To Bop*, discusses some of the "myths" surrounding bebop, and while seeking to dispel some of the more outrageous ideas about this specific subculture, he does speak to the ways in which he and his peers created a unique style and in-group identity. The indulgence in certain behaviors created, for the bebop generation, a sense of community outside the mainstream. In assessing the nature of the community, later researchers failed, it seems, to look beyond them.

Thus we have a juxtaposition of inclusion, based on a person's feeling they have an investment and therefore a right to belong, with a clear sense of exclusion, cultivated from within the community. This duality has been problematic in jazz discourses. Unlike a municipality or nation, with clear geographic divisions that delineate communities (and even these are problematic), clear delineations in jazz are difficult to establish. Some feel that fusion is not jazz, and such a distinction might exclude fusion players from the community. Other boundaries might be drawn based upon occupation (performers, writers, fans, and so on), ability (higher level players as opposed to beginners, who might not be included in the community by some). If membership in the jazz community is truly defined by interest in the music, then where are the boundaries? How is interest objectively measured, and how does it play out in terms of relative identity?

Extending McMillan and Chavis's arguments concerning membership in the community, the authors suggest that membership is further determined by the ideas of "emotional safety," a "sense of belonging and identification," "personal investment," and a "common symbol system." Let us apply these criteria to jazz specifically. In what ways might jazz provide "emotional safety" for its members? Jazz is clearly an emotional issue for many people, if some of the more hyperbolic statements about the music are taken into account. Expressions of liking, passion, and support for jazz often draw upon romanticized language and imagery. As Bill Frisell notes in the recent documentary *Icons Among Us: Jazz in the Present Tense*, a jazz community might involve a shared space "where there's infinite possibilities, and no one gets hurt" (Ratliff 2009, E3). An interest in jazz thus carries both emotional investment and a sense of the community being a "safe space." Members of jazz communities are a passionate lot; they extrapolate philosophical and spiritual aspects of the music, rise to defend it against criticism, and combat apathy toward it. They are, in this respect, advocates for their music. The boundaries that are drawn between it and, say, popular music are not simply a matter of style; they are personal, a point of pride to be in opposition to more mainstream musical and cultural trends. Even within the community, boundaries are staunchly defended in emotional ways, with fans of lesser-liked genres (smooth jazz, as a notable example) sometimes ridiculed, told that it "isn't really jazz." This, by extension, suggests that they are not part of the community, and not entitled to its shared space.

In terms of a "common symbol system," jazz communities also reflect specific criteria for membership. Certain terms, modes of behavior, and assumptions are manifestly present in jazz discourse at many levels, and reinforce a sense of group identity. As McMillan and Chavis note, "Groups use these social conventions (e.g., rites of passage, language, dress) as boundaries intentionally to create social distance between members and nonmembers" (McMillan and Chavis 1986, 5–6). Such ideas can be commonly observed in jazz discourses; most jazz fans will immediately recognize that Bird is Charlie Parker, Trane is John Coltrane, Prez is Lester Young, and so forth. Among musicians themselves, an abstracted musical idea as simple as the twelve-bar blues can be seen as a common symbol; no matter where a jazz musician goes, chances are that if he or she were to start playing a twelve-bar blues, other jazz musicians would recognize it and be able to participate. Colloquial language has often served as a means of establishing the identity of jazz musicians and fans as a group, a point that has often perplexed and fascinated "outsiders." The "cultural separation" (Clark 2001, 319) of the jazz language was an integral part of identifying jazz communities as distinct subcultures in the minds of many, and the frequent peppering of press accounts of jazz musicians with slang terms has long been a motif in jazz journalism. The fascination with jazz's spoken language is underscored by the emergence of texts such as Robert Gold's noted *Jazz Lexicon*, in which the author argues that "the study of the vernacular of jazz is necessarily a study in sociology and social psychology . . ." (Gold 1964, xi).

McMillan and Chavis's research on the sense of community offers us a critical way of understanding membership in this community that is largely a matter of choice, of self-identification with what jazz *means* for each person who engages it, and how those experiences bind communities together and mark them off to the outside. It moves us beyond an emphasis on occupational specialty, role in artistic production and distribution, or print-capitalism. As each individual experience is unique, there can be no one set of attitudes or behaviors that cut across jazz experiences. This is why it is so useful as a means of understanding how relationships between members of jazz communities can be understood as a web of externalized and internalized processes. It also provides us with an expansive model for understanding community. Some might argue that this is too expansive, that a model that is based simply on how someone feels about their relationship to the community falls short of explaining the dynamics of social practice between its members. And indeed, this is a fair point; community is not simply a sense that is "all in our heads," but is a dynamic process of interaction. Language codes, behaviors, and other types of expression may be important, but they are not universally applicable; not all jazz musicians and fans use "jazz lingo" or dress in a certain manner. But interaction can manifest itself in many different ways, and in the following section, I want to propose another model for conceptualizing jazz community in a broad sense, one based on the presence and practice of sound itself.

A Community of Practice

We can certainly observe a number of specific practices in jazz. Chief among these is the act of performance, which one might argue is the central activity in the music. After all, without performance, jazz is simply an idea; performance makes the idea real, tangible, and most importantly for our discussion, able to be shared from one person to another. But what is the role of the non-performer in the performative process? Ethnomusicologists speak of non-Western conceptions of music cultures in which the "distinction between performer and audience" is minimized or, in exceptional cases, nonexistent. Such a continuum of performance-to-audience is often placed in direct opposition to Western norms, in which artist and audience are often segregated by an implicit (or sometimes explicit) barrier. Such tropes are perhaps somewhat romanticized in their presentation of Western and non-Western cultures as being essentially different in terms of the relationship between different parts of the performative moment. There is likely some truth to this idea. Relationships between performers and audiences are physically distant in all but a few cases in contemporary Western cultures in which jazz is practiced.

But does the fact the audiences come to the music primarily via recorded media mean that the relationship to the artist is artificial, or more to the point, that it is imagined? Does the fact that we listen to the music on records, or that we sit in an audience while the performer is on stage, really represent a disconnect between artist and audience as it relates to the practice of performance? If the practice of recording is one that is done with the intent that the resulting artifact (a CD, LP, or MP3 file, for example) will be listened to, then cannot the act of listening be a practice in itself? And, more importantly, is not the practice of listening to this recording an engagement with the original practice of making the recording itself? What I mean to say here is that recording, as a practice, must be understood to include an entire spectrum of activities, from performing the music, to engineering it and manufacturing the media, to distributing it. All these are activities that Becker might classify as being part of the "art world." The listener, however, also plays an important role in this practice. Listening, in essence, completes the process, and the act of listening might be said to represent one aspect of a community of practice.

What then is a community of practice? This concept emerged in the 1980s from cognitive anthropology, particularly the work of Jean Lave and Etienne Wenger. As Wenger argues, communities of practice are distinct from "communities of interest" in that the members of the former consist of "groups of people who share a concern or a passion for something they do and learn how to do it better as they interact regularly" (Wenger n.d.). He outlines three specific criteria for the CoP: "domain," "community," and "practice." Domain is analogous to discourse, the general field around which the practice takes place, around which the community is formed. It is the field as envisioned by its members. The community is predicated on the engagement in specific activities with each other, in an interactive way. The practice implies an active engagement in the field, beyond simple interest. Above all, Wenger argues that a CoP must move beyond a shared interest in a topic: "A community of practice is not merely a community of interest—people who like certain kinds of movies, for instance. Members of a community of practice are practitioners. They develop a shared repertoire of resources: experiences, stories, tools, ways of addressing recurring problems—in short a shared practice. This takes time and sustained interaction" (Wenger n.d.).

Wenger suggests that shared interest in and of itself does not rise to a level of engagement such that it might be designated as a practice. It might, on the surface, seem to suggest that jazz communities are simply communities of interest, involving groups of individuals who share a love for jazz. Talking about recordings within a group of individuals might reflect such a community. At the same time, group listening as a social practice, or a community of practice, is not a completely new concept in studies of music. The late Lise Waxer, in her ethnographic study of salsa in Columbia, writes that records served as a basis for the formation of community groups, a sort of "vinyl museum" in which aficionados of recorded music could meet and listen to music together, creating a space (and community) for a shared practice (Waxer 2002, 111). Jeffery Jackson likewise cites group listening as an important formative element in the emergence of the community of jazz critics and scholars in 1930s France (Jackson 2003, 183). Similarly, Stanley Crouch writes of his own efforts to create a listening-based community, writing, "Before I was out of high school I started a jazz record club to which we would bring our recordings, listen to them, and discuss what we thought we were hearing" (Crouch 2007, 1). Recordings also proved central to the creation of pedagogical communities. Sheila Anderson cites the experience of Milwaukee-based musician Gerald Cannon, who notes, in a discussion of how he learned to play, that "I went berserk listening to records. Once I got hooked on jazz, I spent all my money on jazz records. My buddies and I would listen and talk about the music" (S.

Anderson 2005, 33). Paul Berliner recounts that trombonist and composer Melba Liston and her associates would spend hours "listening to records together, humming the solos till we learned them" (Berliner 1994, 96). Clearly, then, group listening was an important "social activity" (Berliner 1994, 96) in many jazz communities.

Yet accounts such as these, as important as they are to the study of community formation within specific music cultures, do not speak specifically to the relationship between an individual and a recorded artist as a community of practice in itself. Entities such as these are the exception in jazz listening, which is more often done individually. It might seem difficult to think of a single person listening to a recording as an engagement with community. But when we consider the active role that listeners play within the processes of the continuum of recording- listening, we can, I believe, see that listening is not simply a passive act that serves to express an individual's interest in the music. This runs counter to prevailing views on recording technology's effect on the relationships between artists and audiences. Recording is often viewed as a temporal and spatial barrier between the artist and the audience; and mediation is a disruption in the interaction between them, and seemingly antithetical to the creation of community, an artificial and inferior intervention into a more organic relationship based on live performance. Walter Benjamin, in his influential 1936 essay "The Work of Art in the Age of Mechanical Reproduction," argues that mechanical reproduction of an art work serves to destroy the "aura" of that work, the authority it holds for the audience (Benjamin 1968, 221). While Benjamin's essay focused on film, scholars have readily applied his ideas to recorded sound, and to jazz in particular. Karl Coulthard, in an essay on the application of Benjamin's theories of mechanical reproduction to jazz recording, argues a commonly held view that jazz recordings do indeed "lose" something in the transition from live to mediated performance. Coulthard argues:

> One of the most obvious effects of sound recordings is that they radically alter the space of performance, both for the performer and listener. . . . In the studio, however, the jazz musician is removed from this environment, lacking, like the film actor, [quoting Benjamin] "the opportunity of the stage actor to adjust to the audience during his performance," as his "part is acted not for an audience but for a metal contrivance." (Coulthard 2007)

I do not dispute the core argument that listening to live performances and recordings are intrinsically different acts, but I suggest that Coulthard's analysis misses one crucial point: with the exception of "live" recordings, which themselves form a minority of jazz's recorded *oeuvre*, jazz recordings are made with intent, that is to say, with the intent that they will be listened to and reproduced *as recordings*. They are, contrary to Coulthard's claim, explicitly "designed for reproducibility" (Benjamin 1968, 224). There is no aura to be dissipated, as it did not exist in the first place. Or did it? "The audience is also removed from the performance environment and placed in the position of listening to music that is played, essentially, by a metal contrivance. They cannot experience the physical and visual presence, the 'aura' of the musicians, nor can they interact with them and directly affect the music that is being produced" (Coulthard 2007).

At the risk of sounding dismissive, I would suggest that this simply does not matter for the vast majority of jazz listeners, who have never heard, and will likely never hear, live performances by many iconic artists (especially those who are deceased). Their reality as jazz fans is that of the recording, and it is through that medium that they construct their place in community. Recordings, despite whatever flaws they may have, whatever reifying effects they might have for the canon and for the understanding of the music, are the core documents of the jazz tradition. Whether recordings are as "real" as performance is irrelevant. They simply *are*, and the choice between live and recorded performance is a false one. Both exist, both speak to audiences in different ways, and both have a role to play in creating and maintaining different types of communities. To assume that recordings are simply "poor substitutes" for live performance, to dismiss them as not possessing the aura of live music, is to miss a crucial opportunity to understand how relationships in jazz are constructed. Coulthard is correct in stating that "jazz has existed in a kind of dual state developing both inside and outside of the recording space" (2007); where this perspective errs is in its assumption that there is an inherent loss in going between them. Is live performance "better" than recordings? Perhaps, but again, this is beside the point. Recordings are what they are, and they remain an important means of connecting artists and audiences through sound.

Timothy Taylor, writing of the social nature of the production and distribution of technology vis-à-vis consumption (listening) writes: "at the moment of its invention, any technological artifact does not yet have a social history or use, even though it was produced in a social setting. That is, the social production of technology is quite different from its subsequent social uses" (Taylor 2001, 16). Taylor's reference to technology being "produced in a social setting" resonates with Becker's and Martin's conception of the "art world" in which the production of a work of art (in this case a recording) occurs within the context of a web of interaction between many different actors. Like the art world, the world of recording within a social context is distinct from its audience and its subsequent social uses and applications.

I would suggest that the social nature of recordings, as "consumed" by listeners, need not be so clearly segregated from the production and distribution of the work. Taylor's analysis ignores an important social element of the creation of a technologically mediated representation of an art work: recordings, by their very nature, *are* social. What I mean is that a recording's social use beyond the studio or production facility *is* part of the conceptualization of the work itself. Recordings are made with the intent of being listened to, and thus the listening is part of the social process of its production. In a studio recording, what *is* the work of art? It is not simply a reproduction, but it is unique to that moment, at that time. Moreover, the recording, as constituted by performers playing into a microphone, through a mixer, and onto a fixed medium for the purposes of transmission, *is* the art work. It does not exist in any other meaningful time or space; the recording is made for, and exists for, its transmission to the audience. The musical work as performed cannot be separated from the medium. The medium is, as Marshall McLuhan suggested, the same as the message.

Listening can be seen a type of practice in and of itself, or at least a participation in a practice that begins with the act of playing or singing into a microphone in a recording studio, and ends with the listener hearing that same sound. Listeners engage with performers in a way that is very real, very tangible, and very much, I suggest, a type of community that, while not specifically a community of practice as envisioned by Wenger, is nonetheless more than simply a community of interest. Practice involves a network of interactions and relationships between various actors, all of whom inhabit different roles and possess varying degrees of power relative to one another. As Sherry Ortner writes, such a "practice theory" allows us to envision different parts of the "system"—say, artists and audiences—as a single unit in which various forces interact: "A practice approach has no need to break the system into artificial chunks like base and superstructure (and to argue over which determines which), since the analytic effort is not to explain one chunk of the system by referring it to another chunk, but rather to explain the system as an integral whole (which is not to say a harmoniously integrated one) by referring it to practice" (Ortner 1984, 150).

Taylor suggests that Ortner's framework provides a useful way of understanding the relationships between individual agency and the "determinism" of technology. In his view, technology serves the purpose of a "structure" in that it "entails agency" (Taylor 2001, 37). But whether the technology itself is an agent in the relationships between artist and listener may be beside the point. What is more important to the present discussion is the agency of the listener, and their role in completing the process that begins with the making of the recording. In engaging with the sonic representation of an artist's performance, listeners themselves have agency, and are engaged in a practice with both the technology, and more importantly, with the artists who made the recording.

The community of practice of a *recording-listening continuum*, therefore, is not a fixed entity in terms of geography, or even time. Such communities transcend space and time, stretching across boundaries determined only by where and when a recording is played. At that moment, and that moment only, the practice is complete, and the community comes to full fruition, incorporating all of the constituent elements that were involved in the production, distribution, *and* reception of the work. I thus differ with Benjamin in his contention that the reproduction of the work destroys its "aura," its sense of authenticity. In fact, I suggest that the reverse may be true in that jazz records often serve the exact opposite purpose, as a means of creating aura. The experience in listening to a jazz recording is "not a mere surrogate concert" (Small 1998, 76), but an emotional, visceral experience. Listeners feel connected to the artists through recordings, and feel a sense of closeness, rather than the distancing effects of mediation. As Christopher Small notes, "[Listeners] are in fact free to create their own sonic space, their own ambience, and thus their own ritual, centered on the recorded sounds, in a way that is not possible in the highly mediated space of the concert hall" (Small 1998, 76). In creating their own rituals, listeners can also participate in their own communities. Thus a listener who puts on a recording of Armstrong's Hot Fives, for example, is engaging in an act of community with Louis Armstrong that is not simply imagined; the connection between the artist and the listener is not simply on a cognitive level. It is also deeply emotional, and must be understood in ways that move beyond the construction of a shared identification with the genre.

Reactions to hearing recorded jazz reflect this idea. Berliner notes that musicians who listen to jazz often have pointed emotional reactions to what they hear: "[jazz rhythm section] veterans listening to records display their delight at high points in the individual performances of rhythm section players through spontaneous outbursts of laughter, or by miming the precise gesture, a pianist's unusual comping pattern or a drummer's kicks" (Berliner 1998, 388). Similarly, author Quincy Troupe describes his own experience listening to jazz in very strong, personal terms: "The title track [from Miles Davis's album *Bags Groove*] 'Bags Groove,' named after vibraphonist Milt 'Bags' Jackson and recorded in 1954, was the first jazz music that went straight to my heart and brain, not to mention my body. It had something in it that just moved me to my core, something way beyond what I expected to experience listening to a jazz tune" (Troupe 2000, 118). The reference here to "heart and brain" speaks to the dual nature of cognitive and emotional connection via recorded media I alluded to previously; it is, as Constantijn Koopman suggests, a "holistic" experience (Koopman 2005, 88). Accounts such as these are not simply about how one comes to understand the music as a genre, or on a stylistic or technical level, though these are certainly possible outcomes of listening to a recording. They speak as well to the creation of a deep, emotional connection between listener and artist, one that is, I suggest, at the core of the practice of listening-recording. It is precisely for this reason that an artist records, to connect with listeners in such a way.

After performance, the act of listening to recorded jazz might be the most readily identifiable activity among all those individuals who align themselves with jazz.[25] Because of this, I might suggest that this is a more effective and meaningful way to understand jazz community on a vast, non-localized scale, an activity that is not only shared among nearly all the community's members, but also one that in itself represents an engagement between artists and audiences. It is difficult to conceptualize of any self-proclaimed member of the jazz community who would not engage in the practice of listening to the music in some way, at some point. It is, more than any other single activity, that which ties all of the various constituents together. And understanding listeners as critical participants in the processes of recording-listening positions them as crucial stakeholders in the community. The jazz community is not one that is defined by occupation, by production, or by generalized assumptions about race, gender, or performance practice. The shared space between artist and audience is the nexus of a sense of jazz community that binds together disparate constituencies, gives its members a common set of symbols, and allows performers, producers, and fans to both imagine their community and to actively participate within it. Despite Benjamin's suggestions to the contrary, the aura of the jazz art work, and of the artist, is not destroyed through mechanical reproduction, but created anew. This aura has a powerful attraction for jazz fans, and it remains a potent force in jazz discourses.

This community built on listening makes jazz artists and fans, and everyone in between, stakeholders in the same community. But other community structures can also be identified in jazz, and in the following chapters I wish to examine some specific sites where knowledge and claims to authority about jazz are contested, and how communities arise from this process. These communities can take many forms, and almost always reflect some effort to define or otherwise create a boundary between the group and those perceived to be on the outside. In some cases, communities must negotiate a precarious existence relative to traditions and practices not just of jazz, but other institutions and discourses that exert influence upon them. In the next chapter, we will consider a specific context in which these forces come to bear on a jazz community that has often been neglected in jazz scholarship, that of institutionalized jazz education, and how the entrance of jazz into academic life presents challenges of aesthetics, identity, and power for its practitioners, for whom competing traditions require a delicate balancing act.

CHAPTER 2

Jazz Education and the Tightrope of Tradition[1]

The Place of Jazz Education in the Jazz World

There are perhaps few discourses as contentious among jazz communities as those of jazz's move into educational institutions over the last half century, especially at the college level. Jazz education runs the gamut from limited programs featuring a performing jazz group to advanced professional training programs, often housed within established schools of music. Instruction often moves well beyond the ensemble (though big bands still form the core of most university-level programs) into detailed coursework in jazz improvisation, arranging/composition, jazz history, and other areas. In addition, post-secondary jazz students often must complete additional coursework in Western art music history and theory, as well as applied study on their instrument(s), all of which is often a major complaint among both students and teachers. At the highest levels, post-secondary jazz students perform at a level comparable to many professional jazz musicians, and students from such programs often find employment with professional musicians. More often, however, students emerging from such programs must make their own way in an increasingly competitive and economically challenging jazz scene. The numbers of students who graduate with degrees in jazz has become a point of concern for some critics and musicians, who see the jazz world as being glutted with young musicians with no real professional experience, and who perform in very codified, standardized ways. Such attitudes resonate with longstanding tensions between academic and non-academic constituencies in musical study, tensions that are unlikely to go away as jazz programs continue to develop.

Although jazz education has never been fully accepted as part of the larger jazz community, the forces that shape community in jazz are certainly felt within the walls of the music school;[2] communities can be found among the members of various applied studios, within ensembles, and among fields of study or musical approaches. But not all community groups in the music school are determined by self-identification. Students are often placed into course sequences based on grade level, which does not always correspond to the types of social networks common among musicians outside the academy. Student ensembles are determined by audition and, in some cases, by necessity of instrumentation. Any given freshman may have more in common with a doctoral student whose ability levels are similar than to students in their own student cohort. The tension between institutionally defined communities, as determined by major, grade level, and assessment, exist in tension with the seemingly more organic, emergent communities that result from everyday interaction among musicians. Such arrangements often create difficulties for students and teachers who yearn for a more "real" experience than can seemingly be offered within the curriculum.

Indeed, the narratives of jazz education—both from the perspective of individual students, and from that of institutions—are rife with accounts of such difficulties. Students who complain of having to meet requirements of Western art music performance or history often find their teachers in jazz studies to be sympathetic, but powerless to do much about it. The experience of jazz in academia is one in which the distinctions between histories, practices, and communities themselves are brought into relief, often in conflict with each other. As academic communities are those in which the construction, organization, and assessment of knowledge are critical factors in day-to-day life, the ways that jazz educators and students understand their relationship to jazz's histories and practices greatly influence both teaching and identity.

Identity, Community and the History of Jazz Education

The relationship between jazz educators and those within the non-academic jazz community very often has been a troubling one. In particular, academic jazz programs often have been accused of being too far removed from the traditions of jazz as they developed through performance and informal learning situations.[3] The prevailing narratives of the history of jazz education also reinforce the perceptions of a fundamental distinction between academic and non-academic identities. This narrative serves a distinct purpose, in which an institutional identity becomes not only one segment of an historical process, but also a way to contextualize jazz within musical study in higher education. Jazz education has recently come to a self-awareness in terms of its own history, with the emergence of a sub-field dedicated to its own historical development, centered on an "institutional narrative" highlighting developments at important schools. The most widespread version of this narrative is articulated in a 1994 article in the *Jazz Educators Journal* by Daniel Murphy, which has become something of an official history of jazz education.[4] Studies such as Murphy's draw from a limited literature on the subject arising from the 1970s and the 1980s, when jazz educators presumably came to the conclusion that jazz education had a history worth documenting. This was itself a critical step for a field whose roots were somewhat recent; when Charles (Chuck) Suber's survey of the field appeared in *Down Beat*, formalized jazz education was only a few decades old. But there was a growing recognition that there was in fact something worth documenting, that jazz education had a history of its own.

We can identity three periods of historical development in the literature of jazz education's history. The first, from the beginnings of jazz to the 1940s, is usually treated as a kind of prehistoric era, with little or no records of pedagogical activities in jazz. Activities that did take place are treated as prototypical, positioned as events that, in the long run, served mainly as forerunners to later developments. Second, there is a clear chronological boundary drawn during the 1940s with the establishment of curricular activities at a number of institutions, most notably North Texas State College (now UNT) and the Schillinger House in Boston (now Berklee). For many historians, this marks the birth of formal jazz education. Third, jazz education between the 1960s and 1980s is positioned as a period of immense growth, when the fledgling movement of the 1940s comes into its own. Although the specifics of organizational structure vary, what has been described above is repeated frequently in historical accounts of the field.

In jazz education's "prehistoric" period, jazz is squarely positioned as part of the oral tradition. William T. (Ted) McDaniel connects this perception of jazz's orality with early methods of instruction, saying, perhaps somewhat obviously, that it was "highly likely that jazz instruction began with the first jazz musicians, and the historical context of these artists requires examination" (McDaniel 1993, 119). Yet the examination that McDaniel calls for is not readily forthcoming. In fact, the context of which he speaks is, in the next paragraph, relegated to a romanticized oral tradition:

> The jazz tradition was oral, reflecting the African-American music history of passing down songs from generation to generation, group to group, and person to person. The evolution of the blues and the subsequent development of new instrumental expression [one would assume McDaniel refers here to jazz] during the first quarter of the twentieth century by "parlor house professors"—the early jazz artists who worked in the bars and bordellos—wind instrument players indicate that a great deal of teaching must have and did occur. (McDaniel 1993, 119)

Such historical overviews of early jazz education proceed directly from an assumed oral tradition to the inclusion of jazz at certain institutions without drawing a link between one and the other, and these early pedagogical processes are usually forgotten once jazz comes to college.[5] Moreover, the attribution of jazz to a purely oral tradition is itself problematic, as many early jazz musicians were musically literate, particularly those involved with publishing and composition.

A second aspect of this prehistory discussion deals with the development of methodologies, and of early jazz activity on college campuses, particularly historically black colleges and universities.[6] McDaniel, for example, points to the role of musicians such as W. C. Handy as representing an alternative to the commonly accepted belief that jazz education began at certain predominantly white institutions:

> Interestingly, W. C. Handy,[7] the famous "Father of the Blues" and bandmaster, may have been the first jazz educator in a school. In 1900, he was appointed bandmaster at Teacher's Agricultural and Mechanical College for Negroes at Normal, Alabama. While there, he taught many students the techniques and music which, in later years, would be called jazz. Contrary to popular belief, jazz education was not born at North Texas State. (McDaniel 1993, 115)

The reference to Handy presents us with perhaps the first documented account of an accomplished, recognized musician entering the field of jazz education (such as it was at the time). More germane to the present discussion, we can observe that this passage, laying claim to the earliest documented reference to jazz education, clings to an institutionally driven narrative. The emphasis is squarely on the inclusion of jazz within an academic context, with little or no regard for how it got there. Even as McDaniel presents this citation as a counternarrative, he himself reinscribes it by positioning it as *institutional* history. Rather than jazz education being born at one school as in one popular version of the institutional narrative (a version which McDaniel critiques forcefully), it is simply historically relocated to another.

Educator and bandleader Len Bowden is presented as another early innovator in jazz education, directing ensembles and likely some classes at other predominantly black colleges throughout the 1920s and 1930s. Warrick Carter positions Bowden as "the true pioneer of jazz pedagogy" (Carter 1986, 10), as the director of bands at several historically black colleges and universities (HBCUs), though the specifics of his work are not given. During World War II he directed the training program for black musicians at the Great Lakes

Naval Training Center in Chicago. The ways in which his activities at the Greats Lakes center have been interpreted by jazz education historians illustrate how an institutional perspective has affected the field's historiography. Returning to Murphy's essay, Bowden's experiences at Great Lakes are presented as a model for future programs in jazz education:

> In many respects, the Great Lakes program was one of the birthplaces of formal jazz pedagogy. Alumni included such notable performers as Clark Terry, Frank Greer, Jimmy Wilkins, and Major Holly. Educators such as Bowden were the first to define a basic curriculum that is still considered fundamental in contemporary approaches to preparing jazz musicians. . . . these bands were the first testing grounds for pedagogical techniques and a major catalyst for the school jazz ensemble movement. (D. Murphy 1994, 35)

Murphy's use of the terms *testing ground* and *catalyst* imply that such a program is a preliminary or intermediate step toward something presumably bigger and better that is to follow. These activities are validated for their transitional quality, in relation to later institutional developments. Their significance as part of the wider cultural discourse about jazz at the time is not considered. I would also note the changing nature of the content of the passage through a number of reinterpretations. Murphy cites the material in this section as originating from a 1977 article by Warrick Carter entitled "Jazz in the College Curriculum." Carter's original passage (cited by Murphy as a source) reads:

> Typical of these pioneers is Len Bowden, whose involvement with college jazz goes back as far as 1919. . . . Bowden was later to direct the training and education of one of the largest number of musicians ever to be undertaken in this country. As director for the training of the black musicians at Great Lakes Navy Base (1942–45), Len participated in the music education of over 5,000 men, all of whom were expected to function as jazz (dance) as well as military band musicians. . . . The learning environment provided by the early pioneers parallels the courses suggested for today's jazz studies curriculum. (Carter 1977, 52–53)

In a 1986 article Carter refers to Bowden's activities in a similar tone, as does McDaniel later (McDaniel 1993, 120). Murphy's interpretation of Bowden's role at Great Lakes embellishes the accounts upon which his writing is based, but into what, and for what purpose? There is nothing in Carter's original account that would suggest that the Great Lakes center served as the "[birthplace] of formal jazz pedagogy" as Murphy suggests, nor does an oral history project conducted in 1976 by Carter, London Branch, and Samuel Floyd in which a number of musicians (including Bowden) were interviewed (Floyd et al. 1983, 41–60). In interpreting Bowden's work, Murphy constructs an identity that served as a logical precursor to institutional programs. We arrive at a coherent narrative where the development of jazz education is logically connected to later institutional efforts.

What is at issue is not the importance of these individuals as major figures in the development of the field. No one would argue that individuals such as Bowden and Handy were not important to both jazz and jazz education. To the contrary, it is the circumscribed nature of their relationship to the development of the field that makes their historiographic treatment so problematic. These discussions create a counternarrative that claims to challenge prevailing versions of the history of jazz education. Yet the ways in which their roles are constructed also represents a form of marginalization; they are, in this sense, positioned as precursors to the "real thing," when jazz will enter mainstream educational institutions. Moreover, their inclusion does not answer the central question of how the processes and practices of jazz were adapted into an academic context. This concept lies at the heart of understanding the relationships between "the street and the school."

While the emergence of the first major programs gets a great deal of coverage in this institutional narrative, the 1950s present another historiographic gap. Only passing mention is given to developments such as the National Stage Band Camps, or to the Lenox School of Jazz, which ran in the late 1950s. As there were few major institutional developments, the decade is often treated as a period of pedagogical coalescence; the narrative emphasizes the growth of high school ensembles, for example. What are not described are the more subtle pedagogical efforts of people like George Russell and Marshall Stearns. The place of Russell and Stearns (discussed later in this chapter and the following chapter, respectively) in the development of jazz education is important not simply because of institutional links, but because of their relationships to those outside of the academy; both men drew heavily upon their experiences with and connections to jazz musicians outside the academy. Likewise, the activities undertaken at the Lenox School of Jazz would prove important to the development of pedagogical methods later in the 1960s. Running for four summers from 1957 to 1960, Lenox brought together prominent jazz musicians and scholars with promising young musicians for a series of intensive workshops at the Music Inn in the Berkshires in western Massachusetts. With a faculty that represented a Who's Who of jazz in the 1950s—Oscar Peterson, Dizzy Gillespie, Max Roach, Bill Evans, Milt Jackson, and John Lewis are among the artists who taught in the program—Lenox addressed an important issue for jazz musicians in the late 1950s: the need for specialized, mentored learning in a professional jazz world that was facing enormous commercial pressure. While Lenox is often cited as an important influence on later educators, especially David Baker (Brubeck 2002a, 188–89),[8] I underscore its non-institutional role or, more to the point, the place of Lenox as a link between working musicians and the development of jazz pedagogy.

The institutional narrative excludes many of the important processes by which the techniques of jazz were transformed and formalized into a viable academic practice. Intentional or not, this can be seen as an attempt to more closely identify with the *institutional* community rather than the *jazz* community. We should not understate the importance of this, if one considers the overwhelmingly negative attitudes toward jazz that many in academic quarters held. By placing itself squarely within the institutional community, jazz education sought to pacify its institutional critics by emphasizing its relationship to *their* methods and histories, rather than its ties to a larger jazz community. The resulting narratives are, of course, grossly incomplete, and I would like to spend some time discussing how a reorientation of the narrative might restore the important historical links between jazz education and the wider jazz world.

Though jazz was likely being performed at the turn of the twentieth century, the first real boon to the learning of jazz came in 1917 with the release "Livery Stable Blues." Leaving aside arguments about whether the Original Dixieland Jazz Band is an authentic representation of early jazz, recording was a watershed for emerging jazz musicians. Recordings enabled analyses that had been prohibitively difficult, allowing for improvised music to be repeated infinitely (as long as the record held out), and for solos to be broken down into smaller segments. In writings on jazz education, recordings are often treated as method books or textbooks for jazz (D. Murphy 1994, 35). Although this might be another attempt to align practices in jazz with an academic identity, such a conception of recordings as learning tools may not be far from the mark. Although written materials have a place of prominence in the classical tradition, they are only a medium of transmission between the composer/author and the player/learner. Recordings in jazz have a similar role as a medium, and are regarded as a parallel pedagogical breakthrough.

By contrast, most histories pay scant attention to developments in jazz pedagogical publishing through the 1930s, such as the origins of the first jazz-related method books and stylistic studies. Trade magazines, with *Down Beat* being perhaps the most recognized example, published regular columns containing exercises for improvisational study, or analyses and discussions of a given performer, often accompanied by transcribed examples.[9] In the context of the institutional narrative such events are minor occurrences, part of the prehistory of jazz education. But that narrative overlooks the role of such materials in pointing to an increasingly professionalized and commercialized jazz performance industry in the 1930s. Jazz was big business, bigger than it had ever been (or has been since), and the learning of the music had profound economic implications. The increasingly frequent appearance of instructional aids in either trade journals or as self-contained publications likely was an attempt to cash in on this process and the changing nature of the jazz scene itself.

An increasingly professional and competitive jazz performance environment might also be a factor behind the establishment of jazz programs at North Texas and Berklee in the 1940s. In the former case, the administration in the music department surely understood the economic stakes involved with the study of popular music, and the enormous potential for trained musicians in this field. Dance-band music was big business, and the establishment of a dance-band program at the school would serve as an enormous advantage in recruiting students to the school. The fact that the school already had an individual in place (then-student M. E. "Gene" Hall) to institute such a program made matters easier. Indeed, the fundamental orientation of Hall's program was big-band music, a much more commercially attractive proposition than the styles that were emerging from New York at the time.[10] A jazz (or "dance band")[11] program would have been very marketable for an institution seeking a sense of upward mobility in the world of musical academia. The economic trajectory of big bands in the early 1940s certainly accelerated this process. Prior to the 1940s, countless musicians found not only employment in big bands, but also opportunities to receive on-the-job training in music. Even before the war the changing tastes of the public, as well as preparations for mobilization, were making big bands' professional existence more difficult. After the war, schools had a ready market of musicians returning to civilian life after having served in military bands, and eligible for tuition benefits under the G.I. Bill. Thus, in the late 1940s, a program in "dance band" such as that at North Texas was well positioned to respond to these changes in the jazz world. The development of a jazz education program might not simply be a function of stylistic forward thinking, but a reflection of jazz's real-world economics.

Another link between jazz-as-professional-practice and jazz education comes in the area of jazz theory, often regarded as being diametrically opposed to the aesthetic considerations of jazz improvisation. In the 1930s, as the publication of more theory-oriented materials aimed at the community of jazz musicians increased, and as an increasing number of schooled players began to enter this community, abstract theoretical constructs became more common in jazz, but were by no means universally applied or understood. For example, Coleman Hawkins, one of the most prominent of theory-based players on the jazz scene in the late 1920s, is often positioned as an alternative to a soloist such as Louis Armstrong, who displayed an improvisational bent toward blues and riff-based solo techniques (DeVeaux 1999, 84). Nevertheless, many musicians continued to study music theory with instructors in the Western art music tradition, and to apply such methods to jazz (Suber 1976, 367). What we are left with, then, in the late 1930s is a climate in which the increasingly intricate language of jazz improvisation was being related more directly to a theoretical understanding of music, leading to the development of a new knowledge-economy of jazz.

The emergence of bebop necessitated an even more pressing need to function within this context.[12] The complex language of bebop became, in David Baker's words, the lingua franca of contemporary jazz improvisation (National Endowment for the Arts n.d.). Although some would dispute this claim, particularly those who were and still are involved in the creation and performance of contemporary styles, with respect to jazz education today Baker's assessment is appropriate. Nearly every improvisational method on the market is comprised of concepts and/or patterns directly related to this style.[13] Bebop was, like previous styles, grounded in the "aural-written" learning tradition outlined by Al Fraser, employing largely unwritten methodologies, an emphasis on imitation and elaboration of recordings, and at least a basic (and in reality, sometimes quite sophisticated) awareness of musical structures, arising from both jazz and Western art traditions (Fraser 1983, 103–4). And like previous forms, bebop gave rise to a certain amount of how-to methods and instructional aids. These, however, largely were produced after the fact, and their scattered occurrence and lack of coordinated approach to the music made them somewhat unrepresentative of the bebop language as it was emerging. In short, there was no one theoretical construct for bebop that large numbers of musicians agreed upon.

This began to change during the early 1950s, in large part through the work of George Russell. A close associate of many bebop musicians, Russell became familiar with the inner processes of improvisational theory and practice. His theoretical framework for improvisation arose from his desire to develop a system through which musicians could develop a straightforward way of negotiating bebop's complex language. In a 1995 interview with Ingrid Monson, Russell explains the origins of his system:

> Miles [Davis] sort of took a liking to me when he was playing with Bird. . . . And he used to invite me up to his house. . . . He liked my

sense of harmony. And I loved his sense and we'd try to kill each other with chords. . . . I asked him one day on one of those sessions, what's your highest aim?—musical aim—and he said, to learn all the changes. That's all he said [laughs]. At the time I thought he *was* playing the changes . . . he was relating to each chord and arpeggiating, or using certain notes and extending the chord and all that. The more I thought about it, the more I felt there was a system begging to be brought into the world. And that system was based on chord-scale unity which traditional music[14] had absolutely ignored. The whole concept of a chord having a scale—that was basically its birthplace. (Monson 1998, 151)

In 1953 Russell published a pamphlet entitled *The Lydian Chromatic Concept of Tonal Organization*, which was later expanded into a text. This is widely regarded as the first major contribution to music theory from the field of jazz, and today remains a landmark in the development of jazz theory. Russell's concepts were widely known among musicians of the time, especially influential artists who helped to shape development of improvisational and compositional techniques in jazz during the 1950s and 1960s, including Miles Davis, John Coltrane, Ornette Coleman, Eric Dolphy, and Herbie Hancock. The "concept," as it is often called in shorthand, is based on the premise that the Lydian scale provides the basic tonal identity for jazz, at least as was extrapolated from the language of bebop; the raised fourth degree, Russell argued, was a common stylistic device among bebop musicians (Monson 1998, 151).

Russell's watershed development was a theoretical language in jazz that connected harmonic, or "vertical" structures to melodic, or "horizontal" ones. In short, this represents the first systematic expression of "chord-scale" theory, that each harmonic structure within a certain piece of music has a related melodic structure that can be employed in improvisation. Russell's association of chordal and scalar structures allowed improvisers to conceive of solos in a more linear fashion, while still playing the correct chord changes.[15] Within the context of an idiom as harmonically complex as bebop, this was a major breakthrough, but even more so for the burgeoning field of jazz education. As Russell protégé David Baker explains, the concept was a radical step toward an underlying theoretical framework that allowed musicians to communicate about improvisational techniques:

I can remember so vividly the day Jamey Aebersold's eyes lit up, the day I told him about chord-scale relationships, that this chord goes with this scale and vice-versa. I can remember my own eyes lighting up when George Russell had told me that. It's something I think we come to intuitively; but it sure could be expedited when somebody tells us that if I have a $D^{7\,(\#9\,\#5)}$, we can play an E-flat in an ascending melodic minor scale. It also helps us that if we *don't* hear it, we can have some kind of sanctuary that will allow us to survive until we *can* hear [italics in original]. (Brubeck 2002b, 52)

Russell provided jazz educators with a way to communicate about improvisational theory within the academic community, but one that also spoke to nonacademic communities of performers. By the early 1960s, with the tools in place for large-scale instruction in jazz, what was needed for the growth of the field was a climate of acceptance that allowed for the inclusion of what had been considered an inappropriate subject of study in musical academia.

As it turned out, they did not have long to wait, though historians have been equally remiss in fully accounting for such developments. Murphy cites "social changes" in the 1960s as a major factor in the field's growth (D. Murphy 1994, 34), yet never outlines the specifics. Even those narratives that focus exclusively on this period are unclear. Randy Snyder devotes an entire chapter of his dissertation to "cultural aspects," in which he highlights the civil rights movement and educational reform as two pertinent factors, but his research does not demonstrate a clear link that would show why *jazz education* should have been embraced by institutions. Moreover, his argument seems again to be directed toward an institutional narrative; it is the institution, seeing the tumultuous events of the time, which was the primary agent behind the inclusion of jazz in the curriculum. To a degree this is true, as Snyder writes that the "civil rights movement, changes in racial attitudes, and college campus protest did much to soften viewpoints held by white collegiate academics regarding jazz" (Snyder 1999, 49). Institutions *did* decide that the time was perhaps appropriate. However, Snyder ultimately reinforces the institutional narrative by his failure to connect jazz education in the 1960s with important developments in jazz itself, such as the increasingly activist political stances of musicians like Sonny Rollins, Max Roach, and Archie Shepp. Jazz was, by the late 1960s, intertwined with social justice and racial equality, and institutional moves to incorporate jazz need to be understood in this context.

The "social changes" Murphy speaks of did not escape the notice of music educators in general. The results of such a "value reversal" are demonstrated in a 1967 symposium held at the site of the Tanglewood Festival in Massachusetts,[16] the expressed intent of which was the critical discussion of current issues facing the field of music education. Organized by the Music Educators' National Conference (MENC), this symposium served to reevaluate the central philosophies and practices that governed the teaching of music in America. The now famous Tanglewood Declaration, a position statement that articulated the changing orientation toward music that was beginning to be seen in academia, resulted from this symposium: "Music of all periods, styles, forms, and cultures belongs in the curriculum. The musical repertory should be expanded to involve music of our time in its rich variety, including currently popular teen-age music and avant-garde music, American folk music, and music of other cultures" (Choate et al. 1968, 139).

Were those attending the symposium at Tanglewood attempting to establish a pioneering vision for the future of American music education, or was it an effort to catch up to changes that were confronting academia? I would suggest that musical academics were metaphorically dragged to the table kicking and screaming, or at least with a sense of resignation. Some comments from the symposium speak to this idea. Judith Murphy's "interpretive" account of the symposium seems at times overly obsessed with pathological aspects of the societal transformation of the time, suggesting that music educators had better get their collective act together, lest the barrier between "ivory tower and flaming ghetto" be broken down forcibly (J. Murphy 1968, 5). Change, it seemed, was coming whether musical academia liked or not.

Missing from these narratives are accounts of individuals involved in adapting the practices of jazz to the institutional context. The first generation of jazz educators through the 1950s mostly had been products of the educational institution, rather than widely recognized jazz performers. What jazz education needed in the 1960s were individuals who could take advantage of this climate and who possessed a sense of legitimacy not only in terms of their credentials as performers and teachers, but by extension their connection to the jazz community as well. In the 1960s, a number of individuals began to enter the field that satisfied both requirements, possessing credibility within the jazz community as higher-level artists. At the same time, a number of these musician/educators possessed academic training and/or advanced degrees, and thus satisfied a basic requirement of the institutional culture.

The career of David Baker provides us with one important example, highlighting a connection both to the culture of the jazz world and to the academic institution. A native of Indianapolis, Baker began his early studies as a trombonist in an environment that included, among others, Wes Montgomery, J. J. Johnson, and schoolmate Slide Hampton. At the same time, Baker also took advantage of the opportunities afforded him as a student at Indiana University. Given his tenure as a student at Indiana and his previous work as an instructor at Lincoln University, when Baker was appointed to the faculty of Indiana University he was as much an insider to the university culture as he was to the jazz community. Referring to criticisms by jazz musicians outside the academy, Baker simply says "They know better than to say that to me" (Prouty 2002, 151). They "know better" in no small part because of Baker's established reputation as a performer within the jazz community. The importance of musicians such as Baker, Donald Byrd, Jackie McLean, Nathan Davis, and Billy Taylor,[17] to name a few, simply cannot be overstated. On entering the academy, these artists brought a different set of experiences and perspectives to the study of jazz. The ability of such artist-educators to both influence and draw upon their peers in the jazz community was crucial to the field's continued growth. The entry of jazz professionals into the academy not only led to academia's acceptance of jazz, but also to jazz's acceptance of academia. Such individuals provided important links between two different musical worlds that eventually combined to give rise to the field of jazz education as it is known today.

It is worth pausing for a moment to consider the question of race in jazz education. In a 2007 panel on race, jazz, and academia sponsored by Jazz at Lincoln Center, Salim Washington noted the difficulties of integrating "practitioners" of the music into academic settings, especially with regard to tenure-track positions: "You have a lot of people who know as much or more about the music who could never be on tenure track."[18] Concerns such as this have long been echoed by African American jazz educators and musicians. The question of what makes someone qualified to teach jazz, especially in the case of an African American musician, has been hotly debated. In his book *Jazz Pedagogy,* David Baker writes (with more than a hint of sarcasm) the too-often accurate trope that recruited black faculty were expected to be exceptional in more ways than most of their white counterparts (Baker 1979, 37), possessing not only international-level performance skill but also an advanced degree, administrative ability, experience as a conductor, and so forth. In some sense, working musicians were "priced out" of the market without the advanced degrees and breadth of experience needed for tenure-track positions. Following on this is another oft-cited criticism that jazz educators, especially white educators, are often not equipped with the requisite real-world experience to function as effective teachers.

One of the core criticisms of institutionalized jazz studies is that it has moved the music too far beyond the non-academic jazz community, from its roots in vernacular traditions and practices. At times this has been expressed more directly, with charges that the field is overwhelmingly white, especially when measured against the predominance of African American jazz artists. This is a serious charge, and there is very little recent data to demonstrate how racially diverse (or not diverse) jazz studies programs are, but anecdotally, there does seem to be some concern that programs have trouble attracting black students. One study in 1980 did establish that under 40 percent of jazz studies programs had an African American faculty member (I. Anderson 2007, 181). A 1993 study by British critic Graham Collier estimates the number of "minorities" in jazz programs at between 10 and 20 percent, though he offers no specific data (G. Collier 1993).[19] More recently, in a jazz education "roundtable" panel conducted by *JazzTimes*, several participants noted the relative overrepresentation of white students, pointing to economic difficulties for black students in paying tuition, as well as the overwhelmingly white populace of higher education in general (Mergner 2007). In my own experience as a jazz student in the 1990s, it has to be said that there were very, very few African American students, even in one of the largest jazz programs in the United States. It should be noted that, while the presence of black faculty and students in jazz studies programs still seems to lag in many areas, this situation is still light years ahead of schools of music as a whole, where black faculty members are often a rarity. This has forced some jazz studies programs into a situation that is often similar to those of black studies programs on some campuses, of being *the place* for black faculty. I do not want to paint with too broad a brush in making this argument, but certainly some of the criticism of jazz studies programs for not being adequately representative might be better aimed at academia as a whole.

This seeming disconnect between jazz faculty in educational institutions and "practitioners" of jazz resonates forcefully with how the history of jazz education has been written in a way that distances it from its non-academic roots. While developments at the institutional level are important, they only provide a partial description of the ways in which jazz was eventually accepted as an academic discipline. Such orientations toward jazz education's history are, in many ways, detrimental to the field, in that they isolate educational institutions from the jazz community, and from the traditions of jazz itself. Institutionally driven narratives have served to increase the cultural and social distance that many in the field feel in relation to the larger non-academic jazz community. Keith Javors closes his dissertation on the teaching of jazz by stating: "If our [jazz educators'] claim continues to be of jazz performance education, as I feel it should be in at least some programs, then we must strive to bring increased credibility to the profession. Although we cannot replicate the social fabric that nurtured and continues to nurture jazz music, it is not beyond our capabilities to look deeper into our claims, evaluate our labor, and create new possibilities" (Javors 2001, 161–62). Although Javors writes primarily about the application of such "credibility" to the teaching of performance, I believe that a parallel exists in how we can think about the development of the field itself in an historical sense. If the field of jazz education is to have the sort of credibility that Javors calls for, it must be accountable to and inclusive of not just the historical narratives of educators within the institution, but to the historical traditions of jazz as well. In repositioning these historical narratives as a central factor in the development of jazz education, the communities of jazz and academia share a history and heritage. On the level of lived experience for students and teachers, this shared heritage can be problematic, as methodology, like history, can be a site of legitimation and conflict between communities and traditions.

Curriculum and Pedagogy in Improvisation: Constructing Knowledge from Competing Traditions

Though not the only practice that characterizes jazz, improvisation still represents the core activity in the music, and this orientation is manifest in the academic teaching and learning of jazz. To understand how the teaching of improvisation within academic communities is typically structured, it might be useful for us to begin at the end of the sequence, to examine the goals of such a curriculum. While specific requirements for students in improvisation courses can vary considerably, some competence in performance needs to be met. What this specifically requires students to demonstrate also varies. One educator remarked in a class session I observed that students should be able to improvise in a fashion "appropriate to the style." Based on speaking with several students in the class, what exactly this meant to them was somewhat unclear. One interpretation was that students should demonstrate the harmonic concepts presented in class; others saw a statement such as this as implying a deeper level of musical understanding. Such disparities are common in the discourse of jazz improvisation, within the academy and outside of it.

The most common curricular sequences in jazz improvisation last from two to four terms. Prerequisites for coursework in improvisation generally imply some theoretical understanding and instrumental ability before students are allowed to enroll, but again, these requirements display a great deal of variance. During my tenure as a student at the University of North Texas, undergraduates generally completed a two-semester sequence of jazz theory and ear training before being allowed to take the basic improvisation course, which would seem to reflect an orientation toward the mastery of basic theory as a foundation for further study.[20] At Indiana University, by contrast, theoretical structures were viewed as a concept gained through improvisational study itself.[21] Students would be expected to "pick up" the theory in the course of performing the music itself. The continuum of "practice/theory," or "creative/ technical," are at the core of academic improvisational discourses.

In course sequences consisting of two terms of instruction, individual classes usually start with "beginning improvisation," "introduction to improvisation," or sometimes simply "improvisation." Such courses are designed to introduce students to basic concepts of the improvisational language, as well as theoretical concepts and their application to jazz performance. The musical material for such courses is usually drawn from the mainstream jazz repertory, namely, bebop and related forms. In the second term, usually designated as "advanced improvisation," students move on to more sophisticated improvisational concepts, often drawn from contemporary repertories, developed by post-bop musicians such as John Coltrane, Woody Shaw, and David Liebman, as well as sometimes delving into fusion and free jazz styles.

In a four-semester course sequence, the first two courses are often designated as "introduction to improvisation" or "improvisation," while the final courses are generally labeled "advanced improvisation." The pacing of such a sequence is, understandably, slower than in a two-term sequence, allowing for a greater mastery of detailed concepts within improvisational language, as well as concepts tied to specific types of repertories. In relation to a two-semester sequence, the frequency of evaluation is greater; students are evaluated more often in relation to the amount of material covered. Additionally, the examination of repertory becomes an important organizing principle within each course, with techniques specific to certain types of compositions becoming an important consideration. In the advanced courses, the third semester courses generally deal with more advanced types of harmonic schemes, including post-bop structures (harmonic schemes such as those common to the late-1950s music of John Coltrane) and other non-functional types of harmonies. In the final course, material is often drawn from more contemporary sources, or from the repertory of a specific player or group of players.[22] In some cases, students may engage in limited studies of free improvisation in the last weeks of the sequence.

The most common unifying force within these curricular systems is repertory, in which compositions are categorized by their relative complexity and presented in a graded sequence. The most frequent manifestation of this approach is based on a hierarchy of relative harmonic difficulty, with pieces that are identified as being harmonically simple at the beginning of the instructional sequence, such as blues-based tunes,[23] or modal tunes.[24] These types of harmonic structures, it is argued, provide an easier vehicle for students to improvise, as they only require a single scalar structure for long periods of time, and thus students need not be as concerned about "making the changes." From this starting point, students then move on to more harmonically challenging tunes, such as those based upon simple diatonic cadential patterns. Compositions such as Ellington's "Satin Doll" and Sonny Rollins's "Pent Up House" are examples of the repertory at this stage of the curriculum. In each of these pieces, the harmonic structures generally revolve around a single key center, or perhaps two key centers for relatively long periods. In any case, the harmonic challenges presented are kept to a minimum.

In the later stages of a repertoire-based sequence, students are introduced to pieces that present greater challenges in terms of harmonic/scalar structures, with tonalities based on melodic/harmonic minor scales and their related modes, highlighting the use of harmonic extensions and alterations. A song such as "Beautiful Love" or "What Is This Thing Called Love" provides a typical harmonic vehicle, involving chordal structures with extended or altered voices, which the improviser must negotiate. In addition to more complex harmonic structures, repertoire in the advanced improvisation course(s) also introduces students to pieces that represent non-functional harmonic structures, as well as pieces that demonstrate a faster harmonic rhythm. Standard compositions such as pieces based on "I Got Rhythm"[25] and "Have You Met Miss Jones," which features a bridge that modulates between three keys, as well as more modern pieces such as Coltrane's "Giant Steps" or "Countdown," are intended to introduce students to harmonic schemes in which the ability to switch between key centers quickly is an important skill. Many of the songs used in the later stages are those that are considered to be measuring sticks for improvisational proficiency both within and without the academy ("Giant Steps," Parker's "Confirmation," and Benny Golson's "Stablemates" are frequent examples). This grading of repertoire based on relative harmonic complexity is a constant theme in numerous curricular sequences, one that parallels the sequence of harmony-based instruction in the Western canon.

If curriculum represents the large-scale organization of improvisational practice within the teaching of jazz, pedagogy deals with specific methods that educators use to convey that material to their students on a daily basis. The basic goal of all pedagogical methods is the same, namely to bring students through a defined curricular structure or sequence, at which point a student should be able to demonstrate certain skills. Although pedagogical approaches are varied, there are overriding themes that determine how pedagogical methods are developed and applied. Perhaps the most common feature in the institutionalized pedagogy of improvisation is the emphasis on pitch. Put another way, pitch structures, such as scales, chords, and the relationships between the two, are stressed above other factors. As pitch relates fundamentally to both melody and harmony, improvisational pedagogy is, in most instances, concerned with the construction and understanding of these elements. One jazz educator I interviewed indicated that the basic principle behind his teaching is one that deals with "manipulating the pitch."

There are two main pedagogical thrusts in the teaching of jazz improvisation. These can be termed the theory-based and practice-based approaches.[26] In a theory-based approach, musical material is presented as it relates to harmonic/structural components of the repertory. Analysis of chord progressions and the application of chord/scale structures are perhaps the most frequently observed examples of this orientation. In a practice-based orientation, materials are derived from existing musical sources (i.e., recorded and/or transcribed solos) and are intended to be learned and applied to improvisational performance. Pedagogical strategies that involve the use of patterns, clichés, or "licks" are an important example of this approach. The continuum between these two orientations represents something of an intellectual chicken-and-egg dilemma: does theory give rise to improvisational practice, or does practice determine what will be regarded as theory? Most educators recognize that, in fact, both of these viewpoints are valuable, and are not mutually exclusive. Nevertheless, at certain times in the pedagogical process, one or the other approach clearly guides the interactions between student and teacher.

In a theory-based pedagogical system, students use theory (in the academic-disciplinary sense) as a building block of the improvisational language. The demonstration of fluency in the harmonic structures of a certain repertory is often a final objective of improvisation courses. This can take several forms. Obviously, students should be able to demonstrate at least a basic ability to improvise a solo on a certain piece, for example, and be able to "make the changes," to play the correct notes for the chord at any given moment. Additionally, students are often required to demonstrate an understanding of certain harmonic devices and structures, such as cadences or "ii-Vs," showing that they know both how to articulate a certain harmonic structure, and how to successfully move from one to the other. These types of pedagogical strategies emphasize a systematic approach to learning how jazz harmony works, and how melodic constructs relate to harmonic ones, relying heavily on chord/scale theory, with the emphasis on scales and chords as generative devices for improvisational performance. In this context, knowledge of scalar and/or chordal structures serves as a basis for musical creation.

If the pedagogical approaches described above treat improvised solos as resulting from theoretical constructs, practice-based orientations might be described as approaching the relationship between these areas from an opposite perspective. Specifically, such improvisational instruction is concerned with "vocabulary," a concept used frequently by jazz musicians to refer to musical patterns that are prevalent in the repertory of improvised jazz music, as Paul Berliner implies in describing how musicians have engaged in similar processes: "Just as children learn to speak by imitating older competent speakers, so young musicians learn to speak jazz by imitating seasoned improvisers. In part, this involves acquiring a complex vocabulary of conventional phrases and phrase components, which improvisers drawn upon in formulating the melody of a jazz solo" (Berliner 1994, 95). Jazz educators frequently employ similar linguistic terminology in describing the building blocks of the jazz "language." Both "vocabulary" and "language" are often used in instructional contexts, and also as parts of titles of improvisation method books, as can be seen in even a brief survey of such materials.

One manifestation of this type of orientation centers on the practice and mastery of short melodic motifs, variously referred to as clichés, licks, phrases, or patterns. In developing pedagogical strategies based on these types of structures, educators hope to accomplish three basic tasks. First, patterns provide students with a supply of ideas for solos. As David Baker explains, students are able to acquire an "encyclopedic knowledge" of the jazz language, that they may then apply to actual performance situations: "[Students acquire] a repository of ideas; if the ideas don't come they always have something that sounds good. That's what we [jazz players as a whole] do when we play. Nobody can create at the highest level, and I tell people the great players are the ones who have the highest level of bullshit material, because if their bullshit material is better than everybody else's 'A' material, how can you be a bad player?" (Prouty 2002, 182).

Second, patterns provide models for students to build their own musical vocabulary, to understand the ways in which jazz musicians construct melody. In one improvisational styles course I took as an undergraduate, for example, student were required not only to learn patterns from major jazz musicians, but also to write their own in the style of a particular player, to construct patterns that sounded like they might have been created by Louis Armstrong or Charlie Parker. In this way, students are taught to absorb and assimilate patterns, and to connect them historically to the jazz tradition. Third, students can use patterns as exercises to achieve fluency in various situations, by taking a specific pattern and transposing it into various keys and interpolating it into different contexts. The ability to transpose clichés and patterns to all keys, even those which are rarely used in actual performance, is considered a hallmark in separating more advanced players from beginners. In such a case, the actual application of these patterns in various keys centers, while useful in performance, also fulfills the goal of achieving fluency in different key centers.[27]

Theory-based and practice-based orientations toward improvisational pedagogy may simply represent two different ways of understanding the same musical language. What is important to keep in mind is not necessarily any meaningful, applicable distinction between theory and practice. At the deepest levels of musical understanding, the two concepts might be one and the same, the same musical content seen from different perspectives. What defines the distinction between such approaches within improvisational pedagogy is the way in which they are framed within the instructional situation. Put another way, this is the method by which teachers and students *talk* about the fundamental structural aspects of improvisation, and in the pedagogical discourse, at least, the distinction between the two orientations can be made to seem very real.[28] Theory and practice are often seen as very different activities, a distinction that is sometimes reinforced by the introduction of jazz-specific theory courses, spotlighting the distinction between these ideas; this can lead to the adoption of a curriculum in which theory is compartmentalized as a discipline distinct from performance, and not in a positive way.

Distinctions between theory and practice are most often brought into focus during assessments of student performance. As with any other discipline, assessments in jazz studies occur regularly, and in a number of ways. At the most official levels, students are subject to exams by "juries" at the end of each semester, which often determine whether or not a student will advance in or graduate from a program. Testing on specific concepts is also conducted at regular intervals throughout a course. On an unofficial level, students are assessed by both faculty members and their peers on a daily basis, as a result of conversations in the hall, informal jam sessions, and the like. In a context in which student progress is judged against both a technical standard and against the larger historical traditions of jazz performance and creativity, assessment can be problematic. Let me relate a personal example to illustrate this idea.

As I emerged from the room in which my first jazz jury at UNT had just taken place, I felt sick. I had driven thousands of miles, moved to a place that was something of a foreign culture to me (from Maine to Texas), completed an entire semester of study, invested a not-too-small amount of money, only to blow it when the pressure was on. The situation itself had been a somewhat intimidating. As I entered the room, a large rehearsal hall that served as a lecture hall and practice facility for one of the program's many large ensembles, I saw the jury, consisting of five faculty members from the core jazz faculty. One faculty member served as a sort of coordinator, running a video camera, which was used for later evaluation if needed. This faculty member also collected my jury sheet, instructed me as to where to stand, provided a tuning pitch, and so forth. Accompanying the jury performance was a rhythm section of upper-level students who played in one of the top ensembles. Although the students were outstanding players, and I knew them in passing, I had never played with them before.

I was asked to play one selection of my choice. I chose "The Song Is You," played at a brisk tempo. This song is not particularly difficult within the context of the jazz repertoire, although the bridge does modulate from C major to E major. The song was a favorite of mine, and I felt confident that I knew the tune extremely well. During the performance, I missed a few chords, most importantly, the transition back into C major at the end of the bridge. My heart sank in mid-chorus, knowing that I had folded, as students and faculty liked to quip, and I left the room thinking that I would have to re-take the jury at the end of the following semester. Only later did I find out that I had not only passed the jury, but I did so with flying colors. In conversation later, one of the faculty panelists praised the fact that I did not sound like "university jazz." This left me puzzled; if a university jazz student was not supposed to sound like "university jazz," then what are they supposed to sound like?

The answer, of course, lies with the fact that students are always judged against more than what is presented in the classroom, against the jazz tradition itself. This presents a dilemma for students, who often have to determine exactly what it is that they are supposed to do. Students who master technical aspects of the improvisation sequence might still find themselves assessed negatively; the same is true for those who choose to engage in an approach that is seen as being more creative, but is lacking in overt displays of virtuosity and technical mastery. The kinds of pedagogical and curricular orientations discussed previously are intended to negotiate between these two worlds, but success is not always guaranteed. The dynamics of how teachers define what to teach, and perhaps more importantly how to evaluate performance is not easy, nor is it without profound implications for the cultural environment of the music academy. As Henry Kingsbury writes, in his ethnography of a prominent (and pseudonymous) conservatory, the concept of *talent* lies at the heart of evaluations, and thus involves power relations in the music school.

For Kingsbury, talent is both central to Western musical understanding and nearly impossible to specifically define. He relates a tale of a young voice student who fails her promotional jury because she is deemed "unmusical," when she had, only a year before, been lavished with praise by the faculty for her performance (Kingsbury 1988, 64–67). My experience with the jury took the opposite path, an unexpected success, but the issue is the same. In both cases, students were confronted with a pedagogical situation in which the curriculum can only do so much, while the rest is up to them. This disjuncture is frequently criticized by students as unfair, as political, as inconsistent. Trying to figure out exactly what a teacher *wants*, while at the same time negotiating their own place as a jazz performer, is not an easy thing to do.

Similar issues were expressed by another student enrolled in a jazz performance program in the Midwest, whom I interviewed during my doctoral work. The student was well known in the area as a jazz performer, but had left the program in question a few years before. His attitudes toward the program revealed something of the mixed bag that greets many young jazz students; while he recognized the necessity of teaching the "nuts and bolts" of jazz improvisation, he also lamented the idea that, in his view, creativity that deviated from curricular and pedagogical expectations was discouraged. He pointed to the experiences of one fellow student, who like him, had left the program. This individual, who had an "unorthodox" approach to improvisation, got "burned out" from the pressures to conform to a specific ideal. For his friend, a balance between the needs of the jazz tradition and the institution could not be achieved. Teachers too are often cognizant of these conflicts; one educator I spoke with lamented that educators often "stomp on their creativity" in their interactions with students. Others are more pragmatic, or more idealistic. Whatever one's individual perspective, it is at the moment of evaluation, whether in the form of a recital, jury, improvisation class, or a passing comment in the hallway, that the tensions between what is taught and what is expected within the context of the larger jazz tradition come into conflict, and it is not surprising that these are the moments when tensions between students and faculty are at their peak.

Regardless of the approach used to teach or assess improvisation, the types of methods and frameworks that are developed say a great deal about how jazz educators define the process of improvisation within the context of institutional study, and by extension, how they define both jazz itself and communities within which students and teachers are organized. Instructional sequences must be able to be broken down and represented on a syllabus, courses within an instructional sequence must flow into each other, methods of evaluation and assessment must be designed so that they can be applied to a large group of students. These and other institutional pressures on teachers of jazz improvisation are ever present, and while the demands of the academy are satisfied through a sense of structure and curricular/pedagogical regularity, the aesthetic demands of the jazz tradition for individuality and intuition also exert a powerful pull on educators and students who enter this arena because of a deep attraction to the music.

Moments of evaluation are where these varied processes come to a climax, where the demands of different historical forces come into sharp relief. Students whose playing is criticized for being too technical complain that this is what they are taught, while those whose playing does not meet a certain standard for technical or stylistic appropriateness likewise see such evaluations as too rigid. In evaluating student performers, at least two main forces are at work, one of which is under the control of jazz educators (the teaching of technique, for example), while the other largely is not (individual creativity). Institutional instruction has accomplished only so much, yet students are often judged within the totality of the jazz performance tradition, taking more experiential factors into account.[29] Even at an individual level, students and teachers frequently have very different ideas about what constitutes proficient improvisational performance, sometimes with creative ideas being stressed, sometimes technical ones. This is natural, as individual musicians will always bring their own experiences, attitudes, philosophies, and aesthetic values to the table. I do not mean to imply that every student or educator in a jazz program experiences these concepts in the same way. Some students thrive in such an environment, while others suffer. That could be the case for any discipline. In demonstrating the complexity of the language of jazz, educators have made great strides toward demythologizing the music. Yet in debunking such primitivist stereotypes of jazz improvisers, educators may sometimes inadvertently send a message that playing jazz is mostly about technique, and that individual ability or creativity does not factor into the equation. Institutional pressures often force educators to make instructional choices that favor such concepts over what are, in curricular terms at least, less definable concepts. Creativity is more difficult to represent on a blackboard or in a handout than, say, a series of patterns or scales. In my experience as a student, teacher, and observer of jazz education, I have found that such conflicts are difficult to negotiate at all levels. These competing claims to both practice and knowledge make the discourse of the academic jazz community a highly contested one.

Pedagogy and Power in Jazz Education

Improvisation has long been a troublesome concept within musical academia. Techniques of improvisation are found infrequently within the Western art music curriculum, and classical music's legacy of improvisation is often a mystery to novice musicians. The authority of written historical documents (Kingsbury 1988, 87–94) leaves improvised forms with less cultural and pedagogical capital. In Nettl's "heartland" music school,[30] improvisatory music cultures stand apart from those that celebrate "great" works in "large" formats (Nettl 1995, 32). Jazz thus began its academic life with a fundamentally different identity within the academy, at odds with academic musical culture.

At times, the ways in which jazz improvisation is practiced and conceptualized seem "infinite," to borrow from Paul Berliner's superb study; such a musical and social practice might potentially represent a radical move for higher musical education, built on negotiation between teachers and students. Yet formal instruction in jazz improvisation is frequently criticized for producing the opposite result, limiting individual choice and stultifying performance, and thus profoundly influencing power relations between students and teachers. Curricular and pedagogical systems are, as Joan Wink writes, following Henry Giroux, "never just a neutral body," organizing knowledge and the dynamics of social relationships (Wink 1997, 92). But power in this context extends beyond relationships between students and teachers in ensembles and improvisation classes. Historical narratives and traditions themselves have power, determining both musical practice as well as what musics are appropriate for study. In constructing and negotiating individual and community identities, teachers and students must be sensitive not only to the specific demands of institutional and jazz traditions but to the ways these processes affect their interactions on a daily basis. The power to determine just what this community will look like is a constant source of tension for all.

At times, critics of jazz vis-à-vis Western art traditions have drawn on an established literature that positions jazz as a deviant form, a threat to the creative spirit. Anne Shaw Faulkner, writing in 1921, characterizes the genre as a clear and dangerous divergence from more accepted forms of musical entertainment: "Jazz originally was the accompaniment of the voodoo dancer, stimulating the half-crazed barbarian to the vilest deeds. The weird rhythm, accompanied by the syncopated rhythm of the voodoo invokers, has also been employed by other barbaric people to stimulate brutality and sensuality. That it has a demoralizing effect in the human brain has been demonstrated by many scientists" (quoted in Walser 1999, 34). Even into the 1960s some educators would employ this same kind of rhetoric in justifying the exclusion of jazz from the music curriculum. As Harry Allen Feldman writes, "Training a boy to blow a horn no longer ensures that he will not blow a safe. It might blow him into delinquency, for who can deny the close relationship between jazz and delinquency? . . . How can one justify the serious discussion [of jazz] on the college level . . . ?" (Feldman 1964, 61). Here, jazz is segregated from established musical culture (and by extension academia), either due to its perceived vulgarity, or through a sense of derision and dismissal.[31] The idea that European traditions were of higher artistic quality than vernacular traditions is difficult to separate from the widely held assumption that composed music was of superior quality to improvised music.

Such a rejection of jazz is one historical manifestation of a broader rejection of improvisation within musical academia, which has long been tied to the study of the Western classical canon; Timothy Hays refers to the canon and the conservatory as being "interrelated" well into the twentieth century (Hays 1999, vi), though by the 1960s, there was a "tension which developed between the European high art music canon and the forces of American popular culture" (v). Presumably, jazz was part of the latter category; as David Baker argued in an early essay on jazz education, "Because jazz had its origins outside the perimeters of western art music, its lack of acceptance was virtually assured" (Baker 1973, 21).

When improvisation has been included in academic study, it has generally been linked to early music, seldom extending beyond the classic period.[32] Robin Moore suggests that this de-emphasis on improvisation in academia is a relatively recent development, writing: "It is clear that only in the past hundred and fifty years attitudes towards improvisation in Western classical performance have changed drastically. The mandates of compositionally specified interpretation now supersede those of the instrumentalist. To many, improvisatory expression seems threatening, unfamiliar, or underserving [sic] of interest" (Moore 1992, 63). Similarly, Christopher Small writes: "In the western classical tradition, the art of improvisation is today to all intents and purposes dead, and resists all efforts to revive it. The resistance, surprisingly, comes largely from performers themselves, who mostly have little idea of what improvisation is or what it entails" (Small 1987, 283).

In the absence of improvised musical forms, notation was established as the medium of choice for musical pedagogy, following a narrative of "increasing specification"[33]—as musical transmission relied more on notation, performers found their own interpretive choices limited (De Souza 2008). But the power of notation in the academy extends beyond performative interpretation.[34] Describing a session with pseudonymous professor "Marcus Goldman," Henry Kingsbury relates: "A fundamental principle of Goldman's teaching was that students must play what was written on the score, and yet they must not play something simply because it was written on the score . . . everything happened as though the score was only a touchstone in the ongoing negotiation of relative social authority among the persons in the room, an authority manifested in musical and verbal performance" (Kingsbury 1988, 87–88).

In this context, scores are a source of power, both as tangible artifacts of canon and in the formation of the community, the "conservatory culture" of which Kingsbury writes. Teachers, as interpreters of these most tangible artifacts of the canon, become gatekeepers of power/knowledge,[35] and without them, the authority of teachers and the institution as a whole is questioned.

Opposition to jazz from some in academia undoubtedly drew upon a fear of losing such authority in an improvisational idiom. Indeed, as Small argues, improvisation poses just such a threat; in its "freedom from the constraints of harmony and counterpoint" and the "written-out score," improvisation is "closely allied to anarchism" (Small 1987, 180),[36] a musical practice in which, at its extreme, there is no "authority," save for the performer.

Even some arguments in defense of jazz point to obstacles in improvisatory practice. Some see a measure of value in jazz, but only as it contributes to composition. Improvisation is dismissed, while the potential for jazz to contribute to the development of compositional forms is praised. For example, writing in the *Musical Quarterly* in 1926, Edwin J. Stringham argues: "Naturally, there is both good and bad jazz—that is, good or bad from a compositional standpoint. . . . I have in mind only the better type of jazz; that which is composed by understanding musicians, that which is well conceived and written according to ordinary esthetical and technical standards, and that which is really clever in either *composition* or *orchestration*" (Stringham 1926, 191; emphasis added).

This attitude toward jazz, in which the compositional aspects of the idiom are praised, is further reflected by Harvard music professor Walter R. Spaulding, who argues, in *Etude* magazine's famous "Jazz Problem" feature in 1924, that the "good features [of jazz] will gradually be incorporated into the conventional idiom, and extreme mannerisms will be eliminated; for, whatever music is or is not, it is a free experimental art and has always been developed by *composers* [emphasis added] trying all sorts of new possibilities . . ." (in Walser 1999, 51).

Thus, jazz *as* improvisation is seen to be incompatible with academic musical study, or is ignored altogether. David Baker comments on this idea in his spirited defense of jazz education in *Down Beat* from September 1965: "Administrators must be made aware of the difference between jazz and jazz-derived music that bears little more than a superficial resemblance to the real article" (Baker 1965, 29). The "real article" is fairly obvious, with Baker asserting that "the essence of jazz is improvisation" (30). Rather than avoiding improvisation, supporters of jazz education had to argue that improvisation was a musical practice that was as important (and teachable) as those in the Western canon. Improvisation was at the core of jazz as it was understood by its practitioners,[37] and this practice must be reflected in its institutional identity. How to construct such a case was another matter.

Whatever the specific nature of the criticisms of jazz, educators responded pedagogically, creating methods for the study of improvisation and jazz history[38] that drew from the language and approaches of higher education.

Methods were codified and catalogued in a way that presented improvisation as being compatible with the academy. Significant recordings replaced scores as tangible artifacts.[39] Early literature on jazz education attempted to speak the language of the academy, framing the teaching of improvisation in ways that made it accessible to classically trained faculty and administrators. Billy Taylor made just such an argument in justifying the teaching of jazz, linking it with structural and formal elements of the Western canon:

> [O]bserve how many devices of the past can be found in the capsule form of jazz . . . the two part song form, rondo form, and the through composed variation form. The various basso ostinato patterns in use are the direct descendent of the passacaglia, and the twelve-bar blues is a true chaconne. Clear-cut harmonic sequences are the off-spring [*sic*] of the Baroque instrumental style of Corelli and Vivaldi; the majority of harmonic structures are pure Ravelian-Debussyian impressionism or Scriabinesque stereo-types [*sic*], and the roots of the subtle melodic glissandos, snycops, the chromatic embellishments range all the way from the 17th Century bel-canto to the 'elevated speech' of Milhaud's *Les Choephores*. (quoted in Barr 1974, 28)

The development of a canon in jazz is also a result of this kind of thinking. Canon, it is argued, put jazz on an equal footing with the Western art music tradition, as Krin Gabbard explains:

> Because jazz has been treated historically as a "stepchild" of "serious" music, the music's value is usually established with appeals to standards developed for classical music. The project is explicit, for example, in the title of Grover Sales's *Jazz: America's Classical Music*. . . . A great deal of jazz writing implicitly or explicitly expresses the demand that jazz musicians be given the same legitimacy as practitioners of canonical arts. (Gabbard 1995, 2)

The primary project of jazz educators was as much about legitimizing[40] jazz as a cultural form in the academy as it was about preserving musical practice. In constructing methods that accomplished this goal, jazz educators emphasized the language of the academy, and musical structures that could be readily analyzed and classified using common theoretical techniques. They sought to carve out their own place within musical academia that satisfied administrators and critics who were skeptical of or hostile to jazz. Like the institutional narrative that positions jazz education as a function of the institution's history, jazz curricula and pedagogy likewise drew upon academic language in establishing their legitimacy.

These developments have often met with a negative reception from some with an interest in jazz. In his book *Jazz and American Culture*, James Lincoln Collier criticizes teaching and learning of jazz in higher education: "With students all over the United States being taught more or less the same harmonic principles, it is hardly surprising that their solos tend to sound much the same. It is important for us to understand that many of the most influential jazz players developed their own personal harmonic schemes, very frequently because they had little training in theory and were forced to find it their own way" (Collier 1993, 155). Collier articulates a common theme in the criticism of jazz education, namely, that a standardization of pedagogy has led to a stylistic stagnation amongst student jazz performers. Similarly, Stuart Nicholson writes (in his book on the stagnation of American jazz in general): "Today, hundreds of thousands of students and thousands of teachers study [a] narrow repository of stylistic inspiration . . . which for many students has resulted in both a similarity of concept and execution" (Nicholson 2005, 106). Writing over a decade apart, both authors advance a view of jazz education that portrays it as limited, repetitive, and uninspired. By themselves, arguments such as these are not new; jazz improvisation in the academy has been a frequent target of some in the jazz world since its inception. Such criticisms, however, must be considered within the broader context of other developments in jazz over the last quarter century.

The massive growth of jazz education since the 1970s has spurred a cottage industry devoted to the teaching and learning of improvisation. There are hundreds of improvisation texts available, representing both a boost to the dissemination of information about jazz and a significant challenge to the field. The production of method books, as well as those on theory and history, has vastly increased the availability of information for students. Most major sources are easily obtained through mail order or via the internet, and most college-level and pre-college jazz students have used some written text at some point in their studies. The availability of such materials has generated significant debate as to whether they benefit students or not. As early as the 1970s, critics were blaming the publication of pedagogical aids for improvisation for turning jazz into a "written tradition" (Hores 1977, 2), at the expense of a more fundamentally oral identity (Galper, n.d.).

Accompanying jazz education's explosion over the past few decades is the rise of the neo-traditionalists, led by trumpeter and Jazz at Lincoln Center artistic director Wynton Marsalis, and heralded in the press by critics such as Stanley Crouch. The rise of and opposition to Marsalis, Crouch, and JALC are well documented, and I will not revisit these debates here. I would note, however, that criticisms of Marsalis and those of academic jazz improvisation share many characteristics. For example, Eric Nisenson links the rise of Marsalis and his peers with a "clear indication that jazz is fading as an art form" resulting from what he regards as an "increasing diminution of genuine creative vitality" (Nisensen 1997, 13). The development of "canonical" ways of improvising (of which Marsalis's most vocal critics accuse him) are often seen to be at odds with real historical practices, and parallel criticisms of academically trained improvisers. Collier argues: "Jazz musicians, in an earlier day, had to learn for themselves. Bix Beiderbecke . . . worked out a system of cornet fingering that remains unique; Jack Teagarden developed an unorthodox trombone technique that is almost inimitable . . . self-teaching gave them something else, and that was a distinctive, individual quality that made their work instantly identifiable" (Collier, 1993, 152).[41] It is this last passage that interests me the most with respect to the current discussion. The most damning criticism of jazz education is that student players sound alike, that there is little or no individual distinctiveness among them. Performers, not an institution or instructor, have the power to determine their own course through "self-teaching," an essential marker of the non-academic jazz tradition.[42] Such judgments on improvisation are, of course, subjective, but charges such as these are frequent, and are troubling to many educators.

Repertoire is another area that is criticized in jazz education, particularly as it relates to what is seen as a limited approach, emphasizing a few jazz styles and canonical players. David Ake writes in *Jazz Cultures* that such methods reflect a narrow view of jazz's improvisational legacy, emphasizing styles and musicians who reinforce an easily classified and teachable tradition. Examining the academic treatment of John Coltrane, Ake argues that the saxophonist's later creative output is ignored at the expense of the academy's emphasis on "Giant Steps" and similar recordings that are more easily utilized in the academic context (Ake 2002, 129–31). Similarly, Stuart Nicholson laments what he sees as a narrow focus on bebop-based stylistic conventions as a basis for pedagogy: "The problem with basing the educational curriculum on a bebop-styled repertoire is that solos in this style—and it is a style that focuses almost entirely on solos—were becoming so circumscribed stylistically and technically it was increasingly difficult for musicians to say anything original in this idiom" (Nicholson 2005, 107). Peter Townsend quotes Joe Henderson as expressing a similar concern, arguing that through academic study "everybody is doing the same thing, you don't get that individual fingerprint like you used to among players" (Townsend 2000, 179).[43]

These critiques are by no means exceptional; they are, in fact, quite common in the literature of jazz. Some critics place the blame for perceived expressive or artistic failures squarely on teachers and students;[44] for others, such accommodations are the price of doing business in the academy. Such debates underscore the contested nature of improvisation itself, that improvisation cannot be neatly defined, either as a "structured thing" (Berliner 1994, 63) or as "allied to anarchism" (Small 1987, 180). In practice, improvisation has always existed on a continuum between conformity and innovation; the nature of improvisation in academia is one point on this continuum, drawn to either end by the power of historical and cultural practices.

Thus, educators who teach improvisation in the academy have faced two main hurdles. From an historical standpoint, opposition to jazz from more conservative elements of the academic establishment had to be overcome. Such opposition, sometimes in blatantly elitist or racist language, could only be answered by the development of methods that demonstrated jazz's compatibility with academic pedagogy. Systems like Russell's Lydian-Chromatic concept and the work of pioneering educators such as Baker and Jerry Coker went a long way to providing effective and easily replicated models. At the same time, however, jazz educators have come under attack from those who feel that they gave away the store, that too much accommodation has occurred. Jazz educators and students are acutely aware of occupying such a precarious position between traditions, and have long struggled find their place between these two often-competing communities. Power is at the heart of this: the power to determine what is or is not music, how learning should be structured, and how these processes relate to larger questions of tradition and identity. Educators are subjected to this power, and in turn wield power in structuring curricula and pedagogy that seek to serve these competing traditions.

If pedagogy is a practice of power, then instruction and assessment by necessity involve teachers making power-laden decisions that will have potentially profound implications for students. But in a subject such as music, standards for evaluation can be personal and difficult to clearly define; decisions about what constitutes a good performance or good improvisation are contested. Such contestation leads to pedagogical power at times being used to reinforce existing social orders. Power itself, like talent, is difficult to define. It is, following Foucault, not something that is possessed, but rather something that is used or exercised (Foucault 1977, 27). Power has always been an important element in the relationships between jazz improvisers; bandleaders could certainly make (and did make) decisions on whose playing would get them hired or fired. But the academic context implicates a number of different agents; teachers exercise power because they are in positions in which they make assessments of students' performances. Whereas teachers in the Western canon might make assessments based on their roles in interpreting how students should play a score (as Kingsbury argues), teachers of jazz improvisation might make assessments based on the correctness of harmony and melody, whether students have mastered patterns or are interpreting a recording correctly. Jazz educators say "these are the patterns you should practice, these are the people you should listen to," thus "translating the tradition" for students. The authority of the score is replaced by the authority of recordings, or of theoretical constructs and the language of bebop. This might seem at odds with the self-teaching long held as integral to the jazz tradition, where the power rests mainly with the performer.[45] Institutionalized pedagogy can disrupt this tradition, and thus is seen to take power away from the performer, limiting the ability to interpret and apply historical narratives and musical language for themselves.

Power extends beyond the student/teacher relationship, as teachers in turn are assessed by administrators who judge their relative effectiveness as performers and educators. Institutions exercise power because they make decisions on whether someone is hired or earns tenure. Boards of trustees and state agencies have power because they set funding priorities, and so on. All this may seem to get far away from jazz improvisation, but in the final analysis, discourses about jazz education are deeply informed by such discussions of power. Jazz in the academy was criticized by those who disapproved of the music because they feared the loss of the power of the established canon. It is also criticized by those outside the academy who express dismay that pedagogues exert power upon contemporary performance practice. Those within jazz education criticize institutional structures as well as the Western art music system for having too much power. In the discourse of jazz education, there are many opinions as to who has power—teachers, the institution, traditions of jazz themselves; students are answerable to all these. Jazz has often been regarded as a "democratic" form,[46] in which individual voices of improvisers interact in a relatively equal manner. But pedagogy, as Henry Giroux and others have argued, can be a very undemocratic system when it comes to the relationships between students and other actors.

In the previous chapter I argued that jazz communities come in many different forms, comprised of people with converging interests, and ultimately are constructed by individuals themselves in their relationship with jazz artists through the experience of listening. Those involved with jazz education are certainly part of these types of communities. They also form a community among themselves, and it is here that the impact of pedagogy–as-power is most keenly felt. In seeking to form their own community identity as practitioners of jazz within the academy, students and teachers of jazz are constantly finding their place within the communities of the institution and of the jazz tradition, both of which exert enormous historical and practical power. Negotiating the dynamics of such communities is difficult, but both teachers and students have made an effort to accommodate the respective traditions. Be it the creation of an historical narrative for jazz education, the everyday lived experience of improvisational performance, or the larger questions of identity, teachers and students have had to walk a tightrope of tradition, existing simultaneously with communities that at times have rejected each other. But the worlds of musical and academic study have changed, and for jazz studies to remain a radical site in which assumptions about musical and social practice in the academy are called into question, educational methods must by nature evolve as well. All this might be too much to place on the shoulders of teachers who are just trying to get their students to "play the changes," which at the end of the day is a laudable goal in itself. But the nature of jazz improvisation is not, in such a context, "infinite," to borrow from Paul Berliner, and perhaps we should question whether the practice of jazz improvisation in the academy remains a site for contesting the nature of social relationships and musical canons as it once was.

If teachers of jazz performance have had difficulty in negotiating the strictures of the canon, the same can be said of those who teach non-performance areas such as jazz history, perhaps to an even greater degree. In the following chapter, I will examine the development of jazz history's written discourses, with particular attention to many of the same issues that affect performance pedagogy. In particular, jazz historians often find themselves struggling with the same debates over "jazz vs. classical" perspectives, and have relied on many of the same solutions for getting jazz "in the door" of the academy as well. Additionally, historians often have the added burden of teaching a non-performance topic in a fundamentally performance-oriented area, adding yet another layer of complexity to an already contested, conflicted discipline.

CHAPTER 3

Doing and Teaching (and Researching)

In an essay published in the *Black Music Research Journal* in 1988, noted jazz researcher Lewis Porter lamented the prevalence of "problems" in jazz research. Among the issues Porter cites as inhibiting good, solid jazz scholarship are an insensitivity to a black perspective on jazz's history and practice, issues of authority in oral histories, and the role of jazz researchers who, in Porter's view, lack a deep and critical understanding of the jazz tradition, in other words, who do not *know* the music. Porter's essay concludes with the following:

> The recent appearance of the professional jazz scholar—the person who is hired, at least partially, to engage in jazz teaching and research and is not forced to pursue jazz only as a hobby or sideline—is a significant development in the acceptance of jazz in American higher education. But it brings with it certain responsibilities. Jazz scholars should be versed in a variety of research methods, should know music, and, ideally, should be performers. Jazz researchers should strive to produce top quality work. (Porter 1988, 204)

Porter's reference to researchers who study jazz as a "hobby or sideline" might be read as a swipe at non-specialist scholars (indeed, Porter harshly criticizes James Lincoln Collier, and not without justification), but I read the statement more as an intellectual call to arms for young musicologists to bring their talents to bear on jazz. What I am most interested in are Porter's concerns that jazz research comes with "certain responsibilities," and that scholars should "strive to produce top quality work" as if this needed pointing out. Clearly, though, Porter believes it does, and this admonition, appearing at a crucial moment in jazz history's emerging discourse, is reflective of broader currents in jazz in American life. While jazz was no longer popular, it was undergoing a renaissance driven by an overtly historicist clique of performers whose appearance sparked fierce critical debate. At the same time, jazz studies programs had begun to flourish on college campuses around the country and the world, creating a need and an opportunity for trained jazz historians. Porter wrote his article at a moment just before the birth of the "new jazz studies," and just before the appearance of seminal works such as Paul Berliner's *Thinking in Jazz* proved that jazz and musicological inquiry were not mutually exclusive. The character and nature of jazz writing was undergoing dramatic change. But these changes did not appear out of nowhere; debates and conflicts over jazz writing had been going on for years.

Anthropologist Clifford Geertz postulated that a culture can be "read" as a text, that the observed phenomena of cultural behavior can have meaning beyond physical description, applying methods of literary criticism to their interpretation. Such texts are, as Mark A. Schneider notes, "often obscure in [their] meaning and thus in need of interpretation" (Schneider 1987, 809). The texts of jazz have often been read as representing democracy, individuality, the story of American race relations, America's gift to world culture, and other common tropes in the music's discourse. This "story of jazz" has been standardized, canonized, and reified in performance, as have interpretations of jazz as a music of global sensibility and racial transcendence. But jazz also has recorded texts, sonic monuments whose "seductive menace," to borrow from Jed Rasula's excellent essay on recordings in the formation of canon, have fostered a de-historicized understanding of the music. As an experience of communion with performers, recordings transcend time and space; but as products of human agency, they are intertwined with their own historical contexts. Thus, the interpretation of these texts, and of associated historical narratives, can be done in multiple ways—analytical, contextual, semiotic, etc.—each of which speaks to the needs of the interpreter. Such a culture may produce multiple texts, each with a different interpretation.

Unlike Geertz's Balinese community, jazz communities have long existed in parallel with written discourses; these physical texts represent a culture in their own way, subject to similar types of interpretive strategies. Jazz writing runs the gamut from music-focused musicological analysis, to critical opinion-journalism, to culturally grounded studies, and nearly everything in between. Writers in each of these groups (as well as others) frequently cross boundaries from one to the other, making any formal assessment of general trends in jazz writing a mammoth task. Perhaps that is as it should be, for jazz music is itself open to multiple interpretations, and so its written discourse should reflect this. But jazz writing is more than simply an interpretation of the culture; it is a culture by itself, made manifest in the pages of books, recording reviews, interviews, and the like. How do we interpret this culture?

Throwing Geertz's culture-as-text metaphor into reverse, written texts can serve as an expression of jazz knowledge as an act of community and cultural agency. The analysis of these texts becomes a process of untangling how writers have constructed methods and models for knowing jazz, and in the process, how they have created intellectual anchors for jazz communities to define what the music means for them. While jazz's written discourse might be traditionally seen as a commentary and reflection on the "real world" of jazz, I suggest that this written discourse is central to interpreting jazz itself; not only does it construct or reflect the canon, it *is* the canon. Put another way, the act of creating an historical jazz canon through written texts may be as important as the actual musical content of that canon; without the former, the latter has little meaning beyond the reception of individual artists by individual listeners. Canon provides a foundational framework for our understanding of jazz. It does nothing less than allow us to engage in conversations and discourses on jazz—a critical point in the process of positioning ourselves within community contexts.

Jazz History: Birth of a Discipline

A watershed decade for jazz in many ways, the 1950s also saw the development of the modern discipline of jazz history (as distinct from a history of modern jazz). Just as earlier works had sought to establish the primacy of New Orleans jazz,[1] writers by the 1950s were trying to understand jazz in its totality, and as a function of social and cultural currents in American life. The major force behind the codification of a common historical narrative was undoubtedly Marshall Stearns, one of jazz's first intellectual champions. Stearns began his career in jazz writing as a critic for trade publications such as *Down Beat* in the 1930s, most notably authoring a series of columns on the "History of Swing." Pursuing a Ph.D. in English literature (Yale 1942, with an emphasis on medieval works)[2] might seem an unlikely career path for someone who is today regarded as a pioneering figure in jazz scholarship, but jazz at this time was not an accepted field of emphasis within musicology, or the music school in general.[3] Stearns's interest in jazz was reflected in the regular lectures he gave at colleges and universities in the New York region, most notably at the New School and NYU. Stearns's lectures were very well received, as were his lectures as a faculty member at the Lenox School of Jazz, the short-lived summer program in Massachusetts (Yudkin 2006, 62).

Stearns's approach to jazz history is described by John Gennari as a "consensus view" of the discipline (Gennari 2006, 119), a view that could well describe the field today. His major scholarly work on jazz history, 1956's *The Story of Jazz*, which Bruce Boyd Raeburn refers to as "the first great academic survey of jazz history," and "arguably the 'model' for official jazz historiography" (Raeburn 2009, 53), provides important indicators of what such a consensus view entails. But even before the book's publication, Stearns was developing such an approach, as his earlier writings demonstrate. The development of this narrative must first and foremost be understood within the context of an exceptionally racialized jazz discourse during his years as a writer for *Down Beat*, in which articles from the period regularly played up racial identity, focusing on particular qualities of "white" or "colored" jazz. The topic of jazz's racial origins was a frequent theme, as evidenced by a feature on the ODJB's Nick LaRocca, where the cornetist claimed without hesitation that "white man's music started jazz," as the headline proclaimed.[4] Even a cursory glance at the coverage given to popular musicians in the late 1930s demonstrates a notable emphasis on white musicians, with features on African American artists usually focusing on "name bands," or treated as something of a novelty.

It was in this environment that Stearns began to establish an historical narrative for jazz, penning a series of columns between 1936 and 1938 on "The History of Swing Music." For Stearns, swing was not simply the modern manifestation of jazz, it *was* jazz, directly linked to earlier developments and musicians, foreshadowing the "modernist" school led by Barry Ulanov and Leonard Feather in the early 1940s, as Bernard Gendron notes in his essay on jazz "critical wars" of the 1940s. Stearns's articles, which generally featured specific artists or groups of musicians in each installment, presented a more balanced view of the contributions of black artists than one might find in the pages of *Down Beat* at the time, positioning swing as a form that had clear African American roots. In a January 1937 profile of Red McKenzie, Eddie Condon, and the early Chicago school, he claims explicitly that "Colored Musicians Inspired These Boys," linking the development of Chicago jazz to migrant New Orleans musicians, especially Louis Armstrong. Another feature, from July 1937, focuses on the influence of "Colored Bands," highlighting the work of Fletcher Henderson, whose career as a bandleader had largely waned in the years before *Down Beat's* appearance. Stearns's privileging of the African American contributions to jazz served as a corrective to *Down Beat's* extensive coverage of white musicians, paralleling the traditionalist schools of the 1940s, which also sought to give primacy to black authorship of jazz. But Stearns was no "moldy fig"; he was a passionate advocate for swing and modern forms, arguing that jazz was maturing as an art form, and that as important as the New Orleans tradition was, jazz must move beyond its early roots. His focus on black authorship seems designed not as an expression of a primitivism, but mainly as an attempt to establish an accurate historical record.

Stearns's early historical writings in *Down Beat* reflect an approach to the subject that nods to the retrenchment of traditionalist criticism, but is balanced by an acknowledgment that jazz must change, as all styles inevitably do. Thus Stearns began shaping his "consensus view" of jazz history, an antidote to jazz's critical wars, even before those wars were in full flame, not merely as a response to them, and his columns provide important clues as to Stearns's developing perspective which would manifest itself in his later historical work. Most notable is the emphasis on a complete, connected historical development, in which all manifestations of the music, past to present, can be explained logically as part of a single cohesive story. All of the parts make sense; unlike the traditionalist narratives of the 1940s, where modern forms were a betrayal of jazz's roots, or the progressives, for whom the New Orleans tradition was increasingly irrelevant, Stearns occupied a middle ground, privileging neither tradition nor progress, seeing both as essential to jazz's developing historical discourse. It is this middle ground that Stearns is constantly seeking in *The Story of Jazz*, and that effort would codify contemporary approaches to the history of jazz itself.

Given its importance to shaping the jazz canon, that *The Story of Jazz* has not received a more thorough assessment in jazz historiography is surprising.[5] But the book provides important indicators of what characterizes this approach, embracing elements of historiography that are still widely embraced by contemporary scholars of the music. Several overarching themes in *The Story of Jazz* characterize his approach to jazz history, both echoed in later works and foreshadowed in earlier ones. Among these are:

1. A broadly inclusive view of jazz style that incorporates different manifestations of the music. This is important in the wake of the critical debates that characterized jazz criticism in the 1940s (Gennari 2006, 119), of which Stearns was an observer, though not an active participant. His approach seeks a middle ground in these perspectives, drawing upon elements of both, without falling victim to more ideological arguments and conflicts. Stearns's agenda is not the promotion of a specific view of jazz, but of jazz generally.

2. An extensive discussion of jazz's "pre-history" (and an intentionality in the use of that term), with a particular focus on the role of African and African American musical, historical, and cultural forces. While many writers to this point certainly saw blues, ragtime, and other "roots" genres as important to jazz's development, Stearns's systematic and historically grounded treatment is much more extensive and thoroughly documented than most previous work, without emphasizing the primitivist perspectives of earlier writers.

3. The positioning of New Orleans as a focal point, if not the birthplace, of jazz's development up to the 1920s. Stearns clearly shares many of the perspectives of the traditionalists of the 1940s, treating New Orleans as the location from which the first recognizable forms of jazz emerged. New Orleans is, in Stearns's narrative, where jazz "proper" begins.

4. A stylistic narrative in which each decade sees the development of new forms. Stearns's narrative is divided fairly neatly into decade-defined discussions; New Orleans jazz emerges by the 1920s, a decade that is characterized by the development of jazz in Chicago and New York. The 1930s are defined first by a decline in the jazz scene after the Crash of 1929, and later by swing. Meanwhile, around 1940, swing declines, displaced eventually by the New Orleans revival and bebop. The overall narrative juxtaposes periods of stylistic coalescence against those of transition.

5. A discussion of bebop that treats it as a disjuncture in both musical and cultural terms. Terms like "revolution" are frequently employed, and Stearns's narrative emphasizes the perspective that bebop was a musical and cultural reaction to swing and other earlier forms. Stearns also highlights bebop as a generational shift in comparison to earlier forms.

6. A tendency to devote more attention to earlier forms than current ones. Bebop, cool, and other contemporary developments (such as they were in 1956) are included in a single chapter at the end of the narrative, while earlier forms comprise the bulk of the discussion. There is much more coverage, for example, of the period from 1935–1945, for example, than there is of 1945–1955.

Stearns writes with a mix of engagement and affection for the music, but with a clear attempt at scholarly detachment and objectivity. This approach is explicitly outlined in the Preface: "I see no reason to maintain the melancholy pretense of absolute objectivity. I like jazz very much, and I am no doubt biased in its favor—at least to the extent of trying to find out what it is all about" (Stearns 1956, xii). He continues, explaining his broadly inclusive definition of the music: "I find that I have tended to enlarge the usual area covered by the word 'jazz' and to include most of the music created, with the help of the American Negro, in the United States. . . . The aim of *The Story of Jazz* is to outline the main currents of a great tradition" (Stearns 1956, xii).

In his statement about adopting a broad view of the music, Stearns seems to directly address the split in jazz criticism epitomized by the "moldy figs and moderns" debates a decade before. Not all writers shared his views; consensus still needed to be built.[6] This comes as a call for unity for the sake of advancing the cause of all jazz musicians, in what (it must be remembered) was a jazz scene that already had begun to shrink in the face of newly emerging popular forms. This brings us to a second point: Stearns's claim to "include most of the music created . . . in the United States." This is clearly not the case, as by this point in time there were other movements in popular music, from country and western to the newly emerging rhythm and blues/rock and roll continuum. That Stearns fails to include such developments, even while claiming to speak for all "American music" is significant, and represents, I suggest, a growing disdain for new popular music and concern about its gradual displacement of jazz. Stearns's welcoming and accommodating view of jazz, it seems, had its limits.

The Story of Jazz begins with an extended discussion of "The Pre-History of Jazz," the subtitle for Part One of the book. Divided into three chapters, this first discussion is rich in both detail and speculation. Stearns classifies jazz as the "result of a 300-year-old blending in the United States of two great musical traditions, the European and the West African" (Stearns 1956, 3). The most curious aspect of both Stearns's treatment of this idea, and of prevailing historical narratives of jazz in general, is that the main emphasis in this discussion of this pre-history is not actually on the "blending" of traditions, but on the exploration of the African tradition itself. Stearns never explicitly states why this is the case, though he does imply that American culture is "predominantly European." This, then, seems to suggest that the target readership for his book is one that is familiar with the European traditions of folk and classical music that have predominated American musical life. Whether or not this was ever the case is debatable, but from an academic standpoint the predominance of European narratives (especially in musicology) is self-evident. It may also be that for someone whose early interest in jazz was shaped as a record collector of and later writer about a music for whom he had affection, the discussion of African music and culture is simply more interesting. Could it be that Stearns was a bit of an exoticist, favoring the relatively newly discovered (for him) over the staid and boring, enchanted by the lure of an idealized African past?

While not engaging in the kinds of primitivist arguments of earlier critics and scholars, Stearns nonetheless reduces the "qualities that make jazz a little different" as having "something to do with West Africa" (3). This is apparent in his discussions of rhythm (6–7) and "blue notes" (7), and a predilection for call-and-response forms, which for Stearns go a long way toward defining jazz musically. Stearns draws a nearly direct line between African practice and jazz: "The continued existence of the ring shout is of critical importance to jazz, because it means that an assortment of West African musical characteristics are preserved, more or less intact. . . . And an entire way of life has survived with it" (Stearns 1956, 13).

Stearns also emphasizes cultural aspects of the African diaspora, particularly as related to the development of African American communities during the period of enslavement. In chapter 2 he draws a distinction between the experience of slaves in Latin-Catholic colonies to those of British-Protestant ones, arguing that in the former, cultural and musical developments retained more of their African origin, and were allowed to flourish, while those in British areas were forced "underground." New Orleans would thus retain more of an African flavor, directly influencing the course of the music (Stearns 1956, 33). If none of this sounds unfamiliar in the literature of jazz history today, it speaks to the way in which Stearns's core pre-historic jazz narrative still holds.

Stearns's treatment of New Orleans in this "consensus" narrative echoes the traditionalist argument that this was where these different elements would coalesce.[7] The unique qualities of New Orleans are seen as critical to the development of the earliest recognizable jazz styles, having "a special place in the story of jazz" that "led to the birth of a new music" (Stearns 1956, 37). Building on the first section of the book (especially chapters 2 and 3, in which he explores the Latin-Catholic connection), Stearns's portrayal of New Orleans is of a city that is the most "African" of any in the United States. The emphasis on retentions from West African practices obscures other unique aspects of New Orleans music life (such as the minimal attention paid to the flourishing concert music scene). The New Orleans narrative is one of simultaneity of influences: French, Spanish, British, Catholic, Protestant, and above all, African. It is the last influence that again garners the most attention. The primacy of black traditions in Stearns's discussion of New Orleans is reflected in his extensive coverage of Congo Square, positioned as a key factor in fostering the diasporic memories of various groups. Detailing a "transition to jazz" (the title of the fifth chapter), Stearns cites such factors as the Black Code of 1724 and immigration laws (Stearns 1956, 44), the popularity of *vodun* (48–50), and the widespread use of various African-derived drums (51–53) as significant influences, though specific connections are hard to come by in his explanations.

In the sixth chapter, "Jazz Begins," Stearns departs briefly from the African-centered narrative to discuss the role of military bands, spurred on by both their popularity in imperial France and their use in the Civil War (Stearns 1956, 55–56). But these developments are not discussed in anywhere near the level of depth as the African-derived practices of the preceding chapters; presumably Stearns assumes that the readership is familiar with the genre. It is from this point that Stearns (after a brief discussion of African-derived "secret societies") begins to delve into the funeral band traditions. Though he does not make the point directly, it is clear that this is where he draws the dividing line between what is classified as "pre-history" and what can be identified as jazz, the central musical discussion in a chapter entitled "Jazz Begins." It is also in this chapter that Stearns first makes reference to Storyville, and to the roles of Creoles of Color in the shaping of jazz, constructing a narrative in which Creole and black came to inhabit the same musical and social spaces by the early twentieth century. Positioning the Creoles as the melting pot *in persona*, he sees this process as culminating in a form of proto-jazz with direct links to contemporary practices:

> [Creoles] brought their knowledge of European instruments and tech-niques with them and merged with the darker pioneers who thought of any instrument simply as an extension of the human voice. . . . And all of it blended with the thriving brass bands employed by the fraternal so-cieties. The result was a competently played march that also had begun to swing, an *elementary kind of jazz that would still be recognizable as such today*. (Stearns 1956, 66, emphasis added)

This last point is critical to understanding Stearns's "consensus view." All of the discussions of pre-history and early New Orleans lead to this single sentence. Stearns makes an explicit link between the many different musical and social currents running from Africa to New Orleans, and their fusion with European forms. But more than that, he argues that such developments still have rel-evance to contemporary listeners. New Orleans is not merely the birthplace of jazz; it is a tangible link between a distant, largely speculative past and the experiences of the current jazz community. The use of a term like *elementary* positions New Orleans as a start point, an early stage of development upon which later approaches would be based.

To this point, there has been very little discussion of specific musicians. This changes in the next chapter, "Buddy Bolden and the Growth of Jazz." Stearns gathers the scant evidence on Bolden's life and career and constructs a portrait of a figure who was of profound importance to pre-1920s jazz. Though this discussion of Bolden is largely speculative, he serves as a con-venient start point for the construction of a canon, one in which significant individuals are positioned, one after another, in a seamless parade of innova-tion. Stearns's history then takes an odd turn, seemingly moving backwards to a discussion of yet more background developments. Stearns devotes the next few chapters to discussions of religious music, ragtime, blues, and black-face minstrelsy. Specific connections to jazz are hard to come by in some of these discussions; this is particularly true in the case of Stearns's discussions of religious movements and work songs, where connections to jazz are not easily observed in the narrative. Stearns's treatment of blues, by contrast, argues for a deep connection to jazz.

In the chapter on ragtime, we see ample evidence of an orientation toward a developmental view of musical styles. Describing ragtime as an essentially European-derived genre that gradually adopted more African elements (Stearns 1956, 143), Stearns constructs a clear developmental process, evolving through a series of regionally defined stages, beginning in Sedalia, Missouri, the "parent style," which he praises for its "splendid" structure and melody (144). Stearns argues that "the next step in the process" of ragtime's evolution comes from St. Louis, where the "difference is electric" when compared to the Sedalia style (145), the key development being one of rhythmic flow. A "third step in the development of a more complex rhythm" (145) comes from New Orleans, where pianists such as Jelly Roll Morton fused ragtime with the "rolling rhythms created by the popular marching bands" (145). The final step in ragtime's development is epitomized by the New York "stride" pianists such as Willie "the Lion" Smith, James P. Johnson, and Fats Waller. Stearns's interpretation of the history of ragtime and its role in the creation of jazz is less important than the way in which he constructs such a smooth, cogent narrative for its development. One regional style leads logically into the next, each building on the other.

The discussion of jazz's rise to popularity is situated within the context of the 1920s "Jazz Age" (the title of Part Four of *The Story of Jazz*), with chapters devoted to discussions that illustrate a developmental perspective; chapters include "The Jazz Age Begins," "The Jazz Age Flourishes," and "The Jazz Age Ends." In the beginning of this discussion, Stearns outlines two objectives, first linking the rise of jazz in the 1920s to the general social milieu (referencing F. Scott Fitzgerald, Prohibition, the growth of recording, and other contextual factors). Second, from a musical perspective, Stearns ties together threads from his previous discussions, such as the development of the first jazz bands in New Orleans, the emergence of blues singers, and the popularity of ragtime. All the elements are now in place for what would be jazz's golden age. Chapter 14 ("The Jazz Age Begins") ends with a brief account of jazz musicians' activities outside of New Orleans, culminating in Chicago (by way of Los Angeles, St. Louis, and New York), though he does point to the "inadequacy" of the oft-cited "New Orleans-to-Chicago-by-riverboat" narrative (Stearns 1956, 161–62). The "flourishing" of the Jazz Age (chapter 15) focuses mainly on the work of Paul Whiteman and Fletcher Henderson, though Stearns also finds room for blues singers like Bessie Smith, as well as more underappreciated groups such as the Mound City Blue Blowers. As with his emphasis on black authorship of jazz in his *Down Beat* writings, Stearns advances a similar perspective in this discussion, writing:

> A kind of feed-back occurs in jazz whereby white amateurs perform in the humble tradition of Negro song-and-dance bands on street corners. . . . As time passes, the best of them turn professional, joining other professionals who enjoy old-time jazz. . . . Something of this process helps to explain the New Orleans and Dixieland Revivals which have been taking place since 1940 and which have been a powerful factor in the diffusion of jazz. (Stearns 1956, 173)

Stearns again makes an explicit argument that white musicians have come to jazz as followers, rather than as leaders, a theme that echoes his earlier writings.

The "end" of the Jazz Age is characterized by the rise of jazz in New York, Harlem in particular, as well as the Midwest, especially Kansas City. For Stearns, this period marks the end of "jazz" as a widely used term, and the introduction of "swing" (179). The late 1920s marked a period of stylistic chaos, as approaches to the music began to shift along with jazz's racial politics. Stearns argues that this period saw a gradual recognition among white artists that black musicians were the music's pioneers, and that musical ability, rather than race, would dictate the establishment of an artist's bona fides. As much as Stearns has emphasized the African American contribution to jazz, and the white imitation of it, by the 1930s, jazz provided an avenue for a more egalitarian view of American culture, where white and black audiences would be attuned to the same artists. The narrative of jazz as a soundtrack to eventual racial integration and conciliation is thus established.

Stearns's discussion of swing is less extensive than one might expect, given his earlier "History of Swing Music" columns. Stearns sees swing as somewhat different from earlier forms (he compares Benny Goodman with the ODJB), though still fundamentally connected to them. His discussion of swing focuses mainly on Goodman, emphasizing his relationship and stylistic debt to Fletcher Henderson, and his incalculable role in codifying and polarizing the genre. Goodman's fabled performance at the Palomar in Los Angeles in August 1935 is explicitly labeled as the start of the Swing Era (211). But as in many other parts of his narrative, the undercurrent of a white/black dichotomy is ever present. In discussing Goodman's rise to fame, he refers to Count Basie as the "man behind the throne" of the King of Swing's success (211), though Stearns draws no direct link that would justify such a comment. The argument is again one of black authorship of the tradition generally, rather than any specific connection between these two figures. His feelings about swing are surprisingly difficult to gauge; he clearly sees swing as an important development in jazz, but is still somewhat dismissive at the end of the discussion: "Swing music by big bands hit the public eye, made an incredible amount of money, and then faded out; but the music of the small-band New Orleans revival has been growing slowly and surely and seems to be here to stay" (Stearns 1956, 17). Thus Stearns's attitudes towards swing are ultimately conflicted. Unlike the traditionalists of the revivalist school, he does not openly denigrate it. But neither does he offer full-voiced support for it; it seems to be a blip on the radar, a temporary commercial interruption between the New Orleans tradition and what would come later. Discussions of figures such as Ellington are surprisingly minimal. Perhaps if *The Story of Jazz* had been written, say, after Ellington's landmark 1956 performance at Newport, Stearns's perspective on swing might be different.

The place of bebop in Stearns's narrative, as might be expected, is one of abrupt, radical change: "By 1940 jazz had attained enough momentum to stage a revolution more or less on its own. . . . "bop" was a sudden eruption within jazz, a fast but logical complication of melody, harmony and rhythm" (Stearns 1956, 218). He devotes little attention to tracing the development of bebop via an examination of late-1930s soloists, though he does treat Roy Eldridge as a major influence on Dizzy Gillespie, a lineage traced to Armstrong (226). Stearns's attitudes toward bebop, like swing, are difficult to fully assess; he does not offer a ringing endorsement of bop, saying, that of the "cries of anguish" coming from those hearing bop for the first time in 1945, "a good many . . . were justified" (225–26). On the other hand, he refers to Charlie Parker as a "genius," who "had much to do with opening up new elbowroom for improvisation" (231). Another notable aspect of Stearns's discussion of bebop is his combination of it with discussions of cool jazz and the progressive bands of Stan Kenton, Woody Herman, and Boyd Raeburn. For Stearns, these are part of the same general stylistic trend, sharing space with Miles Davis, Gerry Mulligan, Lennie Tristano, and Chico Hamilton, under one stylistic tent, all part of the revolutionary impulse from the mid-1940s. These are important developments for Stearns, if for no other reason than for their role in advancing a view of jazz that is characterized by the sense of evolution—a developmental narrative in which various manifestations of jazz can be seen as sharing a unified narrative.

What is most notable about Stearns's discussion of the prevailing trends of jazz in the 1950s is that it is so brief. That there would be no mention of Ornette Coleman or Cecil Taylor is understandable. More curious is that there is no mention of Sonny Rollins or John Coltrane, while Art Blakey is mentioned only in passing. The most interesting "omission" is Thelonious

Monk, who is barely discussed, and whose name appears in the index on only three pages. Given Monk's role in the development of bebop, one might expect to find a more sustained discussion of his career to that point. Hard bop trumpeter Clifford Brown, today considered a primary influence on modern jazz trumpet, is mentioned exactly once, again only in passing, despite his having co-led a highly regarded quintet with Max Roach by the time of the book's appearance.

The place of bebop and related movements within the jazz narrative speaks to an emphasis on the inevitability of change. This reflects more than the internal tensions within jazz communities; they are representative of a larger process, ultimately beyond jazz itself. One of the most striking passages in *The Story of Jazz*, a perspective that speaks directly to this view of jazz's history, can be found near the end of his historical discussion, in which Stearns attempts to place bebop within its proper historical perspective: "What happened since 1940? In terms of harmony, jazz developed along the same lines as classical music (by adopting the next note in the overtone series),[8] but more recently and rapidly. It still lags behind. Bop represented a stage in the harmonic evolution of jazz roughly comparable to the period that followed Wagner and Debussy" (Stearns 1956, 229). Stearns accomplishes two things here. First, he draws a link between the trajectories of Western art music and jazz. Wagner and Debussy are two figures whose contributions are positioned as having revolutionized the Western canon, and the comparison with bebop would seem to cast Parker, Gillespie, et al. in a similar light. Second, Stearns suggests that jazz, though exhibiting an accelerated developmental timeframe when compared to classical music, still "lags behind," foreshadowing other developments in jazz, though he does not speculate as to their specific character.

For Stearns, it seems, the legitimating value of jazz lay in this broad developmental course paralleling that of the Western canon. Like classical music, jazz history could be traced through a logical progression of stylistic development, an art form with its own path. Perhaps that is Stearns's greatest legacy as an historian, legitimizing jazz through its similarity of trajectory with established art forms. This broad view of jazz has formed the core of legitimating arguments about jazz nearly since its inception, positioning jazz as "America's classical music." Stearns formalized it and gave it academic grounding. Ironically, his identity as a non-music scholar may have given more credence to this idea; if a Yale-educated scholar of Chaucer found artistic value in jazz, then maybe it really *did* have value. In the same way that early jazz educators created methods of instruction that spoke the language of academia, so did Stearns speak the language of canon, and his ability to apply it to jazz is his most enduring contribution.

That Stearns's work provided a foundation for modern jazz historiography is clear; general history texts written since *The Story of Jazz* track remarkably close to his narrative. What is less apparent is the degree to which his work is based in earlier scholarship. Gennari argues that Stearns was notable for "refusing to take sides" in the debates of the previous decade (Gennari 2006, 152). As a developing scholar at Yale, Stearns was influenced by figures in a number of fields, establishing what is best described as an interdisciplinary approach to jazz history. As William Kenney notes, Stearns "consulted with" a number of academics during his graduate years at Yale, gaining some expertise in anthropology, sociology, and musicology from faculty members in different areas (Kenney 2003, 16). With this eclectic approach, not dogmatically tied to musicology, criticism, or his chosen academic career in English, Stearns pulled together numerous perspectives to form a consensus narrative. In his discussion of African influences Stearns echoes much the work of Blesh, Delaunay, and their peers, without the primitivist trappings. But modern developments also form part of his story. The core narrative linking older and newer approaches tracks remarkably close to that of Ulanov. In short, Stearns did not reinvent the wheel—he just made it spin better. By advocating for an inclusive view of jazz, Stearns suggested that jazz, in facing an increasingly bleak commercial future with the rise of rock and roll, could not afford the kinds of divisive debates that took place in the 1940s. Of course, such debates would emerge again with the development of an experimental, avant-garde approach to jazz at nearly the same time *The Story of Jazz* was hitting the bookshelf.

In the wake of *The Story of Jazz*, several other general jazz histories appeared that expressed a similar consensus on the nature of jazz, such as Leroy Ostransky's 1960 book *The Anatomy of Jazz*. Ostransky, trained primarily as a composer, takes a self-consciously outsider's view of the music,[9] constructing his text

> first, to present jazz in its proper perspective to those whose primary interest is in "serious" or classical music, and to relate jazz theory to music theory in general; second, to introduce those whose primary is in jazz to the problems of nonjazz composers and performers by relating jazz to the history of music in general . . . [and] to indicate to jazzmen what I believe to be their present position in music, as well as their musical responsibility to the future. (Ostransky 1960, vii)

Less a history than a primer on various issues in jazz, Ostransky's book makes its own claims about the development of the music, some of which clearly echoes Stearns. In discussing the harmonic intricacies of bebop, for example, he notes that such developments are "not unlike the one[s] that followed Wagner and Debussy in the nineteenth century" (297). Ostransky does not cite Stearns, but merely notes that this fact "has been pointed out many times before" (Ostransky 1960, 297). And like Stearns, Ostransky emphasizes discussions of earlier forms while offering a truncated view of the modern era. Most notable by their omission are developments in the 1950s, in particular the very brief section on cool and the complete omission of hard bop; John Coltrane and Sonny Rollins, both of whom by this time were significant figures on the current jazz scene, are not mentioned at all. These gaps are particularly puzzling given the author's expressed intent to provide a snapshot of the "present position" of jazz musicians, as well as his penchant for prognostication, best represented in the final chapter, "Toward the Future."

Paul Tanner, a jazz trombonist with Glenn Miller and later professor at UCLA, produced (along with Maurice Gerow) *A Study of Jazz* in 1964, rightly seen as the first textbook produced specifically for a collegiate audience. Tanner's jazz history classes at UCLA were the stuff of legend since their inception in 1958, a staple on campus for many years that regularly drew hundreds of students. The narrative of Tanner and Gerow's text follows Stearns very closely, breaking up the subject into similar style-defined sections (though Tanner/Gerow gives more extensive coverage to later developments). Speaking directly to the use of Stearns's book as a classroom tool, Tanner writes: "The Stearns book was more popular before there were others on the market. The consensus of opinion is that Stearns did excellent research, especially in the prejazz area, although he did lack understanding of more modern idioms" (Tanner 1971, 106). Stearns's death in 1966 precluded any further revision to the narrative to include or expand on these modern idioms, limiting its applicability as a classroom text. Tanner's book thus serves as an important step in the shift from jazz history as a critical pursuit into one where pedagogy is of prime concern. With the canon more or less established, writers of jazz histories could now begin to interpret it for use in the classroom. We shall return to this point later in the chapter.

Specialized Scholarship: Gunther Schuller, *Jazz Review*, and *Journal of Jazz Studies*

By the late 1950s, several notable jazz periodicals had appeared. Some, like *Down Beat*, thrived, and were an important avenue of jazz criticism; for others, in particular rival magazine *Metronome*, their days were numbered. But these were mainly trade publications. Few avenues existed for the new generation of jazz scholars whose work was increasingly specialized.[10] In the wake of Stearns and the codification of jazz historiography, scholars began to sharpen their focus, producing academic studies that dealt with narrowly defined topics. Academic articles on jazz were often the purview of social science publications, or those in the humanities. With respect to the former, psychological studies of jazz were common in the 1950s. Jazz was treated as a pathology, and researchers sought to explain what were often seen as deviant, subcultural behaviors. Sociologists such as Howard Becker or William Bruce Cameron examined the social networks of jazz. Such studies were often generalized, essentialized accounts of jazz, with little attention paid to historical process, identity, or musical practice.[11]

The appearance of the *Jazz Review* in 1958 was an attempt to rectify this. Cofounded by Nat Hentoff and Martin Williams, *Jazz Review* featured a balance of scholarly and critical writing, along with letters, feature articles on major musicians, and reviews of both recordings and written publications. Most notable, however, was its role as a venue for focused scholarship, perhaps the first publication to feature what might be called a musicological approach to jazz. *Jazz Review*'s very first article is also likely its most famous, and certainly most controversial: Gunther Schuller's "Sonny Rollins and the Challenge of Thematic Improvisation." Schuller's detailed analysis set the bar for scholarship exceptionally high in his essay, in which he explored Rollins's 1956 recording of "Blue 7" from the album *Saxophone Colossus*, arguing that Rollins had produced an improvised performance that finally approached the melodic coherence in the works of the classical masters. Schuller's treatment was also notable for the reaction from Rollins himself, who was puzzled why anyone would want to dissect his music in such a way. It was, according to Robert Walser, the essay that pushed Rollins to stop reading his own press (Walser 1999, 213).[12] Regardless of interpretation, Schuller's analysis was a watershed moment for jazz scholarship, demonstrating that jazz could be discussed in detailed, analytical ways, that a real jazz musicology was possible.

A short time later he again found himself in hot water with the subject of his writing. In a review of Cecil Taylor's *Jazz Advance* and *Quartet at Newport* albums, Schuller takes a similarly analytical approach, noting that Taylor demonstrated parallels to avant-garde classical composition. Like Rollins, Taylor bristled at Schuller's interpretations equating the works with traditions and techniques of Western art music (Spellman 1966, 30–31). Schuller's intent in these pieces is seemingly resonant with that of Stearns, seeking to legitimize jazz in relation to the Western canon, but with an emphasis on the performance practice of the music. Near the beginning of the Taylor review, Schuller makes the claim the "The history of jazz . . . is taking a course virtually parallel [to the classical tradition]," an assertion that has obvious implications for how future jazz scholars would conceptualize the historical and structural narratives of the music. In detailed, painstaking analyses, he demonstrated the potential of jazz scholarship's emerging discourse; in the reactions to his work by some musicians, he demonstrated the discourse's contested nature.

Jazz Review and *Metronome* ceased publication in 1961, leaving *Down Beat* as the only significant platform for critical debate and discussion of jazz. *Down Beat* has never, however, featured the kind of high-level scholarly study that Schuller contributed to *Jazz Review*, and for over a decade, jazz scholars were left without a dedicated venue for research. Schuller's contributions to *Jazz Review* were, it turned out, merely a warm-up act for his groundbreaking historical studies *Early Jazz* and *The Swing Era*, two of the most detailed and thorough examples of jazz historiography ever published. *Early Jazz* is a scrupulously detailed and thorough account of jazz's first decades, covering the music's pre-history through the late 1920s. He also critically examines existing scholarship, much of which he criticizes for a lack of analytical depth (though he does praise the work of Winthrop Sargeant and Andre Hodier, both of whom he cites as significant influences on his own approach). Of Stearns, Schuller notes that *The Story of Jazz* is "astute and well documented," but suggests that the book suffers from its orientation toward "the layman and general reader" (Schuller 1968, viii). Still, Schuller obviously had a great deal of respect for Stearns, and likely did not want to appear too critical considering Stearns's recent passing. In mitigating his criticism, Schuller suggests that Stearns's book "did not claim to be more than [a general history] . . . as a historian and professor of English Literature Dr. Stearns could hardly have been expected to apply the analytic techniques used by Sargeant and Hodier" (Schuller 1968, viii).[13]

Stearns did not intend to create a detailed analytical overview of jazz, and in the long run, this worked out well for Schuller, in that it gave him the opportunity to establish himself as an expert in this area. Despite distancing his work from Stearns, it is clear that in terms of narrative, Schuller seems to hold many of the same assumptions, that jazz was a music whose different approaches could be linked through a careful interpretation of historical and musical process. Importance is placed on African and African American sources, but white musicians too figure prominently in the narrative. New Orleans figures prominently in the narrative, as do all the usual actors. Schuller in no way attempts to critique or deconstruct the canon, but rather to understand it more deeply, or even to reinforce it. He applies the microscope of analysis and musicological method to the macro-narrative of Stearns and the interdisciplinary consensus view. As such, he represented the first post-Stearns approach to look at the history of jazz that took a different approach to the topic, in method if not in interpretation. This type of scholarship would continue into the 1970s, with jazz studies gaining currency as a dynamic, interdisciplinary endeavor.

As the first director of the Institute of Jazz Studies, Marshall Stearns would have been well positioned to become the leading figure in jazz historiography into the 1970s and beyond. At the time of his death in 1966, the institute was already widely recognized as a vital resource for many emerging and established jazz scholars. But Stearns did not live to see one of the institute's most significant contributions to jazz scholarship. Launched in 1973 under the editorship of Charles Nanry and David Cayer, the *Journal of Jazz Studies* was the first peer-reviewed academic publication devoted specifically to jazz. Though jazz scholarship had begun to grow, publishing opportunities for jazz scholars were exceedingly limited; from the 1950s to the 1970s, the preeminent journal in the field of American musicology, The *Journal of the American Musicological Society*, had not published a single article devoted to jazz; prior to 1950, a pair of articles appeared in 1948: a brief by Lois von Haupt on jazz's "Negroid" origins, and a piece by Richard Waterman entitled "'Hot' Rhythm in Negro Music," both of which are exceptionally primitivist in their treatment of the subject. *Ethnomusicology* had published a few essays, most notably an essay by Alan Merrian and Fradley Garner on the etymology of the word jazz. The scholarly literature of jazz was scattered and without any unifying voice. Nanry and Cayer (speaking for the institute itself, presumably) addressed this problem directly in the introduction to the inaugural issue of the *JJS*:

> For several decades, the article-length literature of jazz has been growing, but its publication has been scattered among a number of periodicals, each of which has considered jazz distinctly peripheral, even if the stature of the authors and the quality of the scholarship was sufficient to overcome the prejudices against jazz. These prejudices—rooted perhaps in the African and Afro-American sources of the music or its status as a part of popular culture—have been fading, but the need for a specialized publication for jazz scholars has remained. (Nanry and Cayer 1973, 1)

The first volume of the *JJS* (comprising two issues from 1973 to 1974) offers a wide variety of topics and approaches to the study of jazz, and the credentials of its contributors speak to the still largely interdisciplinary nature of jazz scholarship of the day. The October 1973 edition (vol. 1, no. 1) features essays on Fats Waller, Billie Holiday, Artie Shaw, the sociology of jazz, and discography in jazz research, as well as a brief tribute to Marshall Stearns. Of the contributors, only James S. Patrick is identified as a musicologist; of the remaining four, two are sociologists, one an historian, and one a professor of English. In the second issue of volume 1, six authors contribute full-length essays, on topics from Buddy Bolden to Charlie Parker to the "Phenomenology of Jazz." Again, scholars in the humanities and social sciences are heavily represented, with only two authors not holding appointments in sociology, history, or English. Subsequent issues reflect a similar interdisciplinary orientation, mixing musicological approaches with those from the humanities and social sciences. The profile of a typical jazz scholar remained difficult to pin down.

By the time of the appearance of volume 6 of *JJS*, in late 1979, the makeup of the editorial board had changed very little, though there were some notable additions, including Gunther Schuller, Rudi Blesh, Dan Morgenstern (later the institute's director) and Frank Gillis, the director of Indiana University's Archive of Traditional Music. Musicologists themselves were still in a minority on the board, though articles by Steven Strunk on bebop harmony and Joshua Barrett, writing on Alan Lomax, are representative of a musicology-oriented approach. This was to be the last issue of the journal; it was succeeded in 1982 by an annual edition (also published by the Institute of Jazz Studies), the *Annual Review of Jazz Studies*. As the editors (Nanry, Cayer, and Morgenstern) note, the shift was due mainly to "reasons of scholarship, broader readership, and inevitably, economics" (Morgenstern et al. 1982, 1). The interdisciplinary nature of both the editorial board and the contributing authors remained largely unchanged; the board listed in the introductory issue was, by and large, the same as for its predecessor.

Those Who Can, Do—Those Who Can't . . . : Teaching Jazz in a Performer's World

As jazz scholarship began to come into its own in the 1970s, jazz history likewise blossomed in academic curricula on many college campuses. Despite the continued use of college-oriented texts such as Tanner and Gerow's, the 1970s also saw the development of the first jazz history textbooks that were intended to address the growing academic market.[14] First and foremost among these was Frank Tirro's *Jazz: A History*, published by W.W. Norton, best known in musicology for its publication of Donald Jay Grout's 800-pound gorilla of musical canon, *A History of Western Music*.[15] For many who anticipated its arrival, Tirro's *Jazz* could potentially provide the still nascent field of jazz studies with a similar unifying, codifying historical text around which to rally, a "jazz Grout" as one of my former professors called it. Like Grout, Tirro's work as a musicologist might have given his efforts more intellectual heft, and as he explained in the book's preface, his work, arising from musicology, filled a particular void in jazz writing:

> The history of jazz is a fascinating subject, and a variety of writers—musicians, scholars, enthusiasts, journalists—have treated it with love and respect. Of all the works presently available, however, no single volume offers the reader an analysis and interpretation of jazz, both historical and musical, which incorporates recent research from allied fields—sociology, cultural anthropology, and American history—as well as from music history and theory. (Tirro 1977, xvii)

In a bit of scholarly self-reflection and honestly, he continues: "Historians try to be objective, but this writer was ultimately forced to include and emphasize those aspects of the historical development which seemed to him to be the most important, most representative, and most germane to present-day teachers" (Tirro 1977, xvii). Like Stearns, Tirro was certainly attracted to the structure and logic provided by the Western canon, and his organization tracks closely to that of earlier studies.

Despite its potential, the reaction to Tirro's textbook was far from enthusiastic. In a crushing review of the book in the *Journal of the American Musicological Society*, Lawrence Gushee attacked Tirro's book on a number of fronts. Highlighting what he contends are mistakes of fact, interpretation and editing, Gushee (also a pedigreed musicologist) is unsparing in his criticism, writing late in his review:

> To sum up: I find *Jazz: A History* an enormous disappointment, particularly because for the past ten years at least there have been appearing more specialized works which are superior in standards of scholarship and clear expression. It may be that, notwithstanding the buzzing swarm of incorrect or imprecisely stated facts and the contradictions and ambivalence of Tirro's broader historical or sociological interpretations, *Jazz: A History* will be found to be a "serviceable" textbook. For myself, I do not believe that compromises of this sort benefit education or public understanding at any level. (Gushee 1978, 539–40)

First impressions are important, and if this is the best that jazz musicology can produce, then the discipline may have a serious problem. These statements speak to what is perhaps a latent fear that jazz is still a sideline, a novelty within the musicological community, one that need not be subjected to the rigors of fact-checking and a groundedness in existing scholarship (all the more curious when considering Gushee's "serviceable" comment).

The debate between Tirro and Gushee (which included a response from Tirro and counter-response from Gushee) represented some of the growing pains of a musicology-based approach to jazz history, a discipline that had, until now, been abdicated to interdisciplinary scholars. In short, the jazz musicologist was just starting to emerge, and Gushee was rightly concerned that the field needed to get it right, lest jazz continue to be relegated to second-class status in academic life. This was underscored by Tirro's defense against criticism that his transcriptions were not accurate, to which he replied that these were the materials with which he had to work. Gushee responded with a comment that stands as a good representation of this entire controversy:

"If Tirro wants a better transcription he should do it himself—this was the point of my criticism—and can begin by hearing that the second chord indicated by Austin is mostly or only in the guitar part, the others hanging on to the subdominant. (This, not incidentally, invalidates one of Austin's basic points.) He can then write the notes at more or less their proper length and position"(Gushee 1979, 598). This is not simply an accusation of scholarly sloppiness. Gushee is accusing Tirro of not being a "real" jazz scholar by not producing his own transcriptions for his book, of being, at some level, an outsider. That Tirro seems to have seen his work as "close enough for jazz" seems to deeply trouble Gushee, and may speak to the nature of the relationship between jazz studies and musicology at the time. As the two scholarly communities were beginning to come into closer contact, jazz historians were under a microscope, much like their predecessors in performance a decade before.

Gushee was not alone in his negative response to *Jazz: A History*, as other scholars took Tirro to task for many of the same problems. In a notable review in *Black Perspective in Music*, Lewis Porter also harshly criticized Tirro, arguing that Tirro's misinterpretations of the "Dippermouth Blues" solo suggests that "[He] is not adequately familiar with one of the most celebrated solos in all of jazz" (L. Porter 1978, 234). While Gushee's comments imply a sense of concern about the impact of poor scholarship on jazz studies, Porter expresses this sentiment explicitly:

> Even in these times of tremendous interest on the part of young people in listening to and learning about jazz, much of academia remains skeptical as to its value. Its popularity among the youth only reaffirms the cynic's conviction that jazz is "pop music." Every book or article that is carelessly researched and thoughtlessly written simply supports this attitude. We who know the music well enough to realize its worth have a

responsibility to help the field by producing work that is as flawless as possible. (L. Porter 1978, 237)

This last sentence is telling, with Porter setting himself and other like-minded jazz scholars "who know the music" apart from Tirro, who by implication does not. The lines of knowledge and, by extension, community in jazz scholarship, were beginning to be drawn. Porter, Gushee, and others understood that the stakes in this discourse were high, and that if this intellectual community was to thrive, their work must not give its critics any cause to dismiss it.

The next major textbook to appear on the college market was Mark Gridley's *Jazz Styles: History and Analysis*. Gridley's is arguably the most widely used jazz history and appreciation text on the academic market, presenting an overview of jazz history that focuses exclusively on characteristics of different styles and genres, rather than on historical or personal narrative. Little attention is paid to the contextual development of jazz styles, or to the ways in which jazz reflected issues of identity or historical circumstance. In finding a place for his own work in the emerging literature, Gridley is both pragmatic and philosophical. On the one hand, he casts his work as eminently usable; the first words of his preface note that he intends for the book to be "intended as a guide to appreciating jazz as well as an introduction to most styles which have been documented on records" (Gridley 1978, vii). As a text intended for "high school through adult readers" (vii) who are not music specialists, Gridley strove to reach a wider audience than Tirro.

Gridley's approach to canon illuminates some of the contentious issues that continue to characterize debates of jazz's history. He notes: "Although it is very difficult to generalize about music, certain recognized styles, such as swing, bop, and West Coast, can be described. . . . It just happened that certain important styles became attached more to musician names than to era names" (Gridley 1978, 4). Canon, of course, does not "just happen," and I find curious his notion that musical styles "just happen" to follow a precise canonical ideal. If Gridley's comments here seem contradictory, they probably are; moreover, they are a reflection of the disconnect between the establishment of canon in scholarship and its application in actual classroom settings.

Such contradictory attitudes are also evident in a subsequent text by Megill and Demory, called simply *Introduction to Jazz History*. The authors purport to employ an even-handed, non-canonical approach to the subject, stating in their preface, "we cannot say one performer is more important than another, and have had a difficult time choosing which performers to discuss" (Megill and Demory 1984, vii). Yet a scan of the table of contents belies this sentiment, as sections are devoted to discussions of Armstrong, Morton, Ellington,

Parker, Monk, Davis, Coltrane, and other canonically established musicians whose work is seemingly deemed more important than that of other players. In fact, there is very little in the text that does not support jazz's "official history," a term used by Scott DeVeaux in his influential 1991 essay on jazz historiography. Despite the authors' claims of anti-canonicity, canonicity in fact pervades the text from start to finish. Thus, in both of these examples of early jazz history texts authors struggle with what canon represents, a simplistic and problematic framework for knowledge, but one that ultimately is too pervasive to ignore.

Lewis Porter seems to have been unsatisfied with the choices given to him as a teacher by the textbook market (though he glowingly reviewed Gridley's original edition); in 1993 he and colleague Michael Ullman produced yet another jazz history book, *Jazz: From Its Origins to the Present*. In the preface, Porter and Ullman write:

> We began this book in 1982 in response to what we—fans, educators, authors, and, in Porter's case, a sometime performer—saw as a need for a literate, accurate, and up-to-date one-volume history of jazz and its major figures . . . to be musically sophisticated and unbiased . . . to give a fair representation of the music that had the greatest impact on musicians and on the general public. When faced with a choice between an obscure personal favorite and a historically significant piece, we have opted for the latter. (Porter and Ullman 1993, vii)

There are several points we should consider in reading this passage. In 1982, the texts on the market included those by Stearns, Tanner, Tirro, and Gridley, among others, as well as the first volume of Schuller's histories. The use of the word *response* suggests that Porter and Ullman consciously constructed their work to address shortcomings in the existing literature. Porter's issues with Tirro are, of course, well documented, as is his praise of Gridley's text. Megill and Demory's text would appear a few years later, and its appearance certainly informed their approach as well. But what is most notable about this statement is in the latter part; here, Porter and Ullman engage the canon directly, not critiquing it, but staking out their own interpretive territory relative to its pervasiveness. Wanting to appear "unbiased" suggests that the authors find bias in other materials, though this is not specified. More importantly, though, they seemingly come down on the side of canon, favoring examples that have "the greatest impact" or are more "historically significant," drawing heavily on the Smithsonian Collection and similar sources. These examples, as a scan of the text demonstrates, do not deviate significantly from previous narratives, though there are some notable differences. For example, Porter and Ullman include specific chapters on Sidney Bechet, Bill Evans, and a chapter on less studied genres of the 1960s, such as bossa nova and soul jazz. But the basic structure of the narrative is essentially the same as other works; Armstrong, Ellington, Parker, and Coltrane are all discussed in depth, and the decade-defined course of jazz is evident. For Porter and Ullman, the problem with jazz historiography does not seem to be the canon itself, but rather the haphazard scholarship and attention to detail that plagued books like Tirro's. Canon, it seems, is not a problem for everyone.

More recently, writers of jazz histories have begun to more explicitly position themselves in relation to the canon in different ways. Critiques of prevailing narratives, implicit or explicit, have begun to influence the textbook market. Perhaps using DeVeaux's 1991 essay as a point of departure, the "official version" of jazz history is increasingly seen as problematic. That does not mean, however, that it has been abandoned. Take, for instance, the remarks of Henry Martin and Keith Waters, whose *Jazz: The First 100 Years* was first published in 2002. In the preface to the second edition (2005), the authors note that they tried to "stimulate fresh thinking about the jazz canon," most notably by including a CD set that goes beyond the Smithsonian Collection (Martin and Waters 2005, xix). But such "fresh thinking" about the canon has its limits, as Martin and Waters themselves acknowledge: "Our chronological presentation of jazz history preserves the customary distinction between stylistic periods, because we feel that this is the clearest method of introducing the material to the student. Nevertheless, throughout the text we continue to acknowledge and emphasize that many (if not most) artists have produced significant work beyond the era in which they first came to public attention" (Martin and Waters 2005, xix). Thus Martin and Waters come face to face with the same fundamental dialectic between the problems of canon, with its limited, circumscribed view of the music, and the necessity of having some way of categorizing and organizing the often messy, contradictory narratives of jazz's past and present. A canon that is based in large part on a clear chronological development provides just such a method of organization. Indeed, the chorological presentation of jazz history in this text tracks closely with that of most previous work.

A similar case might be made for Norton's reentry into the jazz history textbook market. Authored by Scott DeVeaux and Gary Giddins, and simply titled *Jazz*, the book purports to tell the "story of jazz as it has never been told before" (DeVeaux and Giddins 2009, back matter). But for the most part, *Jazz* seems to be organized along the same lines as previous studies, breaking down jazz's history roughly by decade-based stylistic distinction, and emphasizing the contributions of major figures like Armstrong, Ellington (who are described as jazz's "pre-eminent" soloist and composer, respectively), and Coltrane, who headline individual chapters. While the thoroughness of the narrative is impressive, DeVeaux and Giddins work within the same framework of "official history" that has defined jazz scholarship for so long.[16] In the opening to their chapter on New York, they state that "New York City, particularly the borough of Manhattan, has served as the focus for jazz's maturity and evolution since the 1920s to the present." Discussion of women in jazz is still generally relegated to a minor part of the narrative, in this case an inset box on page 203. Bebop is still defined mainly by Parker and Gillespie in the mid-1940s (which is particularly surprising given DeVeaux's superb study *The Birth of Bebop*, in which he advances a far less canonical view of the genre). There are exceptions, such as a chapter devoted to the historical debates in jazz today, the discussion of rhythm and blues in the 1940s, and more extensive coverage of contemporary artists (which may simply be a function of the book's more recent publication). But by and large the book offers a narrative that is similar to the "official version" that DeVeaux decried in 1991.

I say all this not to criticize DeVeaux and Giddins; I am an admirer of both men's work, and in fact, I find their book to be superbly written and documented, a valuable resource that I could easily see using in my own classroom. Rather, my point is to illustrate the difficultly in negotiating non-canonical ways of viewing the history of jazz. For all that we who write and teach in this area complain about the pervasiveness of canonical perspectives, they are very hard to ignore. Could one, for example, imagine teaching a class on the history of jazz without mentioning Armstrong or Coltrane? For the most part, this would be unthinkable. Then again, if we were to adjust our view of what jazz is, it could be done. Traditionalist writers in the 1940s did just that; bebop was simply ignored in their narratives (even as late as Rex Harris's book in 1954). Maybe there is a reason that the canon is what it is, a reason why the same names keep popping up as chapter headings, or why the music of certain decades keeps being called "fragmented" or "revolutionary." Canon is hard to get away from; how we deal with it on a pedagogical level is important, but that is a long way from simply discarding it. Just because it is in the canon, or part of the official narrative, does not mean that it is not accurate. Comments such as those made by Megill and Demory (who expressed "difficulty" in determining whom to include), Porter and Ullman (whose claims to emphasis on "significant" and "influential" recordings speak to their approach), Martin and Waters (for whom the "chronological presentation" of jazz history remains a central feature), and DeVeaux and Giddins (on the pre-eminence of Armstrong and Coltrane) underscore such difficulties. The boundaries of a community of jazz historians permit only so much deviation from the canon; canon serves an important pedagogical purpose. It serves as a common core of knowledge, one that binds this particular community together and sets it apart from others, but also profoundly influenced by outside forces in the academy. In seeking to adapt jazz history from a research project and into a pedagogical method, few other models were available to be followed, and the effects of this are still present in jazz history classrooms.

Writing jazz history textbooks is one thing; putting these historiographic issues into practice in the classroom is another. Aside from his writing, Stearns was also a pioneering teacher of jazz history. His courses at the New School and NYU attracted enthusiastic crowds, inspiring a number of individuals to embark on their own endeavors as collectors or historians. A version of his syllabus,[17] adapted from one of his NYU courses and reproduced in Robert Walser's *Keeping Time*, is organized in ways that seem familiar to contemporary teachers; it is even more notable for his inclusion of guest speakers like Louis Armstrong for the "Chicago and the Jazz Age" lecture, or the following week's session on "Big Bands in New York," featuring Duke Ellington. Later lectures featured appearances by Benny Goodman, Dizzy Gillespie, and Lennie Tristano, among others. Stearns clearly had the respect of many jazz musicians, and this is a crucial point in both his identity as a scholar, and in the connection of historiography with non-academic jazz communities. When Stearns accompanied a group of musicians including Dizzy Gillespie and Quincy Jones on a State Department tour, the players initially saw him as a "white father [sent along] to make sure the brothers didn't get out of control," yet accepted him when they discovered that "he liked to party" (Maggin 2006, 281). As Gennari notes, summarizing an assessment of Stearns's classes in a 1951 *Negro Digest* feature, that his classroom was somewhat loose, characterizing it as "progressive" and relaxed, as Stearns "casually smokes while delivering lectures" (Gennari 2006, 147). Not all early teachers of jazz history had it as seemingly easy as Stearns did. David Baker recounts that upon his arrival in the 1960s at Indiana University to institute a degree program in jazz studies, he had to team-teach the jazz history course with a music historian (Prouty 2002, 272). Within the music school, history was a subject for historians, and only later was it acknowledged that individuals who had actually known many of the musicians who were subjects of that history might be qualified to teach it.

Stearns was also noted for his summer lectures at the Music Inn in the Berkshires, beginning in 1950. Guest speakers and participants at these roundtables included many well-known figures in jazz, from performers to critics and scholars. His work at Music Inn would eventually lead to his inclusion on the faculty of the Lenox School, which was in no small part an outgrowth of the lectures themselves (Fitzgerald 2008, 22). Stearns's lectures at Lenox were very well received by many of the students. Arif Mardin was effusive in his praise of Stearns in an essay in *Jazz Review* from 1958:

> I found Marshall Stearns' lectures on jazz history enormously stimulating. It is obvious that the appeal of this subject to a foreign student is very strong. There were, however, some American students who knew almost nothing about jazz before 1952. I believe we all learned to tolerate and appreciate the jazz of the past as Stearns covered all its phases, liberally illustrating his lectures with records and reading material. (Mardin 1959, 19)

Mardin's enthusiasm for classes on jazz history may not have been shared by everyone, as fellow faculty member Bob Brookmeyer noted:

> On the negative side of the picture, those "know it all" attitudes became distressingly obvious in both composition and Marshall Stearns' "History of Jazz" course. . . . As for not attending that history course; tch, tch! They were cutting themselves off from one of the richest legacies in this world and someday they will realize it. Any man who can evince boredom while being assaulted by Jelly's *Tiger Rag* is a puzzle to be reckoned with (and one I would hardly care to work out). It's his loss, not Jelly's. (Brookmeyer 1959, 49)

Stearns's role at Lenox speaks to the linking of jazz performance and jazz historiography at this critical point. His blending of scholarly acumen with a non-academic sensibility undoubtedly contributed to his success in forging jazz history's place in the academy. What Stearns did for both the institution of a jazz canon, as well as the development of a sensibility toward jazz as a music whose history could and should be taught, is incalculable. But Stearns wrote little about the teaching of jazz history itself, save for the inclusion of his syllabus in later editions of *The Story of Jazz*. The pedagogy of jazz history is, to some extent, still done in a manner that is intuitive and individually determined, as it was with Stearns and the early generation of history teachers. And considering the relative weight given to the teaching of jazz history in the pedagogical literature of jazz, this is not surprising.

In the jazz pedagogy publishing market, little attention is given to instruction in jazz history. David Baker's *Jazz Pedagogy*, perhaps the first significant publication on the teaching of jazz, lays out a sequence of courses based on his own experiences in teaching jazz at Indiana University. For Baker, "[jazz] history courses are among the most important in the curriculum!" (Baker 1979, 45). Indeed, Baker provides overviews of several history courses in his program: general jazz history, contemporary soul and jazz, and two courses on black music in America. The syllabi provided for his general course (80–92) and the contemporary soul and jazz course (93–104) are detailed, addressing topics for individual class sessions. Both provide models for teachers, but Baker provides little commentary on either the reasons for structuring his classes in the manner he does, or on issues involved with teaching. This stands in contrast to his writings on other areas, particularly improvisation, where he gives detailed examples of exercises that he uses (and why he uses them) as well as focused advice for teaching. The book is heavily skewed toward the teaching of performance-oriented topics, despite Baker's insistence that history courses are among the "most important."

Jerry Coker published his pedagogical treatise in 1989, *The Teaching of Jazz*. Like Baker, Coker again cites the importance of jazz history in the curriculum, stating that "History of Jazz is needed early in the curriculum, since even the well-attuned freshman jazz major is likely to have listened to only a handful of jazz performers, and most of those will be current, present day players" (37). But Coker is similarly limited in his commentary about pedagogical considerations or historiographic issues within the discipline. Only a brief syllabus is given, devoid of references to specific topics or genres, keyed only to chapters in the text (which happens to be his own *Listening to Jazz*). The only guidance he offers to potential teachers is that his syllabus is "predicated on the fact that most students will be non-jazz and non-music majors" (56), giving no further discussion of why that presents a challenge. Like other pedagogical materials, Coker's book mainly addresses performance, especially the teaching of jazz improvisation and analysis, offering great detail about different types of melodic classifications for understanding improvisation.

But Coker's discussion of a model jazz history course in *The Teaching of Jazz* is problematic for other reasons. In weeks 2 and 3 in his syllabus, an "overview history of jazz" is presented by way of a "Tape/slide presentation," while in week 14, the content is listed as a "Review of jazz history via recordings." In weeks 11–13, the course covers an "Improviser's Hall of Fame," consisting of "listening and guided analysis of solos by six of the best improvisers in jazz history," a list (drawn from his *Listening to Jazz* text) that includes Louis Armstrong, Coleman Hawkins, Lester Young, Charlie Parker, Miles Davis, and John Coltrane (Coker 1978, 73–134). Canon is one thing, but to distill the development of jazz improvisation to only six figures, significant as they may be, is quite another. Nowhere in Coker's text, which I stress is advanced explicitly as a model jazz history reference, is there discussion of cultural context, alternatives to these "hall of fame" figures, or historical process. The rest of the course is devoted to overviews of the genre itself, such as improvisational devices and the role of the rhythm section in jazz.

In the most recent and expansive of these texts, *Jazz Pedagogy* by Richard Dunscomb and Willie Hill (2004), there is virtually no mention of history, even as part of a larger jazz studies curriculum. Aside from a "jazz history timeline" consisting mainly of musicians' names and dates with a bullet list of characteristics of various genres, there is virtually no mention of history or how it should be taught. The text focuses exclusively on the pedagogical considerations of performance, mainly ensemble direction, but also some material in improvisation. Given the book's implicit focus on pre-college educators (as evidenced by its reference to the MENC national standards), this is not surprising, as pre–college level instruction rarely moves beyond ensemble and performance issues.

In doctoral research, one of the primary venues for the publication of pedagogical studies in jazz education, historical issues are similarly absent. Advanced research on jazz pedagogy generally has been limited to a few main areas: methods and practices in the teaching of improvisation, curricular surveys of jazz teaching, institutional histories, and ensemble direction. There is virtually no attention paid in the research literature to pedagogical or historiographical issues on jazz education. Even studies that purport to suggest "model" jazz studies curricula pay little attention to teaching history. In Walter Barr's 1974 dissertation on teaching jazz, the author includes history as one of six "fundamental categories" of a model jazz studies curriculum. Barr's survey of jazz educators and musicians indicated that of these categories, jazz history and literature was the lowest priority (Barr 1974, 63), and that it was only slightly less important for non-academic musicians than for educators themselves (72). The model jazz history course, argued Barr, should involve a "survey of jazz history, styles, and literature, from its beginnings (ca. 1850) to the present," emphasizing listening skills (103). Dismissal and outright hostility toward the teaching of jazz education was noted in some narrative responses to Barr's survey, as expressed by trumpeter Bobby Shew, who argues: "Studying jazz history can be important only to the degree that it has some practical application to the techniques included and discussed. Who cares who drove the band bus for Woody Herman in 1948?" (qtd. in Barr 1974, 104). Shew's response underscores both a subservient attitude, that history must *serve* performance, and a dismissal of history as being focused on minutiae.

Barr does include jazz history in the curriculum he proposes, and this in itself is significant; his study is likely the first to systematically propose a structured jazz curriculum, and was influential on the development of NASM standards. But nowhere does he discuss the types of decisions and problems with canon that jazz scholars debate. The hegemony of canon is evidenced by its omission from the discussion. It is simply "there." In a similar vein, Larry Fisher's "rationale" for the jazz curriculum, as expressed in his own doctoral dissertation on the subject, devotes a substantial number of pages to jazz history, but the author actually says very little about the reasons for structuring courses as he proposes (in this case, as twelve teaching units based on "major periods of jazz history," which again track closely to the prevailing narrative). Nowhere are issues of historiography addressed in any depth; indeed, the focus is heavily reflective of a canonical approach. Issues of *how* one should teach such a course are not included. What are included are resource lists, proposed semester-long organizations of classes, and similarly-themed "how to" types of discussions. Determining what should be taught is not an issue, seemingly taken for granted.

There remains in the literature of jazz pedagogy a conspicuous lack of critical thought about the teaching of history; this is especially true in the context of scathing critiques of the teaching of performance in many programs. Calls for change in the teaching of jazz history seem to be coming not from within jazz education or its pedagogical literature, but from outside jazz studies programs, even outside music departments generally. What do we make of all this—that within the discourse of jazz pedagogy there is so little attention paid to history, despite repeated assertions of its importance? The literature is rife with arguments that teachers need to be experienced, capable jazz performers, an assessment that is hard to dispute; yet nowhere is suggested the ideal career profile for a teacher of jazz history. Given the emphasis that so many of these pedagogical sources place on performance skill, jazz history is implied to be a subject that could be taught by anyone in the jazz studies program, regardless of experience in historically oriented teaching and research. Indeed, this seems to be the case in many programs. To be fair, many of these individuals are likely outstanding history teachers, with a keen awareness of the kinds of issues that impact historical process. But not all teachers devote this kind of attention of historical process and context. In Coker's *Listening to Jazz*, there is virtually no discussion of these ideas, focusing instead entirely on stylistic considerations. While jazz studies programs at the graduate level devote substantial attention to improvisation and ensemble pedagogy, systematic instruction in the teaching of jazz history is rare. Those who do specialize in academic pursuits often find themselves at odds with the prevailing attitudes of a performance-driven culture, paralleling relationships between artists and writers outside the academic world. While everyone teaches in the academy, hierarchies still exist vis-à-vis an individual's perceived proximity to performance. Individuals associated primarily with non-performance activities are sometimes regarded as a distinct community within the department at large. As Bruno Nettl explains, "performance is seen as central by music school society, and there are those who perform and those who don't. The grouping and status are encapsulated by a frequently heard maxim: 'those who can do; others teach (or write books)'" (Nettl 1995, 56).[18]

It is easy to characterize Nettl's statement as an overgeneralization, but *Heartland Excursions* is essentially a memoir on his own distinguished career as an academic, so his observations are based on personal experience. This is not a criticism, merely an effort to place what he is saying in context. This is also not to say that his observations are unique. John Mangan takes a more systematic and detailed approach to understanding this dialectic: "The divide between the devotees of musicology and performance runs deep, with both sides lobbing charges of intellectual and interpretive heresy at each other" (Mangan 2005, 180). In this discourse there are two separate, yet interrelated issues at stake. First, as Nettl notes, academic faculty are often a sort of "police" whose role is to enforce curricular requirements that often have little application to performance (Nettl 1995, 58). Second, they are often viewed as representing a different type of interpretive process, accused of overintellectualizing music. While these types of issues have played out differently across institutions, some sense of division between performance and scholarship pervades even the most liberal-minded institutions. It is worth noting that neither Nettl nor Mangan fully discusses jazz education; for Nettl, jazz education is both marginalized and corrupted by the academy, while Mangan barely mentions it in his work. Yet those in jazz education face many of the same issues. Many students simply want to perform, and given the fact that jazz students must complete coursework in both jazz and Western art music, something their classical peers generally do not, the sense of distance between them and musicologists, for example, can seem even greater.

If some jazz students and teachers display hostility toward non-performance requirements in Western art music and those who maintain them, others are more pragmatic. David Baker actually sees this as something of an advantage, as jazz students who are forced to undertake studies in Western art music will have a professional advantage over their colleagues who never studied jazz. His own experience as a student at IU, when jazz instruction was minimal at the school, served such a purpose:

> [My] colleagues here at IU saw that I knew as much about their music
> as they did, simply because I came up through the same system as they
> did, which is a system set up to perpetuate the aesthetic out of which

it comes. So I knew as much about Bartok, and I knew as much about Rachmaninoff and Boulez as they did. And I suggest to my students that if they intend to teach, if they intend to work, if they intend to survive, that they do it all. (Prouty 2002, 235)

Indeed, most educators publicly make similar statements, seeking to motivate students who question these requirements; in private, however, many still grumble about these perceived inequities. In particular, jazz educators express a great deal of concern about the increasing academic requirements that their students must complete. The intellectual territory of the music department is clearly defined in the terms and cultural practices of Western art music, and jazz is, in a sense, a visitor.

Non-jazz requirements can thus seem truly foreign for jazz students, and theory classes throw these issues into particularly sharp relief. Western theory often represents a very different mode of thinking for students used to conceptualizing of harmony and melody in jazz. Rules and conventions of four-part choral harmony, for example, are seen to present little practical application for jazz students. In other instances, the study of Western art music theory represents an alternative method of explaining musical phenomena than is common in jazz theory. I recall one such instance from my undergraduate days where, in a session covering augmented sixth chords, several students made the observation that such chords were "just a G7b5," highlighting a disjuncture in the way harmonic devices are classified in the two musical traditions. Students saw the "jazz version" of these chords as being more practical, while those in traditional theory are not. As expected, a lengthy discussion followed as to why students needed to learn seemingly inapplicable ways of representing structures they already used in performance. Conflicts with and challenges to the perceived practicality of one system (or perhaps, a greater degree of familiarity) are met with a degree of hostility and suspicion, or in many cases, confusion.

While course requirements in theory are often thought of as a drain on time that could be spent directly on the cultivation of performance abilities, in other contexts the ability to understand and articulate detailed knowledge about musical processes and structures is positioned as a critical skill for entering today's jazz marketplace. As Bill Dobbins writes, the ability to communicate ideas about musical technique and structure is not a barrier to individual identity and creativity:

Probably the single most important task for the jazz musician dealing with this new environment is the development of verbal skills which are capable of communicating the mechanics and aesthetics of an essentially aural tradition. That such a task can be accomplished is amply illustrated by the tradition of eastern Indian music. The fact that the Indian master musicians can speak in a detailed and highly sophisticated manner about the techniques and vocabulary of their tradition in no way unveiled the music's mysteries nor sapped its creative vitality. (Dobbins 1988, 37)

He continues, cautioning that: "It is not only older, self-educated jazz musicians who sometimes have difficulty in verbally expressing their musical ideas. All too often, jazz students who are aspiring to become professional performers or writers are so obsessed with technical skills that they lose sight of the value of an ability to communicate their knowledge to others, if and when they become involved in teaching" (Dobbins 1988, 37).

Dobbins touches on an important point, in that it is understood that most jazz professionals teach in order to support themselves, given the lack of financial security among musicians today. Exceptional teaching musicians, such as Dizzy Gillespie, Barry Harris, or Lennie Tristano, have always been recognized as individuals who possessed the ability to talk about music in a concise, clear manner.[19] Distinctions between "doers" and "teachers" have become increasingly blurred in recent years, and within the academy, such distinctions are moot, as everyone teaches. Jazz educators have taken it upon themselves to prepare students for this aspect of the professional world, increasingly instituting pedagogy requirements for improvisation and rehearsal techniques as part of the curriculum. The same is not often true for history, however.

Non-performance courses within the jazz curriculum have often been modeled on prevailing currents of Western art music, and unfortunately for teachers of such courses, negative attitudes about Western art music theory and history among some students transfer into negative feelings about theory and history courses in jazz education. In many cases, teachers of such courses are the same individuals who teach improvisation courses or direct ensembles; deeper involvement in non-performance activities can, however, have a negative impact upon the manner in which they are regarded by students. A classmate of mine from graduate school spoke somewhat disdainfully of one particular faculty member, widely renowned as both a pedagogue and performer, insisting that he [the teacher] "sounds like one of his books." In another case, an undergraduate professor of mine (who was the only faculty member to hold a doctoral degree in the program) was described by a former student of the same program as a "non-player." In reality, he was an accomplished performer, but his association with advanced theory and pedagogy courses ascribed to him a specific identity. A teacher such as this becomes, in effect, the "theory guy," or "history guy," a label that has implications for his or her identity within the department, namely that their performance activities take a back seat to their academic considerations.

Jazz might be said to exist in close temporal proximity to its own canon. Most major canonical figures are in living memory, and some are still with us; we also have access to extensive oral histories and other primary accounts, to say nothing of musical recordings of artists themselves. This freshness of historical memory imparts to students of jazz a sense of closeness to canonical figures that eludes the canon of Western art music composers. It might seem odd, then, to construct a jazz canon that mirrors the frameworks developed for musical artists who have been dead, in some cases, for centuries, and I suggest that canonization in jazz history works against such feelings of closeness, sometimes to the detriment of historical study. The sense of distance between student performers and historical jazz musicians is greater with respect to some styles than others, and is often a reflection of the prevailing models of performance within the academy. Put another way, students are not exposed to a great deal of performance pedagogy and experiential activities in early New Orleans styles, or swing.[20] In employing musicological methods for representing jazz history, with "classic" recordings placed at the center of the discourse, historians have created an intellectual climate in which students are detached from the living processes of history-in-the-making. Students may regard Armstrong and Ellington as historically important, but are skeptical when comparing them to Parker and Coltrane, whose impact on current practice is more immediate and measurable. Like theory, the reception of jazz history has a direct relationship to its applicability in a performance setting.

Jazz history courses are unique within the curriculum in that they often attract a significant number (sometimes a majority) of students who are not only non-jazz majors, but often not music majors at all. The appeal of jazz history courses to students outside the department seems to be widespread across institutions, reaching back many years. In the 1940s the appeal of jazz was much more direct to the generation of college students of the time. Jazz was, in effect, popular music, and was not as removed from the popular consciousness as it is currently. Today, students are usually interested in other musical forms, and are not very interested in the technical aspects of jazz's historical development. Thus, jazz history teachers often find themselves applying a wide array of strategies in approaching different student communities. For classes of mainly non-music majors, teachers might focus less on technical aspects of jazz history, emphasizing biographies and social or cultural environments. In classes of jazz majors, by contrast, courses frequently delve into areas of stylistic analysis, in order to demonstrate the ways in which one historical period is connected to the next, or to demonstrate why a certain musician is considered important in the historical record.

Often these different communities are enrolled in the same course sections, forcing teachers to accommodate the needs of both. Such contexts represent a microcosm of historical jazz discourse itself; critical writing that fails to address the music is often treated with contempt by performers, while materials on techniques and detailed musical considerations risk going over the heads of others. Structuring a course in jazz history can require sensitivity in terms of the types of information presented, and even more with respect to the ways in which students are evaluated. Classes must provide a balance of factual (i.e., names and dates), interpretive (understanding historical process), and stylistic considerations, including those that will serve to inform developing performance skills. For most jazz educators, the last area is perhaps the most important. Students in jazz history are expected to become familiar with the various stylistic manifestations of the music, demonstrating a knowledge of musical structures and concepts, and perhaps more importantly, an aural understanding of historical style. The centrality of recordings to the historical discourse means that aural identification of historical recordings usually constitutes a major component of jazz history courses directed toward majors in this field, and evaluative strategies in this area are very controversial with students. So-called "drop the needle" exams are a common vehicle for assessing students' abilities to identify significant styles and/or individuals, and yet such formats are widely unpopular with both students and faculty. Such exams have a long legacy in Western art music history (the phrase "drop the needle" itself historically dates such processes, as tape and now digital music technology have rendered such a method obsolete for a number of years). For many students, listening-identification exams represent everything that is wrong with institutional study, measuring only a limited knowledge of a piece, rather than a deeper understanding of the music. UNT faculty member Ed Soph argues that just such an experience was a negative aspect of his own education:

> But just to give you an idea of how that [desire to study music] was turned off, when I first came to North Texas [as a student], I took a music history course. And I dropped out of the course after my first exam when the instructor dropped the needle on a record and played 30 seconds of music and then asked the class to identify the composer, the year of composition. . . . I said "That's not what it's about." Now if somebody teaches that way . . . they're taking all the joy and beauty and understanding out of music. (Javors 2001, 417–18)

Reliance on such methods is, for some teachers, a function of habit, or of prevailing methodologies. Many teachers in my experience seem resigned to such methods, just as they are resigned to the prevailing methods of historical orientation toward stylistic organization.

The notion of who is teaching a particular class is sometimes important as a marker of the instructor's relative popularity among the university population at large. It also can hold a great deal of significance for students within the program itself. Teachers who have had a more direct experience with the history of jazz as performers or their associates will generally bring a greater degree of authority to their classrooms than educators whom I would term "second generation."

Some time ago, Billy Taylor appeared on a broadcast of *CBS Sunday Morning*, hosting a segment on the Hartt School of Music's Jackie McLean, who was a significant jazz performer long before his initial forays into teaching at a university.[21] One music student interviewee made the point that there was an advantage to studying jazz history with someone "who was there, and didn't learn it out of a book." This can put many contemporary jazz educators in an awkward situation. How does an educator who was not "there" teach jazz history with any sense of legitimacy, other than to reiterate what has been written before? As the ranks of musicians who came of age at the height of jazz inexorably shrinks, how do today's musicians and teachers respond, without simply becoming curators of the canon of jazz history? How can educators help students in jazz education programs to understand their own place with the ongoing jazz tradition, and not to regard jazz as a museum piece?

To be sure, these are not easy questions for educators to address. Specialists in jazz history—who often hold advanced degrees in musicology, ethnomusicology, or other non-performance fields (sometimes even outside music itself)—are often faced with the problem of being labeled "academics" within a performance-oriented department. This, in a sense, is a double-edged sword. As one former classmate put it, when speaking of her attitude regarding academic faculty, "When I went to a teacher's office hours, if I didn't see a piano or a music stand in the room, I didn't think we would be able to relate very well. . . . It made me uncomfortable." While such teachers have generally devoted a great deal of time and study to jazz history, and indeed in many cases are recognized experts in the field, such efforts often have the unintended consequence of de-emphasizing their identity as a performer vis-à-vis others in the program, regardless of their actual experience or abilities. Individuals with a great deal of academic training and scholarly credentials may in fact be seen as being less authentic, not having been in the "real world" to a large extent, and thus, in an ironic twist, bringing a lesser degree of perceived legitimacy to their historical teaching. What this comes down to is what faculty and students know about jazz, and where this knowledge comes from. Among many performers, there is a privileging of knowledge that rises from or is applied to performance, especially outside the academy. If musical academics spend too much time in the library, their legitimacy as carriers of this knowledge is questioned. Most educators do not have Marshall Stearns's ability to invite Dizzy Gillespie to guest lecture. What community within the walls of the music school one belongs to is a function of what one knows about jazz, but possibly even more with how they know it.

Claims to knowledge of what jazz is form the basis of how scholarly communities have forged their own identities relative to the historical traditions of jazz, communities of performers, and to communities dedicated to musicology and interdisciplinary studies. These processes have been difficult at times, but the development of a robust discourse of the history of jazz in both musicology and the New Jazz Studies demonstrates that the efforts have been worth the struggle. Disciplinary debates are far from resolved, but jazz scholarship has come into its own over the last two decades, and many of the concerns expressed by Lewis Porter in his 1988 essay have been addressed. Jazz scholarship now appears regularly in academic journals such as *American Music* and *Ethnomusicology*, as well as specialized publications like the *Jazz Research Journal* and *Jazz Perspectives*.

But as jazz scholars have taken their place in the larger jazz community, others are still negotiating theirs. Thousands, perhaps millions of jazz fans outside of academia, and outside of traditional performance communities, have not had a voice in this music. The gatekeepers of jazz discourse, scholarly and critical, have seldom assessed the role of the ordinary jazz fan as a participant within it, or within the jazz community at large. But just as jazz scholars have found their own place in the community during the last two decades, so too are fans beginning to take a more active role in the jazz world. And just as jazz scholarship has long been a function of the mediating effects of print and recording, jazz fans have turned to technology to assert themselves: the internet. In the following chapter, I examine how electronic platforms are facilitating the creation of new jazz communities, and how they are allowing jazz fans to add their voice to the growing chorus that is jazz discourse.

CHAPTER 4

The Virtual Jazz World

Understanding the Wide World of (Web-based) Jazz

The earliest days of the virtual jazz world were summed up by Bret Primack, who wrote in *Jazz Times* in 1998, "The Internet is the fastest growing phenomenon in the history of mankind. In less than a decade, it has gone from a concept to an obsession. For jazz, Net activity is burgeoning, dramatically" (Primack 1998). One website that was part of this dramatic growth was Jazz Central Station, which appeared in 1996 and was maintained by record label N2K. Most new web-based ventures, however, did not last, and were victims of what would come to be called the burst of the "dot-com bubble." JCS was one of these sites on the bubble. Described in a 1998 *Billboard* review as "the Internet's largest jazz resource and gathering place," the site ceased operating the following year. Featuring current jazz news, artist profiles, audio and video clips, and articles from *JazzTimes*, in addition to its sales offerings, JCS aimed to be a "one stop shop" for jazz enthusiasts. More importantly, it became a focal point for virtual community.

A 1998 study by IBM researcher Jason Ellis highlighted some of the salient features of JCS, and why it was an effective site for the formation of online community. Focusing on the JCS Café, a user-oriented section of the site, Ellis explains:

> The Cafe is really the place where JCS tries to build community and they make a point to let you know . . . . Listed as a "highlight" on the front page is the newest addition to the "People in Our Neighborhood" feature, the full text of which is posted in the Cafe. Finally, there is a "community pulse" out front which links directly into the newsgroup "Jazz Talk" which is found you-know-where. . . . JCS starts from the very beginning trying to pull people into their community. It is also important to note that this begins a self-selection process. For example,

most folks will not click on any of these features unless they have an interest in jazz. (Ellis 1998, 2)

As discussed in chapter 1, self-identification (or "self-selection") with certain attitudes and musical styles is at the core of identity within jazz communities, and community on the internet is no exception. At the same time, the attempt to "pull people in" to the community implies that there is, at some level, an active attempt at community formation. These processes reflect a tension between these two ideas, self-selection and community-selection. Another tension is created through the anonymity of many virtual communities:

There have been countless instances when users posted obnoxious comments anonymously. Many times, these posts will just be generally annoying, but as the disrupters get more familiar with the site, sometimes they do make personal comments. . . . Unfortunately, there is a more troubling problem here: the impersonation issue. This kind of interface not only allows anonymous posts but, worse, anyone can post using anyone else's name, effectively impersonating them. (Ellis 1998, 4)

Though JCS is long gone, the process and problems described here remain part and parcel of the experience of community in the contemporary virtual world.

After the collapse of the web boom of the mid-1990s, a new breed of user-friendly interactive sites emerged that would once again redefine the nature of online communities. One of the biggest developments was the rise of Google, which today is not only the largest (in terms of pages indexed) search engine, but continues to redefine how we think about the connectedness of the internet, and each other. One of the simplest ways to gauge the amount of jazz activity on the web is to simply type the word *jazz* into the search box on Google, click the button, and sit back for the several hundredths of a second that it takes for the results; at present, such a search yields over 200,000,000 hits. Obviously, as sifting through this many web pages would comprise not only the contents of this entire book, but probably several small libraries, I will try to distill these results into something useful.

The order of websites in Google searches says a good deal how internet jazz communities are organized; let us look at the first page of Google results from a search I conducted in December 2008. The sites were, in order:

"Jazz" entry on Wikipedia
All About Jazz

The Official Site of the Utah Jazz
*Video results for jazz**
PBS—JAZZ A Film By Ken Burns: Home
Jazz—PBS KIDS GO!
Jazz Community Site
Jazz.com
A Passion for Jazz! Music History and Education
Jazz—JazzCorner.com jazz websites, video, radio, reviews . . .
The Red Hot Jazz Archive
News results for jazz
Book results for jazz

The same search on July 21, 2009, yielded the following results:

"Jazz" entry on Wikipedia
PBS—JAZZ A Film By Ken Burns: Home
The Official Site of the Utah Jazz
Video results for jazz
All About Jazz
Jazz.com
The Center for Jazz Studies at Columbia University
Jazz—PBS KIDS GO!
Jazz Community Site
Jazz on the Screen: A Blues and Jazz Filmography by David Meeker
The Red Hot Jazz Archive
News results for jazz

A similar search in December 2010 yielded the following:

The Official Site of the Utah Jazz
"Jazz" entry on Wikipedia
PBS—JAZZ A Film By Ken Burns: Home
News results for jazz
Jazz.com
All About Jazz
A Passion for Jazz! Music History and Education
Jazz—PBS KIDS GO!
The Red Hot Jazz Archive
Jazz Online
Book results for Jazz

For the most part, the lists are similar, but there are some changes of order, as well as a few new sites. The method used by Google to determine page rank is based on a complex algorithm known, appropriately enough, as PageRank, determined by a number of factors. Google defines it thusly: "PageRank reflects our view of the importance of web pages by considering more than 500 million variables and 2 billion terms. Pages that we believe are important pages receive a higher PageRank and are more likely to appear at the top of the search results" (Google Corporate, n.d.). The formulae and algorithms used by Google to determine this order are too complex to discuss in detail here, but it is sufficient to say that results are based largely on the number of other sites that link to a particular page, in essence representing a "vote" for the page. As such, the PageRank algorithms might rightly be seen as an attempt to assess the opinions of a virtual community, as expressed in the construction of web pages themselves. In this case, the "community" consists of the web itself, as opposed to the users behind them.

Delving further into Google's search results, I wanted to see what kinds of links would come up "down the list," search results that are lower on Google's hierarchy, so I randomly selected results pages between 1 and 100 (the first 2,000 of the "about" 277,000,000 hits in my December 2008 survey); I clicked over to search page 27, and scanned the results: web sites for jazz clubs (Anna's Jazz Island in Berkeley, Yoshi's in San Francisco, the Blue Note in New York), jazz societies (the New Jersey Jazz Society, the Baltimore Jazz Alliance), record labels (Criss Cross, Bastard Jazz), performers (the Dallas Jazz Orchestra), and pedagogical sites (Just Jazz). On results page 58, I found links for a summer jazz camp at UC San Diego, a news report from the Boston Globe on the Utah Jazz, radio station "Smooth Jazz 107.5, The Oasis" (Dallas), "Jazz Session," a general jazz blog, a jazz society in Erie, Pennsylvania ("Jazz Erie"), "Jazz Promo Services," which bills itself as a service to promote and conduct press campaigns for jazz musicians, the "Jazz in June" concert series in Lincoln, Nebraska, and "Bending Corners," a site featuring MP3 podcasts of acid jazz and related genres.

On the surface this might seem trivial, looking at results of web searches as an expression of community identity and broad statement about jazz. But I suggest that such surveys reveal a great deal about the presence of jazz on the internet, changing by the day, or even hour. Web searches like these often represent the first stop for research, both casual and scholarly, into many different topics. The types of links that appear in a Google search, especially toward the top of the list, reflect the ways in which web users themselves define what is important, and what knowledge holds more value. This is the most critical aspect of the virtual jazz community, that the users themselves determine, in large measure, the structure and practice of the community. Users are able to interact among themselves across vast distances and in nearly real time; and, just as important, these communities are visible, preserved in the digital realm for as long as there is space in the server.

In the remainder of this chapter, I will examine two specific virtual platforms, with an eye toward understanding how the experience of users reflects the processes of community formation and constructions of knowledge that were previously explored. The first example is the article on jazz on the open-source reference site Wikipedia, which just celebrated its tenth anniversary. The development of the article over several years demonstrates how knowledge about jazz is contested and negotiated among members of the community, and how the community struggles to reach the consensus that the website claims to emphasize.

The subsequent study examines jazz message boards, with particular emphasis on the jazz forum on the website All About Jazz. On this site, users regularly engage in debates that heretofore were regarded as the realm of jazz critics and scholars, at least insofar as they are made public. The message boards reveal a virtual jazz community that is fractured, with claims and counterclaims to authority about jazz forming the backbone of discussion. Users can make known their opinions about jazz artists (and each other), bringing into public light what had historically been private. In a concluding section, I assess the role of more recent developments on the internet such as YouTube, Facebook, and twitter, through which users can form communities revolving around themselves, ranging from established jazz artists to middle school jazz students. What happens on these sites is often made obsolete through advances in web technology, and indeed, it is possible that by the time you are reading this, all of this may be passé. These are, however, important as unique ethnographic moments, snapshots of a specific (cyber) space and time that speak to the dynamics of community.

Jazz on Wikipedia: Knowledge by Community, or by Anarchy?

After Google, there are few sites on the web that have generated as much attention as the open-source reference and research source known as Wikipedia. Built around a type of collaborative software known as a "wiki," Wikipedia has radically altered the ways in which information and knowledge about almost everything is constructed and presented in a public forum. As a teacher, I can attest to this firsthand, as the website has become the first, and oftentimes only, resource for student research. Wikipedia grew from an earlier reference work called Nupedia, established in 2000, featuring articles that were constructed collaboratively via email lists and message boards, as cofounder Larry Sanger recalls in a feature on the website Slashdot. The relatively intensive editing process for articles on Nupedia meant that work went slowly—so slowly, Sanger notes, that it eventually was overtaken by a sister site, Wikipedia, which emerged as a response to Nupedia's relative lethargy. Within a short time, Wikipedia had overtaken Nupedia as the preferred destination for both individuals looking for information, and for those wanting to participate in the editing process, in a community of knowledge. Unfortunately, as Sanger argues, the open-source wiki technology also circumvented real, quantifiable standards in writing and knowledge, a critique that hounds Wikipedia to this day. Sanger eventually left the project, leaving it in the hands of James "Jimbo" Wales, now generally regarded as the driving force behind Wikipedia.[1]

Among the most frequent criticisms of Wikipedia is that, without strict editorial control, information presented in Wikipedia articles is suspect. This charge is not without some merit, as a number of recent controversies have demonstrated. In one well-publicized incident, the article on writer John Seigenthaler was anonymously edited by a user later identified as Brian Chase, a delivery service employee from Tennessee, that suggested, among other things, that Seigenthaler played a role in the assassination of John F. Kennedy. The article was eventually corrected, and Chase apologized to Seigenthaler, but the incident highlights the inherent difficulties of open-source platforms, that anyone with a connection to the site can edit an article in nearly any manner. The theory, of course, is that such errors or falsehoods will be self-corrected by the users of the site; but given Wikipedia's widespread use as a first point of reference for those conducting research, false information, even when available for a short time, can spread throughout the internet very quickly. This is perhaps the biggest distinction between Wikipedia and printed sources; in the latter, what one sees is the end result of an editing process in which knowledge ideally is vetted and fact-checked before it is published. With Wikipedia, such buffers are removed. It is as if users are peeking into the editorial process, one which may have no fixed endpoint.

By its own definition Wikipedia is a "community-built" reference, and as such, there is (in the site's own words) a "possibility for error" in article content. Communities often display a multiplicity of viewpoints in the road to consensus, and Wikipedia lays these differences bare. The editing of articles is generally transparent; the history of edits and discussions on the site is archived, where users can see who wrote what and when.[2] But as with most other internet-based communities, Wikipedia provides anonymity to its users and editors, unlike the world of print publishing (for the most part). With some exceptions, no one really knows who is behind all the edits and writing in any given article.

This leads to another frequent complaint directed at Wikipedia, namely that editors, those who write and revise the site's content, may not always have the knowledge or expertise needed for a particular subject. Wikipedia defenders see this as a democratization of knowledge, in which all viewpoints are welcome. In this utopian view, arguments for and against a particular topic are weighed by the community, who will arrive at a consensus knowledge on the topic. But such an idea does not always work in practice. Officially, Wikipedia encourages experts in various fields to contribute to articles, as Wales states in an article published in *Nature* (and cited on Wikipedia's own article on "Wikipedia expert editors"), but the reality is often different. Experts are often reluctant to engage in "edit wars" with someone who has minimal knowledge but can debate effectively, especially when the latter choose not to identify themselves. In a 2007 feature in the *New Yorker*, British climate scientist William Connolley recounted his experience in an edit war with a number of anonymous editors who opposed his views on the subject. Connolley, who always used his real name in making edits to the site, charged that Wikipedia "gives no privilege to those who know what they're talking about." As Stacy Schiff notes, "It can still seem as though the user who spends the most time on the site—or who yells the loudest—wins" (Schiff 2006). Worse yet, the anonymity that Wikipedia affords editors makes the assessment of expertise difficult. In one widely reported incident, a user known as Essjay claimed to "[hold] doctoral degrees in theology and canon law, and [work] as a tenured professor at a private university," and had established himself as a respected editor and mediator in Wikipedia content disputes. In fact, he was a 24-year-old former community college student with no other academic training. This was a major embarrassment for the Wikipedia community, especially as it came on the heels of other well-publicized critiques of its credibility and accuracy.

It is within this environment that Wikipedia editors construct a consensus-based knowledge for a particular topic. Consensus is a critical component of the generation and presentation of articles in the Wikipedia universe. Wikipedia's own article on consensus states: "Editors typically reach a consensus as a natural outcome of wiki-editing. Someone makes a change to a page, then everyone who reads the page has an opportunity to leave it as it is, or change it. When two or more editors cannot reach an agreement by editing, consensus is sought on article talk pages" (Wikipedia contributors, n.d.). But as with seemingly everything else on Wikipedia, this is not always a fixed idea, as the article continues: "Consensus is not immutable. Past decisions are open to challenge and are not binding, and one must realize that such changes are often reasonable. Thus, 'according to consensus' and 'violates consensus' are not valid rationales for making or reverting an edit, or for accepting or rejecting other forms of proposal or action" (Wikipedia contributors, n.d.).

How consensus is achieved on a typical Wiki article is demonstrated on the "Talk Pages," which can be found under each article's "discussion" tab. Here, editors and other interested users discuss specific points and resolve disputes related to article formation and presentation. Determining membership in the Wikipedia community is simple—in theory, anyone who reads or (especially) edits self-selects as a part of this community. But with all community groups, the identity of any one member relative to the community as a whole can be contested. As all communities are based, in some sense, around the demonstration of knowledge, the very act of participating in Wikipedia is an exercise in community. Determining knowledge in such a "community-built" forum can be difficult, and often contentious. Credentials are both touted and questioned, from the perspectives of whether they actually exist, or are necessary or even desired.

All of this should be kept in mind as we examine Wikipedia articles devoted to jazz. The amount of writing on jazz in Wikipedia is substantial. Granted, some of these articles do not relate specifically to jazz as music. Articles about the Utah Jazz, Jazz Airlines, a Transformers character named jazz, a female professional wrestler, a motorcycle made by Honda, and a defunct Finnish soccer team called FC Jazz Pori are also tagged by this search, to give a few examples. But most results deal in some way with jazz as music, and it would take months, perhaps years, to sort through them all. The default site when searching Wikipedia for jazz is the general article on the music,[3] which serves both as an overview of the genre, and a gateway to numerous sub-articles devoted to musicians, genres, national style, and other related topics. The earliest version of the article, as logged in the "history" page for the article, is dated to November 28, 2001. The main text of this version comes in at around 950 words, about the equivalent of three typed pages in Microsoft Word, and gives a very general overview of jazz's historical development. The first line of the article reads, in its entirety: "Jazz, a musical form that grew out of roots in the blues, has been called the first American art form." Subsequent paragraphs reference various styles and musicians, without much analysis or commentary. Following the main text is a list of links to essays on representative musicians broken down by historical period—early, middle, and modern—as well as a list of sub-styles and "notable figures" by instrument. Clicking on the link for Louis Armstrong brings up another article, which itself appeared on Wikipedia on October 21 of the same year. The Armstrong article consisted of a personal appreciation, which begins "Louis Daniel Armstrong was to my mind the greatest musician of all genres in the 20th century." The ending to the original 200-word article is equally gushing: "In conclusion the best ambassador of hot music and a wonderful human being." Early manifestations of articles were often akin to message boards, in which users chime in with opinions and personal observations, activities that are officially discouraged on Wikipedia.[4] The Armstrong article was not edited until February 2002, when a few users, most notably jazzoctopus and Robert Merkel (the latter a "real name"), began to clean up some of the text. Merkel's edits, in particular, began the transformation of the original, anonymous, praise-ridden text to a more encyclopedic style of writing; his work, as indicated in his edit tag from February 23, "removed the more meaningless bits of fluffery" in earlier versions of the article.

In processes such as these, the transformation of an article from a short, effusive entry into a text better suited to a reference source, are replicated on countless other article pages throughout Wikipedia, and this process can be traced specifically. During late 2005 and early 2006, the article was heavily edited by numerous Wikipedians, with users adding sections, fixing language, addressing "vandalism," and generally trying to improve the article and make it more authoritative. By March 2006 the article had expanded to nearly 2900 words, with sections devoted to Armstrong's early life and career, his personality, aspects of his musical style, and his legacy in jazz and popular music. By October, five years after it first appeared on Wikipedia, the Armstrong article was up to 3300 words, with little change to the basic organization from March. In February 2007 the article was frequently and heavily vandalized, leading Wikipedia administrators to "protect" the site (preventing further unauthorized editing); anonymous users had inserted text such as "LUOIS [sic] WAS SOOO UGLY THAT EVERYBODY DIED IF THEY MET HIM!!!! plus he smelled bad." Further vandalism was seen later that year, as evidenced by the insertion of the text "DARNELL MARTIN IS THE BEST BASKETBALL PLAYER IN THE WHOLE WORLD. HE TRAVELED OVER SEAS AND WENT TO MARS HAHAHAHAHAHA U DUMBYS" on October 18 by another anonymous user.

Informative as the edit logs are, we can learn even more by reading the attached discussion pages, in which editors debate various perspectives on the topic. For example, a brief discussion began in January 2005 concerning Armstrong's supposed hypochondria and advocacy of laxatives. Though not extensive in terms of coverage, the discussion stretched into August of the following year. Other discussions revolve around his birth date, relationship with Joe Glaser, accusations of "Uncle Tomming," and Armstrong's role in transforming jazz. Despite the massive amount of editing, at least in statistical terms, consensus on Armstrong as evidenced in the Wikipedia article seemed to emerge fairly quickly and without many problems.

The same cannot be said for the article on jazz itself. Since its first appearance in November 2001, the article has generated enormous controversy and debate, as reflected in both the edit logs and the discussion pages. In terms of edits, the article had been edited around 6,000 times as of summer 2009, by around 2,500 editors (again, the vast majority of whom are anonymous, making minor edits). In the jazz article we can see the type of discourse that lies beneath the surface of a Wikipedia entry. For example, one of the fiercest debates on the article's discussion pages took place over two weeks in July 2008, concerning the wording of the lede (opening) of the essay. One user, identified as Editor437 in a post from July 10, 2008, took issue with recent discussions and edits which seemed to de-emphasize the connection of stylistic elements in jazz to West African origins: "These [edits] do not seem to be helpful—I doubt any serious work on Jazz would deny that Jazz originated, at least primarily, in African-American communities in the South and that 19th and 20th century American popular music was based upon (with, of course, further developments) European music." Another user, with the screen name Verklempt, responded the same day:

> There are many jazz scholars who argue that the music arose in a variety of locales, and some of these scholars are covered in the source cited. . . . Since most of these elements have other origins in addition to Africa (which is also addressed in the cited source), it's misleading to attribute them to Africa alone. In general, the lede section should be strictly accurate, and should maintain strict NPOV[5] on issues that are disputed in the scholarly literature.

The debate that ensued, conducted mainly between Verklempt and another anonymous user, ran until July 22 and, when finished, totaled around 3,600 words—seventy times longer than the lede under discussion and only about 1,000 words short of the entire article. A number of issues were raised in the course of this debate, from charges of bias, complaints about procedures in editing, citation and use of sources, personal attacks, and the true nature of jazz's origins. In other words, this one discussion represents in microcosm the dynamics of negotiating community. I will return to this point later.

Certain users seemingly have a lot invested in this article, as a review of the article's archived discussions indicates. Users see themselves as leaders in this virtual community, and debates involving their work are often very personal. As Benjamin Keith Johnson notes, users who invest time and effort into

editing articles have a sense of ownership, even within the borderless community of Wikipedia: "Reputation was an important part of editing activity
of Wikipedia, in a way that was integrated into the underlying structure of
the project. . . . There is enough of a sense of ownership of articles that respondents would keep close track of articles they had started or contributed
to via their watchlists" (Johnson 2007, 35). This is reflected in the case of a
user/editor referred to as deeceevoice who spent significant time beginning
in 2004 working on the jazz entry. Her experiences speak to the contested
nature of jazz historiography in the virtual community. One of deeceevoice's
earliest discussions involves the characterization of jazz in terms of race. She
wrote, on July 8, 2004: "I'll probably catch a lot of flack for this, but as an
African-American, it galls me when people try to act like black folks aren't
the originators of jazz. I've edited this article extensively to reflect that fact."
Shortly thereafter, deeceevoice also posted to the discussion page with a sense
of discomfort about assertions in earlier versions of the article that refer to
"mixed-race" musicians and the application of "conservatory standards" as
a result of the tightening of segregation in 1890s New Orleans (discussions
on July 8 to September 8, 2004). Throughout most of the summer of 2004,
deeceevoice was one of the only Wikipedia users regularly editing the article.
Her extensive work (and that of others at the time) did not go unnoticed;
by September, the entry was nominated to be "featured" on the Wikipedia
site, meaning that it had been determined to have reached a standard of
writing, editing, and research. This is an envied status among Wikipedians,
as featured status represents a public expression by Wikipedia that an article
reflects what is best about the site. These are the articles that Wikipedia wants
the public to see.

But there is seldom a "final product" in the Wikipedia universe. Articles
change, and when they are at their beginning stages, that is expected. But
change in an article that has been highlighted as an exemplar of the virtues
of the community means something entirely different, especially to members
of the community who have invested a great deal in its creation. Consider
the following passage from deeceevoice's user profile. On September 2, 2007,
the following passage was added: "I recently revisited Jazz, once a featured
article. It's now an utter mess and has been de-featured (is that a word?). It's
been so whitewashed, so gutted, the subject is barely recognizable. I've rein-
serted some language here and there. I simply don't have the patience to read
the entire thing, let alone attempt a thorough rewrite." The distance from
being a primary (maybe *the* primary) editor of what had in the past been
a featured Wikipedia article to perspectives espoused in the passage quoted
above is startling; of particular concern to deeceevoice was the de-emphasis on

African American origins and artists, championed by the previously cited user Verklempt, who advocated a perspective emphasizing European (read: white) contributions more prominently, and advocated a more "colorblind" approach to the discussion of jazz. In a post to the article's discussion page from October 25, 2007, Verklempt wrote: "I still object to the 'African American communities' phrase. The history is quite clear that early jazz was performed on riverboats, at resorts on Lake Ponchartrain, and in the Storyville brothel district. It is inaccurate to describe these locales as 'African American communities.'

Throughout the fall of 2007, Verklempt's posts to the discussion page of the article were a catalyst for intense debate about not only the procedures and practices of editing Wikipedia sites, but also the nature of the cultural identity of jazz. With Verklempt seemingly on one side of the debate, and deeceevoice on the other, the contested cultural identity of jazz was argued and counterargued over a period of several weeks. The central question came down to whether jazz should be classified as an historically African American idiom, or whether discussion of the music should be more race neutral. This debate seems to have been instigated by this comment from deeceevoice from September 1, 2007:

> What I discovered upon revisiting this page was far from an improvement. Talk about a whitewash. . . . Wikipedia—unfortunately—seems to be the site most consulted for information on jazz. Why unfortunately? Because it's the only site where one can go and read about how un-black jazz is and read a long, long list of ALL white and Jewish, many relatively obscure, band leaders of the 1920s. WTF? How's *that* for cultural appropriation?

This comment elicited a spirited response from Verklempt (later the same day), which stated that "Wikipedia is not a venue for racial politics. . . . musicians are important because of their artistry, not their race." Going back and forth over the next couple of days, deeceevoice and Verklempt waged what might be termed a "flame war," in which users taking opposite perspectives mixed intellectual discourse with personal insult.

Here is where the real tension in community-consensus knowledge formation comes to the fore. Two prolific editors, neither of whom will back down from their positions, engage in a fierce, sometimes bitter discourse, all of which is archived by Wikipedia. What happens to consensus and community when two vastly different perspectives on the nature of the music cannot be reconciled? Despite the vastness of the web and the seeming openness of a venue such as Wikipedia, there are some conflicts that will not be resolved.

There is only one "Jazz" entry on Wikipedia, only one text that can be read at any given time. Whose perspective "wins"? Who gets to speak for the community, and thus, whose knowledge defines it? At a certain point, deeceevoice seemed to throw in the towel; her editing activity on the article decreased substantially after 2007. Verklempt also seems to have largely abandoned the jazz entry, reducing his editing shortly after the debates with Editor437 and other anonymous editors in July 2008. The intense debates that lay behind the scenes may seem to be resolved when one reads the article, but as we see, in some cases, editors simply give up and absent themselves from the process, and from the community itself.

A frequent complaint on the article's discussion pages is that certain styles, artists, or perspectives are not included. For example, an anonymous user (identified by IP address only) complained that Art Tatum, "described as one of the greatest jazz pianists of all time by many top rank musicians and critics" (to quote this user), is not mentioned in the article. Another user (also identified by IP address) indicates that the article should include information on jazz's relationship to society, suggesting on November 23, 2008:

> Beyond discussing genre and form in a chronological fashion, this article is devoid of sociological perspectives on the relationship between jazz and white society. We need more on mainstream white perception of the evils of jazz in the early twentieth century, Pat Robertson's recent odd comments, its adoption by universities and NPR, etc. In the comments above, there's a little bit on race, but let's keep going. Music is far more than form.

Earlier, a user identified as Vb calls for a greater inclusion of European jazz artists, specifically citing Django Reinhardt, Stephane Grappelli, and Toots Thielemans. Inevitably some discussions come to the topic of various artists that may or may not be jazz. Take, for example, this exchange between users A.M.L. and Mütze from September 24, 2006. Commenting on the appropriateness of including audio samples of the Mahavishnu Orchestra's "Birds of Fire" and Courtney Pine's "The Jazzstep," A.M.L. states: "If 'Birds of Fire' is jazz (or at least has something in common with it), then I am Charlie Parker. And how 'The Jazzstep' can be called modern jazz, while it is just a simple tune played over a synthesized background?"

Responding, Mütze writes: "Well, if you are Charlie Parker and/or haven't read the article, you indeed wouldn't know that the development of Jazz didn't completely halt after the exploration of Bebop. The Mahavishnu Orchestra's Fusion is just as much Jazz as the first Dixie bands and Ornette Coleman's free experiments." To which A.M.L. follows up with "I don't judge the whole jazz fusion genre. I just state that this particular audio sample of 30 seconds isn't ever jazz fusion, it's straight rock. The caption says "this piece by the Mahavishnu Orchestra merges jazz improvisation and rock instrumentation into jazz fusion." The guitar solo can be called improvisation, but what makes it *jazz* improvisation? As to me, it is played in a typical rock manner." Again, the idea of consensus building is important here, with two seemingly opposed arguments, both equally plausible, vying for inclusion. You cannot both include and exclude John McLaughlin or Courtney Pine from a single article, so while a decision must be reached at some point, the debate rages on. The community, as expressed in the main text of the article itself, has to come down on one side or the other.

Controversies over authorship and commentary on the relative strengths of knowledge, experience, and credentials of editors are also frequent points of contention among editors. During the previously mentioned debate between deeceevoice and Verklempt, the latter user deleted some material that he felt could not be easily verified. In justifying his actions, he wrote on September 2: "Material that cannot be substantiated needs to be deleted. I am well-read in jazz history, and I know that most of what I deleted can never be proven. (E.g., the notion that spirituals, blues, and ragtime trace back to the Sahel is simply absurd. I have traveled all through the Sahel. They don't have many pianos there, much less a history of ragtime.)" Verklempt is making a clear claim to expertise, based on his being "well-read in jazz history" and having not seen any evidence of ragtime, etc., in the Sahel. But what does being "well-read" mean here? How can we assess the qualifications of someone who does not use his/her real identity? This is perhaps the most enduring aspect of controversies like that of Essjay: that there still is no way to objectively verify the authority of anonymous users. After Essjay was exposed, Wales proposed a system for verification of claimed expertise and credentials that was met with a mixed reaction among Wikipedia editors, some favoring the reliability and quality this move would potentially bring, others fearing that it would damage what was best about Wikipedia, the sense that all opinions are valid.

If the touting of one's own credentials does not happen very much, the invocation of other scholars' work happens frequently in support of various positions. Users are frequently asked to back up or justify conclusions with hard evidence. The problem with this type of discussion, in which one user presents sources to support a claim, only to be countered by another, is that these debates tend to spiral on ad infinitum. Ultimately, the emphasis is placed not on creating a consensus of knowledge, but something more reminiscent of those high school policy debates in which participants try to pack in as many bits of supporting evidence as possible. It is not quality of argument and knowledge that wins the day, but the skill at finding and employing bits of information to make a point.

It is not uncommon for editors to openly question the expertise of outside sources whose work they may not agree with. For example, this comment from Verklempt on August 15, 2007, demonstrates his disdain for a certain well-known jazz critic: "I enjoy [Gary] Giddens [*sic*] as a journalist, but I don't consider him an expert. He has never taken a PhD in music history, nor published in peer reviewed journals. He doesn't appear to have ever done much if any primary source research, save for listening to records. Jazz history has long been polluted by poorly informed amateurs." That Gary Giddins might not be an "expert" due to the fact the he "has never taken a PhD in music history" is notable, given Wikipedians' (and many musicians' and critics') frequent dismissal of advanced degrees as a necessity for expertise. Conversely, *not* claiming expertise can also be a strategy for establishing oneself in the community, as deeceevoice notes in a comment on the discussion page for the "Blues" article: "The use of blue notes and note bending as a vocal technique is common throughout non Muslim Africa, as well. Guess I'd have to hear the piece of music referred to in the article—but right now, I'd have to say I don't see a definitive link. But, again, I'm hardly an expert." It is difficult to ascertain exactly what the credentials or expertise of deeceevoice are. Her extensive editing would suggest that she does see herself as something of an expert; yet this claim could also be read as an attempt to, shall we say, "keep it real," to establish bona fides in the Wikipedia community by standing apart from overt displays of expertise.

The users who created the jazz article have engaged in a collective construction of the knowledge, as defined by this particular community. Debates over the article's formation, from disputes over inclusion and exclusion, to ethnic, racial, and national identity, are manifestations of debates that have been raging for years within jazz communities. The difference here is that these debates are not just being played out by professional critics and scholars in the pages of major jazz publications; they are conducted by everyday people with an interest in the music and a desire to contribute to the fostering of jazz knowledge. Are they "citizen scholars," whose role is to wrest jazz from academic and critical discourses? Or are they just people who have listened to a few jazz records and have too much time on their hands? Both of these are represented in the Wikipedia community; sorting out who's who is the problem.

Jazz Message Boards: Fan Communities Online

As with the early community sections of sites like Jazz Central Station, message boards provide an important forum for jazz fans to engage in discourses on the music. Of all the message board sites devoted to jazz, three stand out in terms of popularity. The largest and most active jazz message board is associated with the website All About Jazz (AAJ).[6] As the name implies, AAJ is a clearinghouse for many different types of information about jazz, providing (as the website states) "information and opinion about jazz from the past, present, and future." Established in 1995 by Michael Ricci, All About Jazz is arguably the most commonly visited website on the internet devoted to jazz, containing reviews, original feature articles, profiles of member musicians, and a wealth of other information on every conceivable aspect of jazz. As of late 2010 its discussion board has over 11,000 members, making it by far the largest jazz discussion forum on the internet. The Organissimo Jazz Discussion Forum, established in 2003 by Jim Alfredson, is linked to the website of the trio of the same name, based in Lansing, Michigan (Alfredson is the group's organist). The Organissimo forum boasts over 3,700 members, substantially fewer than AAJ but still significant considering the forum's relatively short existence. A third website, the "Speakeasy" on the website JazzCorner, shares many of the same features as the other two. JazzCorner is similar in a number of ways to AAJ, but arguably on a smaller scale. Billing itself as "the largest portal for the official websites of hundreds of jazz musicians and organizations," JazzCorner is, like AAJ, a site that gathers interviews and news, as well as a roster of affiliated musicians. With around 7,500 members as of late 2010, the forum sits somewhere between All About Jazz and Organissimo in terms of membership.

Message boards are typically subdivided into sub-forums of varying depth or breadth. For example, the forum at All About Jazz has five subcategories: "All About Jazz," for discussion of issues relating to the website itself; "Talk Jazz," devoted to general jazz-related discussions; "Play Jazz," which includes more focused topics geared toward working musicians, and other topics of interest to performers; "Open Air," a general forum for non-jazz topics; and "Promote It," which as the name implies, serves as a vehicle for artists and others to promote gigs, buy/sell/trade items, and otherwise engage in the business of jazz. Within each of these subcategories are numerous other forums. In the "Talk Jazz" area, for example, there are discussions devoted to "General Music Discussion," "Artists and Bands," "Sights and Sounds," and a forum for jazz "newbies" to ask questions, to list a few examples. "Play Jazz," meanwhile, contains discussions devoted to audio/video samples, theory and analysis, and networking with other players. "Open Air" is devoted to discussions of topics that may not relate directly to the website's mission, and serves as a general clearinghouse for forum members to talk about different topics.

The Organissimo forum is similarly organized into sub-forums, arguably less specific than those on AAJ: "About Organissimo," devoted to discussions of the band itself; "Music Discussion," focused mainly on jazz; and a non-music "General Discussion" area. The discussion board on JazzCorner, called the "Speakeasy," is based on the same vBulletin platform[7] used by AAJ, and thus displays a similar structure, though without specifically labeled sub-forums. Speakeasy discussions are generally similar to those on other websites, with discussion areas designated for "Gigs," "Live Music Reviews," and "Musicians Resources," among others. The general jazz discussion section, "Speak Out," and non-music area "The Alley," are usually the most active discussions. Compared with AAJ and Organissimo, the Speakeasy does not seem to host as many contentious debates or controversial topics, and generally is geared more toward discussions of new releases, and news about jazz artists.

Within these discussion areas occur the real, focused interactions among message board users. One of the most heavily populated areas of the All About Jazz forum is the "General Music Discussion" (GMD) area under "Talk Jazz," second only to "Get the Word Out" discussion under "Promote It!" (the latter, however, features very little discussion, only listings which are akin to classified ads). The GMD discussion is a freewheeling, open-ended forum for users to post messages on nearly anything in which users might be interested. Discussion "threads," individual topics to which users post and reply to messages, are created relatively frequently in the GMD section, and posting occurs in many threads on at least a daily basis. Topics in this section represent a broad cross section of popular discourses on jazz; a brief scan of active topics toward the end of December 2010 showed discussions related to "Where is jazz going in the coming years," "Any jazz under your tree," "Favorite albums of 2010," "current jazz guitarists," and "Billy Taylor—RIP," to name a few. A similar survey of topics in July 2009 saw threads related to "Live Jazz from the 50s," "Billie Holiday Fifty Years Later: A Tribute and Reassessment," "Favorite jazz drummer," and "Flamenco-Jazz Guitar." There is no real barrier to what users may post, though forum moderators may move a thread to a section of the site that is deemed more appropriate.[8]

In general, the three message boards discussed in this section are relatively harmonious places, with users sharing thoughts on recordings, concerts, and other jazz-related matters. Most threads deal with listening, favorite recordings, local scenes, and the like, and the general tenor is one in which users are glad to have a place to exchange ideas about the music. Occasionally conflicts arise on the boards that become contentious, and it is at these times that message boards reveal their full potential as sites of community formation and maintenance, of contesting and negotiating knowledge. What follows are two case studies of threads that have generated a good deal of discussion, and make clear the ways in which message boards serve to underscore differences between various constituencies in jazz cyberspace.

Case Study 1: "What the F**k happened to Black Popular Music"—The Long and Winding Road of a Discussion Thread

Topics that generate heavy viewership and participation often deal with more complex and controversial topics. One example from the AAJ board was labeled "'What the F**k happened to Black Popular Music' Article," concerning a discussion of an essay by pianist Kenny Drew Jr.[9] In his essay, Drew takes issue with what he sees as the declining state of black poplar music, specifically rap, ending with a call for a boycott of the music. Originally posted by Drew as an AAJ article in April 2006, the ensuing discussion in the AAJ board was intense and spirited. What follows is a brief summation of the thread's creation and the discussions that ensued throughout the spring of 2006. I have reproduced a number of passages that illustrate some of the main viewpoints and issues that are manifest in the thread. The initial post in the thread, by a user called "jazz man" on April 6, commented on Drew's piece:

> I'll freely admit, I have very mixed feelings on these sort of topics. On one hand, people like Herbie Hancock have openly embraced rap and have incorporated the latest electronics and other devices into their own recordings. Also, from what I know, when be-bop was in its early stages in the 1940's, many of the established jazz musicians, Louie Armstrong included, dismissed be-bop as noise.

User Artmaus responded later the same day:

> I'm sick of people defending rap. It sucks and aside from some obsure [*sic*] artists who the general public never has and never will hear of it will continue to suck. Music is supposed to be made up of melody, rhythm and harmony.

By contrast, user Stopbobby notes, also on April 6:

> I find it rather ridiculous when people say rap sucks. There are a lot of hip-hop artists making great music (K-OS, Aesop Rock, The Roots,

Hieroglyphics, etc.)—and yes they tend to be less popular, but it's generally true of all music styles (including jazz) that mediocre work tends to reach the widest audience.

Finding a middle ground, user Jakeweiser chimes in:

> I am torn on this subject. Firstly because I don't think anyone has the right to tell anyone what music is good or what music is bad. We have our own desires musically and to tell me that my musical tastes are lesser then someone elses or greater then someone elses [*sic*] really gets me upset. Music is music, and there is so much music out there in so many genres that there is no one 'genre' that can encompass music listeners . . . That being said. I do not agree with a lot of the messages of Rap music.

Meanwhile, Copper Scroll writes (4/7/06):

> The question arises: Need rap be so threatening and confrontational? No, but look at where these kids come from. **Telling them that they are stupid and that their music sucks won't make them less confrontational—won't help them to listen to what you have to say.** They, first, need to know that their artform is respected as an artform. Find common ground. From that point, they can be reasoned with and be called to a higher moral standard. [boldface in original]

By midday on April 7, users had begun addressing each other directly, although still in a relatively civil tone, as user clave notes to fellow user Copper Scroll on April 7:

> Copper scroll "yeah, that!" [with a thumbs up symbol]

User jazzofonik gives a similar nod to Copper Scroll:

> Mos' Def!!!

Some were not as civil in their comments to other users. Tritone Sub sends the following advice to artmaus, concerning his strong opinions on this subject on April 7: "Don't drop the tablets on your way down the mountain." By April 8 the discussion had meandered into other areas, touching on politics and social issues. A particularly pointed exchange between users Copper Scroll and stopbobby centered on the connection between rap and inner city communities. Copper Scroll writes:

> Individual poor people pulling themselves out of poverty won't change the conditions in the communities they leave behind. I said they need to change their socioeconomic conditions, and most raps don't further this goal.

User stopbobby responds later that day:

> Black people living in poverty are a minority of the entire U.S. population, so they can't force the government to do anything. So the suggestion that it's within the power of poor Blacks to change their socioeconomic conditions is implausible to say the least. The point remains that it's offensive to suggest that poor Blacks don't have to be poor if they don't want to be.

The exchange between these users, and a few others, would stretch into the following day. By April 11 the discussion had moved onto topics as wide ranging as John Cage and Marcel Duchamp, and by April 12 the nature of the discussion had begun to wear down some users. Alexander argues, on April 12:

> Jesus Christ. I can't believe some of the things I've read in this thread. The narrow-mindedness and snobbery is really sickening . . . I love jazz. I love rock. I love hip-hop. I love country. I love blues, punk, funk, folk, bluegrass . . . you get the idea . . . It's all MUSIC. And it's all good. You like what you like, and that's fine, but those people who say, "I will NEVER listen to (fill in genre)" are depriving themselves of some kick-ass sounds.

Newly registered user Jeffery Newton, Esq. writes on April 13, commenting on what he perceives as the out-of-place nature of the debate in this forum:

> I just joined this forum, and this thread caught my eye. This *is* a Jazz forum, is it not???

This comment bears some further exploration. Jeffery Newton, Esq. suggests that a boundary has been crossed, that a discussion of hip hop has invaded a jazz community forum, and that such a discussion is out of place. This is a fair point: why *is* this topic so actively and forcefully argued on a jazz message board? The question indicates that some users see the boundaries between jazz and other forms, especially popular music, as important enough to be argued, or to be defended. No one throughout this entire thread ever asks the question about why jazz musicians and fans should really care about rap, yet so many users have opinions on the subject. In this context, talking about the "state of black popular music" is an exercise in which *this* jazz community can define and redefine itself in opposition to other forms. Drew's article may say less about rap than it does about jazz, which stands in implicit opposition to pop. The pragmatic comment of Jeffery Newton, Esq. seems to cut to the core of this issue.

April 13 saw the peak of argumentative activity in the thread; the first post of the day, from user Visitor13, is at 1:32 a.m., responding to a message from Skipster, who notes that this debate is nothing new in jazz discourse. By 9 a.m. thirty posts have already been added to the thread, continuing debates from the previous day (bringing the total to over 240 in the week since the thread started). Posting continues for the rest of the day and into the evening, one message coming on top of another, in some cases, "passing" each other in the process. A review of post times from late in the day shows that users involved in this debate were sometimes posting literally minutes apart, seemingly waiting by their computers. By the following day, there were 361, up from 213. There was a sense of engagement and investment in this thread, but also a sense of concern that the post was taking a negative turn, and some users reminded others that a sense of decorum was needed to maintain it. User clave asks, later in the day on April 13:

Anyone taken a look at the Welcome! and Board Policies threads yet? (For the newbies.)

A short time later, however the same user posted this:

This thread is a first—we've been talking *with* each other about about [*sic*] the subject. (For the most part.) It's refreshing!

This is a telling comment, as clave explicitly references the message board's function as a site for discourse, and therefore, a site for community formation and discourse.

Posting continued regularly on this thread through May, though the frequency of posts began to decline around the end of April. By mid May, posting became less frequent, with a slight uptick around mid-July into the end of the summer. Between August 14 and October 19 there were no posts to the thread, and the October post was a single entry by a newly registered user who had just encountered the thread. Over one year later, two users summed the situation up nicely in a pair of succinct posts on December 6, 2007, writing simply, "Legendary thread" (user 3Q15) and, in reply "wow. i can't believe it's over a year since that thread has been posted in. time flies . . ." (user thedwork).

Case Study 2: Attitudes Toward Musicians

Disputes or controversial comments about (or in some cases from) jazz artists similarly polarize users on the board. Perhaps not surprisingly, topics concerning Wynton Marsalis generate substantial discussion among board users. In one post from a student seeking advice in writing a research paper on topics in jazz, user spitfirepete put the angst over Marsalis into context, advising the student "If you search the Wynton Marsalis Threads on this site . . . you will find very heated opposing views . . ." (10/8/08). One thread on the AAJ forum concerning Marsalis's appearance on Comedy Central's *Colbert Report* from October 21, 2008, generated fifteen responses in three days, as well as over 350 views; by the end of December, there were 1,050 views (but only five additional replies). Most posts in the thread alternated between discussions about Colbert's on-screen persona and not-so-subtle jabs at Marsalis. One reply by user jookyle stated simply: "He was a prick. And not in a funny way. Just a prick" (10/23/08). Some confusion ensued as to whether the "prick" in question was Marsalis or Colbert, whom several users pointed out adopts this persona as part of his act, but jookyle put this matter to rest, posting the next day, "No, I meant Wynton." As with most threads on Marsalis, there are those who defend him. User Berzin writes, on October 26:

> I thought the bit with Marsalis was hilarious. Call him what you want, but he has done much good with his fame at such a young age, and to have achieved international fame in such a niche genre like jazz I think is incredible. So he may come across as pompous—he has every right to be.

To this, user Borys Pomianek adds:

> There are always two sides of the M problem. . . . When it comes to my personal opinion, from the audience perspective i have no problem with Marsalis. I listened to his records, its good playing. I do not consider him to be on the level of his fame but that is the case with life in general

and thus not a problem for me. He is not a guy i would transcribe
though. . . . From the musicians perspective, him doing good for himself is of no use for me so i can only wonder if he does good for me. . . .

A thread on the same topic from the Organissimo forum (though attracting
only 377 views and nine posts) covered much of the same ground, some specifically praising Colbert for his performance, while others again pointed criticisms at Marsalis. One user, The red Menace, stated simply: "I watched the
first three minutes and thought him rather an ass!!!" Though it is not specified,
one assumes the user refers to Marsalis. User md655321 noted the reactions of
him and his "lady friend" to Marsalis's "demeanor" in a post on October 24:

> Me: Wynton is the most famous "jazz musician" on earth.
> Music, but not jazz, inclined lady friend: He sure acts like it.
> Smart girl.

User Hot Ptah, meanwhile, seems to offer some suggestions for Marsalis:

> As I watched Colbert, I thought that it would be nice if Wynton had
> more of a light touch, was more likeable and engaging on TV. Since he
> seems to get most of the very rare opportunities for a jazz artist to appear
> on TV in the U.S., if his personality was more like, say, Barack Obama's,
> just to pick out a random example, it might actually be positive for jazz.

In another thread at AAJ, a user asks whether Marsalis is a "friend or foe" of
jazz. The thread was initiated on February 9, 2008, by user bluenote82, who
quotes from Marsalis's biography in the *All Music Guide*, and then ends with
the following inquiry:

> I know he's a very controversial jazz musician, but what do think about
> his music? Not his opinions. Let's forget about all the stuff he's said and
> talk about his music. What do you guys really think of his playing?

What begins as an attempt to focus squarely on Marsalis's playing quickly
veers into the relatively predictable debate over Marsalis the person. A few
early posts do stick with the expressed theme. User apricissimus opines:

> I actually really like a lot of his music, even if he comes off as extremely
> narrow and parochial at times. He does what he does very well, and I
> think people get put off by him because he's not someone who pushes

the boundaries of the music. Of course his rhetoric also puts people off, but I think if people were able to put that out of their minds, you'd find that a lot more people would be able to appreciate his music.

User modalbopo8 agrees, stating:

> Wynton is the man. people say that he is not an innovator, but albums of his like "Think of One" may contest such statements. his standard time groups have a very definitive sound.

On February 10, bluenote82 posted the following, anticipating the debate that was sure to follow:

> I haven't heard from anyone that dislikes him yet. Most of the comments made have been good or neutral, so this should be interesting. And now we wait. . . . .

Later the same day, user Alexander obliges:

> But, and even some of Wynton's admirers will admit this, Wynton didn't quite live up to his own hype. Now, was this his fault? Not really. He'd been built up by critics and PR-men . . . So, is Wynton a friend to jazz? Of course he is. But, many would note that with friends like Wynton, jazz doesn't need enemies.

That same day, user justHerb made the following observation, which I have edited here:

> So if we all agree that Wynton is a Friend of Jazz who would one consider a foe? Even someone like Kenny G holds a semi important place in the Jazz World . . . So who IS a foe? . . . The Media? Today's schools? Jazz snobs?

I want to pause for a moment on this post, because it highlights an important aspect of the formation of jazz communities in the virtual environment. In his comment asking about who is a "foe" of jazz, justHerb engages in an exercise at the root of self-identification with community—who's in, and who's not. That *even* Kenny G is important to the community suggests that members' classification of who belongs can be measured by shifting criteria. Kenny G, perhaps one of the most reviled artists among those who consider themselves serious jazz fans can in some sense be considered a jazz musician. Debating whether Marsalis is a "friend or foe" can be yet another expression of this exercise. Other comments in this thread were less cryptic in their positions on Marsalis. User Jay Norem advances the following argument on February 10:

> It seems to me that anyone who says that jazz is only jazz when it contains characteristics X, Y, and Z is a foe of jazz. Because even if someone's music does contain those characteristics, it may not be rendered in a way that meets the approval of the definers.

What I find most interesting about such a comment is that Jay Norem is accusing Marsalis of engaging in precisely the same activity that is at the heart of community formation, of establishing boundaries. The user accuses Marsalis of engaging in exclusion in defining jazz, and therefore jazz community, in a manner that may not include those whom the user feels should be "in." Drawing boundaries is an exercise in relativity and perspective; the very fact that one is participating in a forum on a site called All About Jazz contains a particular view that jazz *is* bounded at some level.

Subsequent posts in the early days of the thread (the flurry of posting activity that took place between February 9 and 11), went over many of the same issues, in addition to discussing specific recordings, as well as those of Wynton's brother Branford. By February 14 (ironically, Valentine's Day), more personal comments began to emerge in the thread. Much of this revolved around posts by user Aggie87, who posted the following in the early afternoon of February 14, responding to a comment from another user praising Marsalis as an innovator:

> It's a good thing "good" music is subjective, because my ears don't hear anything innovative from Wynton. He's playing a style of music that was innovative 50 years ago . . . Nothing wrong with you finding it highly entertaining, of course. But I fail to see how it's innovative. Wynton hasn't done anything that previous trumpeters haven't already done, and did better.

This message led to several other posts, some agreeing with this sentiment, others opposing it, including the user who initiated the thread, who in retrospect seems to have been itching for a fight. Striking a relatively uncivil tone, he addressed a comment to Damon_Smith early that evening:

Damon, you're about as open-minded as any "Wynton Basher" I've ever met. Most of the "Wynton Bashers" say they're more open-minded, when the sad reality is their actually some of the most narrow-minded people you'll ever meet . . . I think you're a tired, bitter, unforgiving person who can't let go of the past.

Aggie87 responded:

Please demonstrate where Damon has said anything that would suggest he's close-minded. Your argument has no basis in anything he's written. In fact, what he's written suggests quite the opposite. And this is a thread about whether Marsalis is a friend or foe, so both opinions should be valid. It's not a thread for only Wynton fans.

Later that evening, bluenote82 wrote:

. . . Cut the bullshit and start talking about the music. Nobody gives a shit what Wynton thinks, believes in, has thought about, or what he has said in the past 20 years. I sure as hell don't. I listen to the music, not the person's opinions making it. Get over it, man.

Bill_McCloskey then addresses a comment to bluenote82 concerning the tone of the debate:

I have to say that, while you are certainly entitled to express your opinion, I can't help but wish you could develop some restraint. It often feels like to me that the adults are talking and suddenly a kid runs in throwing a tantrum. I believe the level of discourse was rising in this thread and that your comments add nothing constructive.

Not heeding this advice, bluenote82 posts a few minutes later:

Every damn thing you've said Aggie 87 has been negative. If you don't like Wynton's music that's fine state your opinion. . . . move on somewhere else. You have made yourself quite clear that you don't like Wynton. That's fine, so why do you continue to talk crap about Wynton when it's clear to everyone that you don't like him?

By 10 p.m., the thread has devolved into a full-fledged conflagration, a "flame war" that continued over the next several days, in which the venom that had been directed at Marsalis was turned against posters themselves. The point of all this is to illustrate both the passions with which members of the community identify with specific constituencies, and to demonstrate how untidy the processes of community formation and maintenance can be. Do users like bluenote82 and Aggie87 see themselves as part of the same community? What is the responsibility of other members of the community to maintain order and decorum (as Bill_McCloskey attempted to do)?

The thread continued with users actively posting replies until February 22, when there were 463 messages (for an average of over 30 messages per day), at which point posting stopped. On July 19, user CoyotePalace posted the following, seemingly trying to coax the debate back into the open:

Ahhhhh, yessssss! Time to drag this old chestnut back out into the cold light of day. Considering the current thread running, this should be a great place to beat on a very dead horse one more time from the top of the form!

No one obliged. As of the end of 2008, this was the last post on the topic. Was there a weariness to go over all this again? Is the "Wynton debate" really a dead horse, as CoyotePalace states? If so, one wonders why such debates continue to appear. Positions seem entrenched, seemingly little changes, opinions are reinforced among members of the community. Perhaps the experience of participating in such debates is really what this community is all about.

Lest we think that Wynton Marsalis is the only jazz musician whose music and behavior is debated in such forums, consider the behavior of pianist Keith Jarrett at the 2007 Umbria Jazz Festival. Jarrett, upon walking onstage along with trio-mates Jack DeJohnette and Gary Peacock, proceeded to berate the audience about snapping photographs, a practice that has raised Jarrett's ire (and to be fair, that of other musicians as well) on previous occasions. Little would have been made of this incident if not for the fact that someone, clearly in violation of Jarrett's directives, recorded the incident on video, which found its way to YouTube and other file sharing sites. Jarrett concluded his tirade by insulting the organizers and host city, which earned him, according to the organizers, a lifetime ban from the event. Against this backdrop, a number of threads began to appear on various internet forums. At AAJ, there were a number of threads that discussed Jarrett's behavior at Umbria 2007. One thread, started on July 11 (one day after the performance) and titled "Jarrett opens a concert dissing the audience," the vast majority of the responses to the initial post by user sergio were not supportive of Jarrett's actions, with many declaring their intent to no longer patronize him (avoiding performances, not buying recordings, etc.), and more than a few suggesting mental help. He (sergio) himself ends his post by stating "I swear it's the last time I pay to listen to this bastard egomaniac." User artmaus suggests that discourses such as these will have little impact on changing artists' behavior, saying in a post on July 12:

> Jarrett doesn't care in the least what you have to say. He doesn't have a web site (neither does Peacock for that matter and DeJohnette has one but with no contact link). The only thing that will get through to him would be declining sales. So talk all you want, it just not going to change anything.

This message raises an interesting question: within the larger context of the community, and of artist/audience relationships, what is the point of this? Does an artist read these posts, and do the posters believe that they are really going to have any impact on either an artist specifically or the perceived community generally? Obviously, such discussions are important to those who are participating in them, and that in itself is an important part of the life of the message board, of this *specific* jazz community. On a broader level, fans want to feel as if they are contributing something to a larger discourse—that they, in essence, have a voice.

Such sentiments are evident in a second thread, initiated by AAJ founder Michael Ricci (user xricci) on July 27, beginning with "An open letter to Keith Jarrett," in which Ricci links to an essay by French musician and writer Daniel Biro that chides Jarrett for the incident at Umbria.[10] Most of the users who posted on the topic echoed the sentiments expressed by Biro (including, presumably, Ricci). User James posted, on July 27, the same day the thread was initiated:

> I get really vexed when so-called fans of the music disrespect the musicians, but demonstrating respect is a two way street. I'll never pay to see this clown live, and will not support him with cd purchases either. Have enuff Jarrett in my collection to scratch my itch when the itch appears.

Posting later that evening, thedwork speaks of putting words into action:

> yeah, i thought the letter was ok. but your point of getting it *to the people* (jarrett or the community . . .) is key. when i wrote my letter about Peacock's arrogant/elitist behavior i brought it to the trio's Carnegie Hall performance and handed it out directly to the patrons. putting stuff up

here at AAJ is a good way to get it out as well, but i still believe in *"hard copy"* or *"print media."*

papsrus later adds:

> Pretty restrained letter, really. The guy's a child, and because of his be-
> havior deserves exactly zero respect from me as a listener. I could frankly
> do without ever listening to him again, and it's unlikely I'll buy another
> of his CDs. He's a freak show at this point.

User dandan takes a seemingly more sympathetic tone, writing:

> It is the mad genius thing. It is not that uncommon for genius to be
> mixed with madness (and Mr. Jarrett certainly is a genius).

In subsequent posts, users speculated about whether Jarrett is really a "genius," (even bringing up his supposedly high I.Q.), whether he may be afflicted with some disorder (Tourette and Asperger syndromes were both mentioned) that affected his onstage manner (with varying degrees of sympathy), to whether Jarrett would be able to survive as an artist and if people would keep coming to his performances. But the most telling comment was on July 30, by user 128Bit Encryption, who writes:

> Outstanding! I think you did the right thing by voicing your opinion
> and displeasure with Jarretts [*sic*] offensive and obnoxiously disrespect-
> ful behavior. Jarrett is a fine musician, but he is not that important
> or major. But actually, it really doesn't matter. *Disrespectful and rude
> behavior is no excuse.* I can understand his displeasure with flashes and
> possible taping. But there is a manner in which you can communicate
> this concern in a stern but respectful way. From all accounts, Jarrett has
> failed to grasp this concept. Best way to deal with it is not to attend his
> live performances and let everyone know why you refuse to see him live.
> *People have a right to boycott being disrespected.* [emphasis in original]

A parallel discussion (as part of a larger thread on Jarrett) occurred in mid-July at Organissimo, and again, while most users condemned Jarrett's comments, some rose to defend him. On the former point, user Clifford Thornton re-sponded to a post of a link to the video of Jarrett at Umbria with a succinct observation: "Yes, he is indeed a twat," a view echoed by several other users in relatively short order. On the other hand, user skeith offers some qualified support for Jarrett:

> After viewing the video—I have to say that although Jarrett said it in rather over the top fashion I basically agree with him. IT is not clear whether they had already started playing or not, but am I the only one who gets annoyed at concerts by photographers constantly making the clicking noises with the lens shutters and the lights flashing.

User Van Basten II seems to take a middle ground:

> Watching the video, i did not mind the complaints about the people who were taking pictures, however to say that it's a goddamn city because of a few bad apples shows that this guy is living is his own world and should learn about diplomacy.

The importance of discussions like this is not, I believe, in these users' attitudes toward Jarrett's behavior, but because they underscore a shift to a more fan-centric view of jazz discourse, in which they have an ability to exert power and control over the discourse of artist/audience relationships. The strong sentiments expressed by users indicate that fans feel a certain personal investment not only in the music, but the personas and activities of jazz musicians, especially those whose activities might reflect on the jazz community (as they perceive it) in general. We can see this in the comments directed at Marsalis, whose statements in interviews about the nature of jazz cause consternation mainly because he is one of the few public faces for the community at large. The same can be said for Jarrett, who while not as well known among the general public as Marsalis, is certainly known to most casual fans of jazz. On this point, the perceived transgressions of one person are a reason to be marginalized, even ostracized by others, who strongly assert that these opinions do not reflect the community. As user mingusfingus writes in the "open letter" thread on July 27:

> Sorry to hear about such a poor experience. *Glad he's not important enough to represent the entirety of the art form.* I believe strongly that the entirety of music is really about commune. It's from and about all the people who are involved, from the casual listener and appreciator all the way to the writers and producers and performers. [emphasis added]

As with Wikipedia, message boards provide an avenue for jazz fans to speak for themselves, to construct their own communities, in which they can exchange, debate, and generate what it is that they know, or think they know, about the music, its history, and its practice. In other virtual environments, individual users can take an even greater role in asserting their own identities, influencing discourses, and constructing their own spheres of knowledge about jazz.

Virtual Communities and Individual Agency

Leaving aside arguments about copyright and legality, it is beyond dispute that the advent of file sharing has radically altered the ways in which individual listeners see their place within the music industry. So called peer-to-peer (p2p) platforms allow fans to easily and quickly share audio files, and for the better part of the last decade, the established recording industry, through its main trade organization, the RIAA, has been playing catch-up, filing lawsuits against the most egregious offenders and targeting YouTube sites for DMCA notices. It comes as no surprise that most of the attention has been focused on popular music as opposed to jazz, as the latter still represents only a small percentage of overall record sales.[11]

Jazz's limited commercial role may inadvertently benefit the sharing of the music online. YouTube videos featuring jazz performances, live and recorded, are found in large numbers on the site, but as of the time of this writing, I have yet to encounter a notice that a video has been removed due to a copyright claim. Searching YouTube by artist also yields a plethora of videos of live performances, clips of documentaries, and tribute videos put up by fans, many of which feature copyrighted audio tracks (to say nothing of video and still images). For example, searching for "Charlie Parker" yields over 5,000 results. One of the top results is a capture of Parker and Dizzy Gillespie's famous 1952 appearance on the television show *Stage Entrance*, in which host Earl Wilson refers to them as "boys." Another video shows Parker with Coleman Hawkins from a 1950 Norman Granz production. A video marker appears constantly in the upper middle of the screen, clearly indicating that this clip was "ripped" from a DVD. Videos such as these provide a valuable and eminently accessible historical document, searchable by even casual fans. They also, in many cases, are posted illegally, but given their widespread availability, it seems that the recording industry and artist management have more pressing (or profitable) targets for its policing of copyrights.

Another phenomenon on YouTube is the creation of "tribute" videos to various artists, in which an artist's music is combined with images, artwork, or still photos to create a collage of sight and sound. Staying for the moment with our search on Charlie Parker, one video[12] presents a recording of Parker playing "Bird of Paradise" set against a photo of the album cover for the *Complete Dial Masters* set. Toward the end of the first chorus of Parker's solo, this fades into a second picture, of the cover for *Bird of Paradise*. As Miles Davis begins his solo, another fade takes us to a still of bassist Tommy Potter. The audio track eventually shifts to "Dewey Square," as more photos of Parker fade one into another. In another Parker themed video tribute, a single photo of Parker (smiling and looking away from the camera) is set to the music of Parker and Miles Davis's recording of "My Old Flame" from 1947.[13] The single image does not change throughout the recording. A third tribute video sets Parker's "strings" recording of "Summertime" against a pair of photos, beginning with a well known shot of Parker in a polka-dot tie (which moves for in a lingering close up over a few minutes), then to a new shot of Parker, and finally back to the original photo.

YouTube's role in disseminating jazz videos is evidenced by the appearance of satellite sites such as Jazz Tube, which identifies itself as a repository of jazz-related YouTube materials. In a feature on the website All About Jazz in August 2006, "jazz video guy" Bret Primack outlines the potential YouTube holds for jazz: "Video is the hottest content on the web right now. . . . Of course there's plenty of stupid pet tricks, but you can find Coltrane, Cecil Taylor and Lee Morgan on YouTube, as well. It's a great place for all artists to showcase their work as more and more people are searching for Jazz content" (All About Jazz Publicity, 2009). Primack himself has worked in collaboration with artists and record companies to produce original content for YouTube, including a large number of mini-documentaries and features of specific musicians. All About Jazz has its own section of the website where embedded YouTube videos can be seen, often of pre-existing performances. AAJ is careful to note, in a disclaimer accompanying each video: "All rights reserved. The video footage is for individual personal usage only; no other rights are granted or implied." As a commercial site, All About Jazz undoubtedly has to take greater care in adhering to copyright laws than does, say, an anonymous user, but it is likely that authorized content forms only a fraction of video on YouTube.

Not everyone is pleased with the role YouTube has played in the sidestepping of traditional methods for accessing jazz video, such as actually buying them, or failing that, borrowing them from a library. As Bruce Klauber writes in the community forum section of the *Jazz Times* website:

What I absolutely fail to understand is just how the folks who post all this stuff, complete with original on-screen titling, yet, can ignore just where this material came from. Would it hurt to at least credit Hudson Music, Alfred Publishing or JazzLegends.com as the source? When I confronted one YouTube poster about this, he claimed he found the video "Gene Krupa: Jazz Legend" in an unmarked box and had no idea where it came from. The credits, of course, clearly spell out the source involved. (Klauber 2009)

As Klauber notes, the posting of these types of videos online makes producing them (as he has done) less profitable, and potentially could lead to them being abandoned altogether. A fair point, but users still do not seem deterred from their use of online clips. Judging by the sheer numbers of videos available, users seem to have decided to ignore such trivialities, with its "netizen" members taking the distribution of the music into their own hands, and this is the point I want to underscore. Where in the 1940s, small groups of enthusiasts might gather in a tiny apartment to listen to the latest records, today's turntable is the internet, the small apartment has become a global network, and everyone is invited.

YouTube and similar platforms also provide vital outlets for a new type of do-it-yourself, grass-roots pedagogy.[14] As a site of pedagogical interaction, YouTube allows developing musicians to post clips of themselves performing or practicing and, due to users' ability to leave comments, solicit feedback. Users of the site can post comments that range from praise, to offers of specific musical and technical advice, to comments that are more negative, sometimes shockingly so, again a function of web anonymity. Posting self-performance clips on YouTube provides musicians an opportunity to engage with a larger community than they would be accustomed to in their own "real world," but it is not an exercise for the thin-skinned or the faint of heart. All YouTube video sites come with a comments section, where users may respond to the videos they are watching. Merely the act of "putting yourself out there" takes some courage, but combined with the comments feature of the site, it can be a frightening exercise. The open and anonymous exchange featured in the comments section of YouTube spotlights what is both best and worst about the web. Anyone can be a star, and anyone can be an expert on the topic. YouTube provides the opportunity not only to be a student of anyone who may be watching, but also to be, in some sense, a teacher or critic of anyone you see. What is most important about all this activity on YouTube is the *You*, the agency of the individual jazz fan or amateur musician. Here, jazz fans can be "citizen filmmakers," like their "citizen scholar" counterparts on Wikipedia. But unlike Wikipedia's eschewing of individual control or authority, YouTube offers, in theory at least, a chance for the individual to carve out their own virtual territory, to be at the center of their own community in jazz, bounded only by the speed of the broadband connection.

In a similar fashion, web logs, or blogs, have allowed for the rise of "citizen journalists" in the virtual jazz world. Such virtual journals allow writers, whether seasoned veterans of jazz performance or criticism, or amateurs just getting their feet wet in jazz writing, not only to communicate their own views on the subject but, perhaps more importantly, to provide a forum for a continually expanding, increasingly global internet jazz discourse. As trumpeter-cum-blogger Dave Douglas notes on NPR's "A Blog Supreme": "Blogging is big in the jazz world, and growing fast. (I've got a blog at greenleafmusic.com, and here I am guest blogging . . .) In a way, blogging in the jazz world has become like having living, breathing liner notes. But blogging is not going to move the music forward. It's just the megaphone, albeit a good one" (Douglas 2009). Douglas's experiences are instructive, in that they point to the fact that the virtual world is not simply a means for fans to assume a greater role in the discourse (important as that is), but for established artists to engage directly with their public without the intervention of an intermediary. Historically, artists who wanted to "get their message out" often had to do so through the efforts of a critic or journalist, traditionally the gatekeepers of this kind of knowledge. This is a role that is becoming increasingly endangered in the new virtual world. As Stephen Humphries writes in the *Christian Science Monitor* on August 29, 2008, "amateur music critics" are increasingly making their professional counterparts irrelevant:

> The blogosphere and chat forums, meanwhile, have spawned the garage-band equivalent of music reviewers as thousands of fans express their opinions. Call it the era of vox pop music critiques. With all those voices, are professional music critics still relevant? As consumers become more attuned to the wisdom of the masses, a once-elite cadre of professional music writers is facing a new reality: They aren't as influential as they once were. . . . But critics are being squeezed out. Over the past year, dozens of newspapers and news magazines have laid off movie, TV, book, food, and music reviewers. Zagat-style criticism gives ordinary readers an alternative to the musings of ordained connoisseurs. (Humphries 2008)[15]

Indeed, the effects of such shifts have already been notable in jazz journalist communities. At the end of 2008, the *Village Voice* laid off three staff writers, including legendary jazz writer Nat Hentoff, in a downsizing move. Hentoff's dismissal is likely due in large part to the general downturn in the newspaper industry, but it should also be seen in light of the argument made by Humphries (and indeed, Hentoff's writing covered much more than just jazz). The move startled many, however, and has led to an increasing sense of insecurity among many in print jazz journalism.[16] Circulations among jazz periodicals are relatively small, and seem to be shrinking. Howard Mandel reports that *Jazz Times* has an estimated circulation of 100,000, which he speculates is a high figure. *Down Beat*, meanwhile, has a circulation that is estimated at around 70,000 (Mandel 2009).[17]

There is nothing remarkable about fans and musicians expressing opinions about recordings, concerts, debates, and their own experiences as musicians and listeners in jazz. However, blogging provides an opportunity that heretofore did not exist in practical terms, to make an individual's voice heard (or seen) anywhere in the world with a computer and an internet connection. I contend that the growth of the jazz blogosphere has begun to radically reshape the dynamics of jazz writing, moving the journalistic discourse of jazz away from its historical centers such as New York, or even the United States in general. In this new environment, the jazz community is truly becoming globalized in the real, twenty-first-century sense of that term.

It is distinctly possible that by the time you are reading this book, all of what I have been arguing in this chapter will be passé, given the speed with which virtual platforms are developing. In December 2010 the social networking site Facebook overtook Google as the world's most used web platform.[18] With the growth of Facebook and the "micro-blogging" site Twitter, the ascendancy of individual agency in the virtual world may be approaching its peak. Facebook, in particular, is rapidly becoming a first-stop portal for many jazz artists and fans, allowing both groups to connect as "friends," and creating what might be the closest thing to a virtual neighborhood the web has yet seen. Nearly every major (and minor) jazz artist has discovered Facebook as a means of disseminating information. Even long-deceased artists somehow find their way online; Louis Armstrong has several Facebook pages, including one that seems to be official. In most cases, fans can post comments on the site, often addressing the artists directly about their music and other activities. Despite its ubiquity in online discourse, Facebook is still in its infancy as a virtual platform, and its role in creating a web of community connectivity is yet to be fully assessed.

The same could be said for what has come to be known as "micro-blog-ging," best represented by the platform called Twitter, which functions on short text-based messages, referred to as "tweets," that allow writers to connect with their audiences on a near instantaneous basis. Twitter has recently been adopted by a number of artists to inform fans of what they are doing. Wynton Marsalis, for example, has his own profile on the Twitter site, where one can see an archive of his posts. For example, in a note posted on July 20, 2008, Marsalis notes that he was "in the recording studio with Chano Dominguez and the JLCO to record the suite I wrote for Vitoria." Another post from July 17 stated that Marsalis was "Getting ready to hit the stage in Valencia, Spain. The guys are rested and ready to swing"; while another opines "Swinging in Paris, the city of lights http://bit.ly/3aqxd."[19] Other posts direct users towards his website: "I released Big Train 10 years ago. . . I'm giving away a signed copy of the score to celebrate! Sign up to win http://bit.ly/CulLp" (the URL redirects to Marsalis's website). In the summer of 2008 Marsalis had 4,000 followers on Twitter; by the end of 2010 the number was over 13,000. On the other hand, Lady Gaga had nearly eight million.

If this last statistic is somewhat depressing for jazz fans, that is not my intent. On the contrary, I suggest that as jazz continues to struggle for public attention, we should understand the increasingly important role of the virtual world as a space for exchanging information about jazz, of engaging in critical discourses that used to fill the pages of *Down Beat* or even regional newspapers and television programs. But virtual platforms are not simply a replacement for traditional media; they have a fundamental transformative quality, reshap-ing the discourses of jazz into those that are not dominated by a particular class of critics, filmmakers, or scholars. This fundamental decentralization of jazz discourse, and of the ability of its actors to determine how they come to know the music, is an inevitable function of both Web 2.0 and its inextricable links to an increasingly globalized jazz scene. I will take up this theme in the next chapter: how globalization,[20] enabled in large part through advances in information technology, has ushered in a new and contested understanding of just what jazz is.

CHAPTER 5

The Global Jazz Community

Jazz and Globalization

Jazz is a music whose identity has long reflected a tension between American and global influences and perspectives, with jazz often serving as a metaphor for globalization itself, reflecting in sound America's identity in the world. In this view, jazz *is* globalization in its purest form. Taylor Atkins writes that "practically from its inception, jazz was a harbinger of what we now call 'globalization.' In no one's mind have the music's ties to its country of origin been severed, yet the historical record proves that it has for some time had global relevance" (Atkins 2003, xv).

As a "harbinger" of globalization, the processes by which jazz arose in various cultures parallel later economic and cultural developments. Yet much of Atkins's study *Jazz Planet* deals with the local, assessing jazz "in" various locales (India, Zimbabwe, Cuba, Brazil, and so forth). I say this not as a criticism, but as an observation that so much research on globalization focuses on what is often termed the "glocal," a portmanteau of "global" and "local" that came into common usage in the 1990s. Atkins's view of jazz-as-global-music tracks very closely to other studies of global jazz, focusing on the unique adaptations of jazz in specific environments. Glocal studies of jazz are a critical component of scholarship in the New Jazz Studies, but reflect a particular view on globalization, as will be discussed later.

Others argue that the globalization of jazz is reflective of a more unifying paradigm, a "jazz consciousness" as evidenced in the title of Paul Austerlitz's acclaimed study. Austerlitz sees global jazz as expressing a "planetary humanism," reflecting both a "holistic aesthetic" of universalism and a worldview derived from African American experience: "A *creative tension*, resulting from African Americans' equivocal position both within and without modernity speaks eloquently to the contradictions that all free people face . . . jazz creates a virtual space where we can confront, learn from, and even heal the contradictions resulting from social rupture" (Austerlitz 2005, xvi). "Global" is thus about more than just the music, representing a way of living born of a specific, historically defined cultural experience, but applied universally. It is worth emphasizing that in neither of these studies is the ultimate American origin of jazz called into question, and on this point, the merits and effects of globalization are hotly debated within and outside the United States. For many Americans, globalization represents a challenge to American ideals and the exceptionalist foundations of much American historical thought. For many others around the world, globalization heralds not a challenge to American hegemony but an extension of it.

National and global identities present a relatively new and increasingly contested layer in the discourses of jazz, one that individuals and communities are finding difficult to negotiate. The emergence of virtual networks and other global forms of mediation tend to exacerbate this, as the development of global broadband networks and interactive web platforms levels the playing field, destroying traditional discursive and aesthetic hierarchies. The jazz world is "flattening," to borrow from the parlance of *New York Times* columnist Tom Friedman, who suggests that globalization is leading to a global environment in which traditional flows of the knowledge economy are replaced with truly collaborative lateral relationships, a "Globalization 3.0." Within this framework, what it means to be American will be vastly different. I suggest that discourses on jazz have begun to reflect a similar tendency, that American perspectives are no longer granted the critical, scholarly, and aesthetic deference they once were, and that jazz's globalization is not simply a function of jazz being exported as American's "greatest contribution to world culture." In this chapter, I wish to highlight specific cases in which such contestations of identity are manifested in thinking about jazz and community formation. In the first case—an examination of the now-defunct International Association for Jazz Education (IAJE)—identity on the global stage was constructed from a largely American viewpoint, which led, I contend, at least indirectly to the organization's eventual demise. Although IAJE is dead and buried, its growth and eventual collapse provide an important opportunity to examine how the forces of American hegemony in jazz discourses, jazz education, and changing jazz industry, and the reorientation of global politics in the post 9/11 world all collided at a specific moment. The subsequent discussion examines the interconnections between American exceptionalism in the early twenty-first century, the neo-classicist jazz discourse, and efforts to counter the hegemonic influence of American perspectives in jazz. I conclude with a look at the different perspectives on national and global identity expressed in two films, Ken Burns's *Jazz* and the more recent *Icons Among Us: Jazz in the Present Tense*, and how these films reflect the contested nature of identity in global jazz discourses. At the center of all these discussions are claims to knowledge of what jazz is, and efforts to define or disrupt common community structures that are built upon it.

The Rise and Fall of IAJE: A Tale of Global Jazz Community

The notion that the entire scope of jazz activity around the world could be represented in one singular community formation might seem absurd on the surface. Traditional definitions of jazz community, however, do not account for any distinctions based on nation or location at the global level, and claims to a worldwide jazz community were as easy to make as any other. One organization that very visibly placed itself at the center of this worldwide community was the International Association for Jazz Education. At its peak of influence around the turn of early twenty-first century, IAJE positioned itself as the focal point for an increasingly connected "global jazz community," as referred to in its own literature. IAJE's story underscores a number of issues concerning relative power relations among various constituencies in jazz, as well as its identity within a global context. The changes that IAJE underwent throughout its forty years speak directly to these ideas.

As I approached the Long Beach Convention Center in January 2002 for the annual International Association of Jazz Educators convention, I noticed a banner suspended over the entrance: WELCOME, INTERNATIONAL ASSOCIATION FOR JAZZ EDUCATION. My first reaction was "they screwed up the name of the group on the banner," but in fact the name had been changed, almost without notice. My curiosity piqued, I surveyed the pages of the conference issue of the *Jazz Educators Journal*; on closer inspection, I discovered that the name of the magazine had also been changed, to the *Jazz Education Journal*. I surveyed a number of back issues, and discovered that the change had been instituted several months earlier. According to then-president Ronald McCurdy, this change allows the organization to "address [jazz] education in the broadest sense, to be more inclusive rather than exclusive" (McCurdy 2001, 4). IAJE's name change and comments such as those made by McCurdy raised several issues. How did such a move reflect changes in the organization that had already taken place over the years? What did it mean to "address jazz education in the broadest sense"? It was around the same time that IAJE began referring to its conference as the "world's largest gathering of the global jazz community," including not only educators and students, but many others. These changes are best understood within the context of IAJE's history, and with how its growth reflects important shifts in the world of jazz.

The group was founded in 1968 as the National Association of Jazz Educators (NAJE), as an ancillary organization to the Music Educators National Conference (Music Educators National Conference 1971, 59). A critical point in jazz education's rise to acceptance in academia, NAJE filled a distinct void in the field, providing a place where educators from around the country (and eventually the world) could meet to exchange ideas and, as one early member noted, "to cry on each others' shoulders." NAJE's founding members included some of the important early figures in jazz education, including David Baker and Gene Hall. According to Hall, his selection as president was, in a sense, "academic": "I was selected as president because I had the only doctorate in the group of people that formed the association, and at the time we were trying to display as much responsibility as possible.[1] It was ironic, but on the day we affiliated with MENC, we immediately became respectable, although none of us had changed any from what we were the day before" (Scott 1973, 130). The organization's name was as much of a concern, as Hall continues:

> The name of the organization, Dr. Hall says, was at best a compromise. "We spent the best part of the day at our organizational meeting trying to decide on a name that would reflect the broad scope of music we were trying to represent—American music, as differentiated from other types. This would take on jazz, pop, rock, folk, country and western— everything, but we couldn't come up with an umbrella term that would cover everything, so we became the jazz educators." (Scott 1973, 130)

In a 1969 article, Hall outlined seven aims of the organization:

1) To foster and promote the understanding and appreciation of jazz and popular music and its artistic performance . . .
2) To lend assistance and guidance in the organization and development of jazz and popular music curricula at schools and colleges to include stage band and ensembles of all types . . .
3) To foster the application of jazz principles to music materials at all levels . . .
4) To foster and encourage the development and adoption of curricula that will explore contemporary composition, arranging, and improvisation . . .
5) To disseminate educational and professional news of interest to music educators . . .
6) To assist in the organization of clinics, festivals, and symposiums at local, state and regional, and national levels . . .
7) To cooperate with all organizations dedicated to the development of musical culture in America (Hall 1969, 45–46)

Compare this with a similar list of goals printed in the January 2002 issue of the *Jazz Education Journal*:[2]

1) To expand member benefits and programs to meet and exceed member needs and expectations . . .
2) To advocate for superior jazz education . . .
3) To internationalize the products and services of IAJE in order to better serve an increasingly global jazz community and membership . . .
4) To create an effective communications strategy that embraces technology . . .
5) To evaluate and strengthen the governance and membership structure of IAJE . . .
6) To solidify the administrative capacity and resources of IAJE (International Association for Jazz Education 2002, A63–A64)

There are a number of important differences between these two documents, with an earlier emphasis on advocacy and outreach replaced with language that seems to focus inward, on the organization. Most strikingly, the term "popular music" does not appear anywhere in the latter statement, demonstrating a clear ideological shift toward a strict identification with jazz. Later conference programming, in fact, reflects little of the broadly inclusive approach of which Hall spoke.

Early membership numbers were fairly modest, though by 1970 the organization included around 2,000 members (Music Educators National Conference 1971, 59). The first few meetings of the group were small-scale affairs, with members gathering at a conference-within-a-conference at the MENC conventions. In 1973, however, the organization began to break away from MENC and, under the auspices of new president William Lee, the first standalone annual meeting was held the following year in Chicago. Since then, meetings have become massive affairs, regularly drawing in excess of 8,000 attendees by 2006. One significant boost to the IAJE conference was its 2000 merger with the annual *JazzTimes* industry conference, regarded as the most important meeting of jazz artists, record labels, and media. The "industry" had actually had a significant presence at IAJE meetings for a number of years, but the official embrace of the two organizations brought them together in a more tangible way. Such an arrangement was not without its critics, however, as a number of musicians, particularly those not affiliated with one of the major industry record labels, lamented IAJE's alliance. Noted pianist and educator Hal Galper, writing in an essay on his website, argued that this arrangement was an example of "selling out" to industry pressures (Galper, n.d.).

Despite Galper's well-intentioned concerns, the dynamics of power between the jazz industry and the field of jazz education have shifted significantly over the course of the last few decades, and jazz education (and IAJE by extension) was at the center of this readjustment. Today, those involved with jazz education—students, teachers, institutions—comprise a significant portion of the consumer base for the music, buying recordings, attending concerts, contributing advertising revenue to publications, and contributing talent to the pool of professional musicians. As jazz record sales continue to hold flat at around 3 percent of the total record market, any new base of consumers is important. Education-related activities are increasingly important to the financial success of an artist, and even such individuals and groups began to advertise and purchase exhibit space at IAJE conventions, touting their abilities to offer students something unique and worthwhile as a guest performer and lecturer on campus. Even artists like Hal Galper, while denouncing much of what takes place within jazz education, and particularly its standardization and industrialization, devotes a significant portion of his time to what he terms the "college lecture circuit."[3] At some point, nearly every major jazz performer in the world performed at the IAJE conference (many performed regularly), even those who have spoken with disdain (sometimes publicly) for what the organization has come to represent. Jazz education has grown to the point where it cannot be ignored, as either a creative or economic force, within the jazz community. It has been, as David Baker put it, the "saving grace" for jazz performers (Prouty 2002, 291), echoing statements by Stan Kenton and Dave Brubeck a half century earlier, and IAJE positioned itself to capitalize on this shift.

Another shift came with the change to the term "international" in the group's name which was adopted in 1989. In making such a change, IAJE staked its claim to leadership of an increasingly global jazz education community, and the annual meeting regularly included presentations and performances of students and professionals from around the world. Yet despite the "I" in IAJE, most of its activities were still geared toward an American audience. This may have been a natural tendency for those who view jazz as an historically American musical form, but there are many who find this idea problematic. This has in fact been a frequent criticism of the organization, that while it claimed to be the champion of a global jazz community, IAJE in fact reflected the classic American exceptionalist view of jazz, that the United States was still the center of the jazz world, and that American viewpoints still mattered most. The tension between IAJE's professed international identity and its overwhelmingly American membership did not appear to be headed toward an easy resolution.

In seeking to define the global jazz community, IAJE created a role for itself as an organization at the forefront of the internationalization of jazz, and for jazz education as an equal player (or even a dominant force) within this community. Those who wished to be a part of this community, whether as internationally known performers, industry reps, publishers, and others (to say nothing of educators), had to deal with IAJE or jazz education in some way. This itself represents a remarkable shift in the role jazz education plays. But the inclusiveness of which Ron McCurdy spoke is relative; the organization was certainly inclusive in bringing together students and educators with performers and industry execs, but was seemingly less inclined to be fully inclusive of a truly international identity. Through IAJE's actions, jazz was implicitly defined as an American music, and despite overtures toward internationalization, there is little to suggest that IAJE ever really embraced an identity in which its global identity was emphasized.

Given the importance of IAJE and its mission to jazz education, many members were shocked in the spring of 2008 to receive news that the organization was in dire financial trouble. Most IAJE members, I suspect, had little idea that was coming. IAJE newsletters from February and March 2008 mentioned nothing about any financial or organizational hardships. In fact, both messages touted upcoming events, including the 2009 conference in Seattle. If there was turmoil in IAJE's offices in Manhattan, Kansas, it was not yet being communicated to the membership. Despite this, there had been rumblings of problems with IAJE's management. I had heard anecdotally for years that IAJE simply could not continue operating the way it was, that its financial situation was somewhat suspect, that the future was in doubt. There were never any specifics; IAJE's financial information was held close to the vest. But the 2008 conference, held in Toronto for the second time (the city had also hosted the 2003 conference), brought many of these sentiments into the open. In Toronto, I overheard more than one comment by vendors whose reactions to the relatively low turnout (estimated at between 5,000 and 6,000) ranged from resignation, to shock, to real worry about the survival of not only IAJE but their own businesses, many of whom depended on IAJE to generate sales throughout the rest of the year.

The first official sign of IAJE's troubles came in the form of an email from Chuck Owen, president of IAJE's board of directors, informing the membership of a financial crisis. Owen called for IAJE members to contribute funds to support continued operations, "to enlist [member] support in what is clearly the most challenging time in the Association's history." Owen continued his dire message by highlighting some of the challenges IAJE faced:

Unfortunately, IAJE presently finds itself facing significant challenges that threaten its ability to continue to meet its vital mission.

* IAJE's Campaign for Jazz, envisioned over 5 years ago as a means of endowing IAJE's programs and thus (ironically) assuring its fiscal stability, has not performed as hoped or expected. . . . In short, IAJE invested heavily in this campaign and has not come close to recouping its expenses, resulting in the accumulation of significant debt.

* The Toronto conference, while an incredible event (and the usual great "hang"), experienced very poor attendance—down by nearly 40 percent from previous years. Many factors beyond IAJE's control influenced this: the high cost of airfares, the weakness of the American dollar, and new passport requirement for U.S. citizens. Nevertheless, this situation left us with an additional debilitating financial loss.

In addition to calling for immediate emergency donations (with a "suggested" $25 minimum), Owen also outlined steps designed to help stabilize IAJE, including the suspension of:

* Search for a new executive director
* Park City Jazz Summit in Park City, Utah
* All scholarship programs
* Production of the *Jazz Education Journal*

He also stated that a "transition team" would be assembled "to help guide IAJE through this difficult time," though it was not stated what this transition would actually be. Owen's email spread around the jazz world like wildfire, posted and discussed in numerous message boards and blogs, and it soon became a hot topic in the jazz world. Speculation swiftly mounted; many blamed the Toronto conference turnout, while others took aim at IAJE's leadership, accusing them of mismanaging the group's accounts. As it turned out, there was probably truth to both.

On April 18, 2008, a second email was sent by IAJE board president Chuck Owen to the organization's membership. He began his message stating:

It is with a great sense of loss that I inform you that despite drastic efforts to cut expenses and raise emergency funds, the IAJE Board has voted to file for bankruptcy under Chapter 7 of the Federal Bankruptcy Law. I want to thank profusely those who responded with their generous donations and offers of assistance following my last communication. While over 250 individuals contributed just over $12,000, this, along with the many other efforts and contributions of IAJE staff, Board members, and association partners, was simply not enough to address the accumulated debt of the organization or its urgent need for cash relief.

No information was given about how much this "accumulated debt" was, but given the relatively small number of donations (250 contributors out of a membership that is conservatively estimated at between 7,000 and 10,000), there was likely a sense among members that giving money to IAJE might be a futile exercise. Owen's message concluded with the following:

> Today, we, the members of IAJE and the global jazz community, face an extremely important task. For, as we all recognize, the opportunities, impact, and work of this association are too vital to simply disappear. . . . it is clear the mission of IAJE still resonates and its advocacy is needed today more than ever. We must, therefore, look at this as an opportunity to refocus the mission, scope, programs, and vision of IAJE (or whatever succeeds it) to better meet the needs of our members and the jazz community not only today but looking toward the future.

In its very death throes, IAJE was still clinging to the notion that it was the representative of the "global jazz community,"[4] and that its demise was a challenge not only to educators in America, but for the global jazz scene in general.

Even before the emails from Owen, indications of turmoil were emerging, and hints of IAJE's problems had started to come to light. On January 28, 2008, the IAJE board announced that Bill McFarlin, executive director of IAJE for over twenty years, was stepping down, ostensibly to take a position at the Blue Lake Fine Arts Camp in Michigan. The announcement did not receive a great deal of attention at the time, but in retrospect it is clear that this was an important warning sign, though the release included nothing about IAJE's financial situation. IAJE's news release, which effusively praised McFarlin's service, ended on a retrospectively ironic note: "Please join us for our 36th Annual International Convention in Seattle, Washington, January 8–11, 2009." No details were given for McFarlin's departure from IAJE. But in an April 4 post on his blog The Independent Ear, jazz industry jack-of-all-trades Willard Jenkins, himself a longtime supporter of IAJE and participant in its programming, claimed that

> The bill seems to have come due (pun intended) with the post-conference "resignation" of former long time IAJE executive director Bill McFarlin. For years boards came and boards went, presidents occupied

figurehead chairs and the beat went on—all with Bill McFarlin wielding an unchallenged iron hand with zero oversight. Well folks, the bill has come due. Fact is McFarlin took a powder in lieu of being canned. Once his dust cleared and the *real* books [emphasis in original] were examined, the rosy picture he painted for years was revealed to be as counterfeit and bankrupt as a proverbial house of straw. (Jenkins 2008c)

There are real accusations here of malfeasance; Jenkins seems to be directly accusing McFarlin of "cooking the books" (note his emphasis on the "*real* books" being examined).Many colleagues who are seemingly "in the know" on these issues have been reluctant to speak about them publicly, probably for good reason.

Other news began to emerge that demonstrated IAJE's precarious position. A piece posted to *Down Beat*'s website on April 4 reported that Mary Jo Papich, a highly regarded jazz educator from the Chicago area and IAJE's president-elect, was also resigning. As the first woman to be elected in IAJE's history, Papich's elevation to the post was significant, which made her decision to leave all the more startling. According to Jenkins, Papich left "due to insurmountable differences on direction with the current board—members of whom [*sic*] apparently have their own series of agendas, IAJE and jazz be damned" (Jenkins 2008c).

As the IAJE post-mortems began, interviews with many jazz educators began to appear, addressing what the loss of IAJE meant. Educator Dave Yarborough, a public arts school teacher from Washington, D.C., described it to an NPR reporter as a "shocking, shocking loss," a sentiment surely shared by many for whom IAJE was an important avenue for networking and resources. Yarborough continues, speaking of IAJE's networking opportunities: "[IAJE] gave that opportunity. It also gave me an opportunity to meet with the college band directors, so that I could tell them about what juniors and seniors I had. It also presented the platform where all the summer camps that were going on, they generally had a booth or something there, so, you could talk to everyone and see what's best for the kids that you work with" (Contreras 2008).

Reactions among my own colleagues were mixed. Some were saddened by the collapse, echoing many of the same sentiments as Owen. My friend and colleague at MSU Sunny Wilkinson, a noted jazz vocalist and educator, lamented both the loss of community and the extensive work that she personally had invested in the group. Others I spoke with were less distressed, some even expressing a satisfaction the IAJE was finally gone, that the organization had collapsed under its own weight.

So what killed IAJE? In the wake of board president Owen's bankruptcy announcement, accusations flew and fingers were pointed in many quarters. The same day as the announcement of IAJE's bankruptcy filing, *Down Beat* reported that IAJE's debt, according to "sources," might have totaled more than half a million dollars. Speaking informally with colleagues, I have heard figures in excess of a million. Willard Jenkins, as we previously noted, was not shy in his assignment of blame primarily to the organization's leadership, especially executive director McFarlin. McFarlin himself, in the NPR story, stated "I think you have to compile the blame," seemingly shifting responsibility away from just himself. And certainly, one person cannot shoulder sole responsibility for the collapse. IAJE general counsel Alan Bergman adds, in the same report: "That's not just a mystery. I know who's going to take the fall for it. I am and the board is—and the officers are, and Bill. . . . It happened on our watch" (Contreras 2008). Some assigned blame more directly to McFarlin. As Willard Jenkins posted on his blog entries in April and May 2008, McFarlin should be held primarily responsible for the accumulation of debt, as well as the failure of the capital campaign. As for Bergman's statement in the NPR report, Jenkins writes the following: "In the Chronicle of Philanthropy IAJE legal counsel Alan Bergman, himself a wannabe drummer, amazingly blamed the demise of IAJE on the organization's *musician* leadership; cavalierly dismissing the causal factors as if to say, *what could you expect from an organization led by mere jazz musicians*" [emphasis in original] (Jenkins 2008a). For Jenkins, IAJE's problem was that it was, in fact, too closely associated with jazz educators: "It seems from this 25-year member's standpoint that for far too long, even in the wake of the absorption of the old Jazz Times Convention's industry-oriented model coaxed into the IAJE conference . . . IAJE has continued to be ruled by the tight grip of jazz educators" (Jenkins 2008c).

I find this complaint profoundly ironic—as if an educational organization should be ruled by some other entity. But Jenkins reveals an undercurrent of disdain for those who identify themselves as jazz educators by others in "the industry," seemingly in this case, those who would know better (musicians and industry figures like himself). It also speaks (not positively) to the increasing role that jazz educators play in the shaping of jazz discourses, and the discomfort that others in the jazz community feel about those developments.

The reasons for IAJE's downfall became clearer, at least from a public perspective, following a summer "post crash course" by Paul De Barros in *Down Beat*, which painted a none-too-flattering picture of IAJE's management and oversight. According to him, IAJE's demise began after 2001, when the organization had assets of $800,000 and "no significant debt." The aftermath of the September 11, 2001, attacks did impact IAJE, as attendance at the following conference dipped, contributing heavily to a growing debt. Spending was increasing, De Barros reports, but income was not. By the summer of 2005, IAJE was "effectively wiped out" (De Barros 2008, 13). Many of his accounts seem to confirm some of the arguments made by Jenkins, Howard Mandel and others, regarding what they perceived as at best incompetence and, at worst, malfeasance. IAJE's conferences have always been, compared to other organizations, somewhat lavish affairs, attracting top name headline performers, gala dinners, golf tournaments, and similar events; they are also massively expensive to stage. As De Barros reports, IAJE operated conferences at a loss in 2002, 2003, and 2005 (De Barros 2008, 13). Failure to generate sufficient revenue from conferences is a critical factor in IAJE's collapse, and the massive failure (in financial terms) of the 2008 conference brought the whole enterprise crashing down.

This brings us to our most important question: why was IAJE's attendance down so dramatically in 2008? Many reasons have been offered: high airfares, passport requirements for traveling to Canada, the slumping economy, a perceived less-than-stellar lineup, the fact that the conference is in a foreign country—all of these have been given as reasons for the conference's failure.

But this speaks to another important issue, which has gone largely unnoticed in the IAJE post-mortem discourses. The idea that holding IAJE in a foreign country (and to be sure, with no offense intended to my Canadian colleagues, Toronto is not exactly a "foreign" culture to Americans) presents logistical problems so great, or a destination so unattractive for jazz musicians and educators, that so many members choose not to attend, contradicts the "international" identity of IAJE. Despite the change from "N" to "I," IAJE remained a predominantly American organization from cradle to grave, an identity that contributed in no small way to its inability to function as a truly international organization. International membership, while officially encouraged, was in practice marginalized. No serious organizational efforts were ever mounted to hold an annual conference outside North America. As Willard Jenkins noted in his blog post in January, "And let's not forget how notoriously lazy and provincial certain members of the New York-centric jazz industry and intelligensia [*sic*] are about traveling to the 'provinces'" (Jenkins 2008b).

If I may be forgiven for delving into a more personal account for a moment, from the perspective of one who has attended numerous IAJE conferences in the past, I actually found the Toronto conference to be among the best I have attended. Without the massive crush of people,[5] I was able to engage in longer, more meaningful conversations, to actually see people I had not seen in years, to hear many outstanding concerts without having to wait for headline performances in what amounted to a cattle pen outside the ballrooms, to have more time to give and discuss research presentations. I am sympathetic to the vendors, whose livelihoods are put in jeopardy both by the organization's demise and by the low attendance at the conference. But from my own perspective, I found Toronto to be immensely enjoyable, and certainly much more "international" than past conferences.

I return to the question of what, precisely, this all means for the constituencies that comprise the "global jazz community." Does the world no longer have a central organization through which the construction of community can take place? Perhaps a better question is, did it ever? In the grand scheme of things, was IAJE really that important to both the health of the music, or as a means of connecting various elements, various communities, in common place and purpose? In the years since IAJE collapsed, I have sensed no massive decline in the amount of jazz activity. Schools have not closed, jazz has not stopped being produced around the world. In questioning IAJE's centrality to the contemporary jazz world, in no way am I denigrating its work. There are things that IAJE could have done better, but on balance, it is hard to argue that it was not a positive force. After all, if one did not like IAJE, they did not have to participate. But that is exactly what happened. "Global" individuals (those from outside the United States) frequently stayed home, no doubt due in large part to the difficulties and expenses involved with travel. When the tables were turned, and the conference was held in Canada, Americans acted in generally the same way, seeing increased airfare and enhanced security and customs requirements as barriers to their participation. This put the notion that IAJE was somehow the center of the "global jazz community" to rest— and suggests, moreover, that there really *was* no global jazz community in that sense.

Given the criticism of IAJE over the years, not everyone was buying their message. To attempt to represent global jazz is both futile and undesirable; as De Barros suggests, such a strong, centralized institution might not be a good thing, an idea that is "getting some traction around the country" (De Barros 2008, 13). The attempt to create a global community, overwhelmingly comprised of members from one country who did not seem inclined to engage in international meetings, had to overcome a wide chasm that, as it turned out, was simply too big an obstacle. The pronouncement of IAJE as a global jazz community, and its reality as one based in the United States, represented a fundamental disconnect, and points us toward an increasingly contentious view of the role of the United States as a dominant force in the world of jazz.

"A Rare and Valuable National Treasure": Jazz and the "Myth" of American Exceptionalism

If IAJE represented a particularly America-centric view of a global jazz community, this view is certainly not shared among international jazz scholars, especially considering the relative paucity of organized jazz conferences in the United States itself. The early twenty-first century has seen an increasingly aggressive critique of jazz-as-American music, perhaps a function of the ways in which American culture and identity are themselves coming under sustained criticism. *USA Today* reports in an article from March 2003 that ordinary tourists had begun to bear the brunt of much of this sentiment, and in ways that seemed much more unsettling for those involved:

> If European criticism of the United States was previously limited to newspaper headlines and kaffeeklatsch debates, the tug of war over Iraq has unleashed a torrent of frustrated invective on the streets. Laurel Scapicchio and her 13-year-old daughter were waiting for a train in the Paris metro a few weeks ago when their conversation was interrupted. Two men in their 20s overheard their American accents and shouted, "Pigs!" (Della Cava 2003)

To my knowledge, there have not been any documented instances of American jazz performers subjected to boos or shouts of "Pigs!" at performances, at least not as directly related to anti-American activity. In fact, the well-worn notion that American musicians have found greater success abroad than at home is still commonly heard. As Marc Ribot writes in "The Care and Feeding of a Musical Margin," Europe still provides an important avenue for many American performers, especially outside the aesthetic mainstream: "European touring, heavily state subsidized, has been the real economic motor of experimental jazz/new music for decades, the light at the end of the tunnel of months of scarce and/or poorly paid NYC gigs. The fact that access to Europe was easier and cheaper for NYC musicians than for their LA counterparts is an important factor in the historical productivity of the NYC new music scene as compared with the West Coast" (Ribot 2007). Ribot's assessment provides a counterpoint to the view of jazz's influence as a one-way flow to Europe from the United States. Still, American-dominated jazz narratives represent a hegemonic force in global discourses, and international critics have begun to more aggressively call into question such assumptions about jazz's identity—assumptions institutionalized in the United States and exported, and I use that term intentionally, to the rest of the world.

Traditionally, the identity of jazz in international musical discourse has been constructed as both an American idiom, and as something that is uniquely American in development, reflective of a particularly American quality of thought. Quasi-public statements about jazz within the United States are often laced with such sentiment, as evidenced by Ken Burns's epic PBS documentary *Jazz*. Public institutions frequently draw upon such sentiments; jazz has for some years now been institutionalized by organizations such as the National Endowment for the Arts, the Kennedy Center, and the Smithsonian Institution, all of which have at some point engaged in jazz programming that reinforces canonicity and American identity. The most official expression of this came with the 1987 passage of House Concurrent Resolution 57, authored by Michigan Democratic representative John Conyers. The full text of the resolution easily can be found online, so I will not reprint it here; suffice it to say that HR 57 casts jazz explicitly as a "rare and valuable national American treasure," emphasizing links between jazz and democratic principles and aspects of American history and identity. The resolution has absolutely no force of law, nor does it demand (or even suggest) any type of public funding to support jazz (though the National Endowment for the Arts and the Smithsonian Institution, both independent federal agencies, do provide funding for jazz programming). Nevertheless, HR 57 does provide a tangible, vocal statement in support of the claim to jazz's identity as American music par excellence.

It might seem odd, then (or not, depending your view of the effectiveness of American congressional actions), that jazz artists in other countries are often supported in their work at levels substantially more generous than in the United States. *New York Times* jazz writer Peter Watrous noted this irony in a June 1990 article, reporting that avant-garde saxophonist David Murray had recently received a Danish award and substantial cash prize ($30,000), the Jazzpar, whose purpose was to "[promote] greater recognition of jazz in society," presumably starting with Denmark. Of public jazz funding in the United States, Watrous notes:

> Jazz does get institutional support in this country, but not much. The Thelonius [sic] Monk Center for Jazz Studies in Washington has recently begun awarding a $10,000 piano prize annually and plans to start a Louis Armstrong Prize for trumpeters. The National Endowment for the Arts distributes several Jazz Masters Awards a year worth $20,000 each. And though the Endowment spends roughly one-eighth of its yearly $16 million music budget on jazz, jazz in the United States is still mostly dependent on the marketplace for its daily bread. (Watrous 1990, 24)

I would note that while Murray (and his Jazzpar award predecessor, Muhal Richard Abrams) is highly regarded as an experimental musician, most of the NEA jazz masters recipients are older artists whose work fits more easily into the jazz canon. Watrous continues: "Why leave it to Denmark to bestow prizes on American musicians? It's time to question why so little mainstream music financing goes to jazz, and why the Pulitzer committee has never awarded a prize to a jazz composer.[6] It's time for the *jazz community* to demand equal billing" [emphasis added] (Watrous 1990, 24).

Let me make a few observations here, at the risk of reading too much into what Watrous has written. First, the phrase "Why leave it to Denmark" suggests that Americans ought to be taking the lead in creating and promoting these kinds of awards, that *Americans* should be recognizing *American* music. Second, there is a "yes, but" quality to Watrous's reference to the NEA Jazz Masters program. A survey of the list of NEA Jazz Masters points to a rather canonical view of the genre. Some avant-garde musicians are included on the list, notably Cecil Taylor, Ornette Coleman, and Abrams, a newly named recipient. But the most telling part of Watrous's argument is the call to the *jazz community* to demand the same types of support and recognition given to classical artists and institutions (earlier in the article, Watrous referenced the Van Cliburn competition, and the Naumberg and Grawemeyer awards). Watrous argues that the jazz community is still marginalized, despite the resurgence of the music in the decade preceding the writing of his article. Jazz in 1990 was likely, in terms of commercial viability, in much better shape than it had been in 1980. But recognition is not all about money—it is also about defining one's place within both the artistic community, and society at large.

Mark Ribot makes a related argument regarding the subsidizing of American artists in Europe. In his perspective, however, it is experimental jazz musicians who are marginalized, a distinction Watrous does not explicitly make:

> The idea behind European public arts subsidies, the reason why NYC jazz/new music artists for at least the last 40 years have played Paris, Cologne and Zurich many more times than they've played Hartford (and how many have ever played Des Moines?) is a doctrine called "the European cultural exception", a set of government policies based on the concept that, even within a market economy, art/culture is to be treated differently from other commodities. (Ribot 2007)

For Ribot, the problem is not a lack of arts subsidy per se, but rather the lack of subsidy for music that has difficulty competing in the commercial marketplace. To some extent, this is true. Jazz at Lincoln Center seems to have little trouble attracting sponsors; major donors are certainly aware of what JALC stands for, both as a musical institution and what it represents as an expression of a particular American worldview. While it may not be "sucking the life" from the jazz community (Nicholson 2005, 76), JALC and institutions that similarly affirm American-ness may be sucking up funding on this side of the Atlantic. This is certainly true of funding at the federal level, which has long employed jazz as a tool in fostering American interests in foreign policy.

The importance of jazz in advancing American political interests is evidenced by the significant role it has played in American cultural diplomacy. From Willis Conover's broadcasts of jazz to audiences behind the Iron Curtain on the Voice of America to government-sponsored tours by jazz artists during the Cold War, jazz has long been officially conflated with American identity. It is, as former Secretary of State Madeline Albright suggested at a White House conference on diplomacy and culture in November 2000, "an example of how our free nation has made something new and incomparable out of really diverse roots. Jazz is Americanization at its best." But the character of American jazz today, if we are to judge by critical discourses emerging from non-American voices, seems to be dominated by a particular perspective that moves beyond the simple Jazz-as-America trope, and into what we might call an American exceptionalist view. Dorothy Ross defines American exceptionalism as "The idea that America occupies a place in history significantly different from that of any other country in the world [and is] at the core of nationalist ideology in the United States and at center of debate and reflection over the American experience."

An "edifying myth central to American democracy," American exceptionalism helps create and maintain an historical and cultural center for a nation that is new in relation to its forebears, without a clear global historical legacy until relatively recently. As an expression of American exceptionalism, jazz was crucial in constructing a positive image of American culture. As James Q. Wilson writes in conservative news monthly the *American Spectator*, jazz's role in fostering such views stands in stark contrast to American cultural influence today: "As Martha Bayles and others have pointed out, this is not what we exported right after the Second World War when, with government aid, we sent abroad artists, jazz musicians, and gifted writers to show what America could produce. Our earlier efforts at public diplomacy were a success; our most recent efforts at consumerism confirm in the minds of many leaders that we are a corrupt, violent, and mindless people" (Wilson 2009, 15).

Indeed, if there was one thing that conservatives and liberals could seemingly agree on in the Cold War, it was that jazz had a role to play in bringing the world into an American cultural orbit. And in large measure, it worked. Duke Ellington's band represented the country on a renowned State Department tour in 1963; the band's performances were not only well received by local audiences, but were also highly praised by the diplomatic corps. Later, his group would tour the U.S.S.R., which speaks to the important place of jazz within the Eastern bloc; the Soviet Union's last leader, Mikhail Gorbachev, was known to be a jazz fan himself.

The rise of an American exceptionalist perspective on jazz can also be contextualized within the emergence of the political neoconservatives. Rising from the aftermath of "internecine liberal conflicts" (Dionne 2004, 57) in the 1950s, the early neoconservatives crystallized around discontent over the liberal social policies of Johnson's Great Society programs in the 1960s, as well as the so-called New Left, which represented an activist, radical strain of liberalism. The hallmark of this political "persuasion" (a term favored by pioneering neoconservative Irving Kristol) is an aggressive foreign policy that has roots in anti-Communist activism in the 1950s. Today, neoconservative foreign policy emphasizes a worldview in which America's role in the world is unapologetically dominant, some might say imperial, citing the need for interventionist actions and unilateral, preemptive use of force to ensure the national interest. Neoconservatism's view of the world cannot and should not be separated from American exceptionalism. As Mark D. Froese writes, "Neoconservatism, as a set of ideas and organizing principles, draws extensively on the philosophy of American Exceptionalism," and that "The Neoconservative ideational universe is built upon a retelling of the myth of American Exceptionalism, which first gained global currency in the 19th century" (Froese 2007). In applying these ideas to the discourse of jazz, American exceptionalism provides a clear intellectual and ideological model for establishing jazz as an expression of "something American," while the neoconservative model provides a newly energized platform for its dissemination. The rhetorical trope of "jazz as democracy," for example, links these two ideas. Historical narratives which not only privilege American perspectives, but argue that America is the only place where jazz could have developed, are key to these philosophies.

Such attitudes about jazz-as-America are manifest in the emergence of the neoclassical jazz musicians since the early 1980s, with musicians such as Wynton Marsalis and critics like Stanley Crouch leading the way. The very word neoclassical points us to the parallel discourse about American exceptionalism and the image of America in the world. Neoclassic conflates all too easily with neoconservative, and indeed, both movements can be seen as expressing an exceptionalist ideology; just as neoconservatism expresses a particular perspective on America's place in the world, neoclassicism expresses a particular view of the identity and role of jazz as "America's classical music." A number of jazz writers use the term *neoconservative* explicitly in talking about Marsalis, Crouch, and company. Mike Heffley, in his book on European jazz, refers to Marsalis's efforts as "neocon preservationism" (Heffley 2005, 246), while Ken Waxman, in a review of Leslie Gourse's biography of Art Blakey, refers to the late drummer as nurturing a "neo-con version of jazz" (Waxman 2003). Musicians, too, have adopted this term; avant-garde saxophonist David Murray refers to Marsalis et al. as "neo-con artists" and "little dudes in three-piece suits" (quoted in Prestianni 2006).

So does this mean that Wynton Marsalis is the George W. Bush of jazz? And if so, who is Stanley Crouch (perhaps a certain former vice-president)? All this might be overstating things a bit—and in fact, in Marsalis's recent and pronounced political turn, his album *From the Plantation to the Penitentiary* sees him rapping (yes, you read that right) about some decidedly non-neocon themes:

> *After 9/11 the whole world*
> *Was ready to love us*
> *Now everybody can't wait to rub us*
> *We runnin' all over the world with a blunderbuss*
> *And the Constitution all but forgot in the fuss*

In a post on his blog The New Partisan from October 2004, Eric Adler questions the use of the term neoconservative to refer to these artists and critics, noting a passage from an essay by Michael Veal on the reception of jazz fusion. Veal writes the following on the relationship between commercialism and the reaction against it by many jazz "purists": "Those who criticize fusion for its commercialism fail to note that the corporate music agenda underwrites the neoconservative movement in a much more insidious and destructive way [than with fusion]" (Veal 2002, 156). Veal suggests that the "stodginess of the neoconservative revival" is a major influence on American jazz today. Adler's basic complaint with Veal's assessment of these musicians as "neoconservative" is that the term is not appropriate:

> Neither Marsalis brother was a radical who became conservative due to what he perceived as the excesses of the 1960s New Left. Neither has become an outspoken champion of the liberation of Iraq. And Wynton Marsalis' views on jazz as inherently African-American do not jive with political discriminations that could earnestly be called neoconservative. Clearly, Veal—like so many critics—is using the term neoconservative

inappropriately. These days it seems that neoconservative has become a synonym for bad. (Adler 2004)

But Veal's article, which was written in 2002, and Adler's post, written in 2004, are the products of vastly different social and political climates. In short, in the aftermath of the 9/11 and the invasion of Iraq, a more muscular and unilaterally exceptionalist foreign policy has changed the way we think about the term "neoconservative." I doubt that Veal's intent was to compare musicians such as Marsalis with the likes of Paul Wolfowitz or Bill Kristol, but what occurred from 2001 to 2004, and to the present, informs all subsequent utterances of this term.

The point here is not to argue that neoclassicists somehow share a political kinship with the neocons. But the reception of both neocons and neoclassicists outside the United States, and in Europe in particular, is strikingly similar. Just as neoconservatism came to represent America in the world in the first decade of the twenty-first century, neoclassicism came to represent American jazz on the global stage. And as America's image in the world has suffered, so too has American jazz borne the brunt of a sustained, consistent critique. These types of critiques have been around for many years, but the changing nature of America's relationship with the rest of the world has brought to these debates a new sense of urgency and forcefulness. Critiques of American jazz are no longer just about the interpretation of the music and its history, but about the ability of jazz communities to define the identity of music and their place within it.

At the same time, local narratives have become more and more common in recent years, de-centering American perspectives in the discourse of global culture. Taylor Atkins's edition *Jazz Planet* offers histories of jazz in a number of different areas—Cuba, Brazil, Zimbabwe, Sweden, Australia—emphasizing their distinctiveness as national traditions. British writers, in particular, have been active in recasting jazz in the U.K. as a distinct entity with its own history. Works by Catherine Parsonage on early British jazz[7] and George McKay's work on the cultural politics of jazz in Britain[8] are indicative of this trend. These works, while not ignoring connections to American roots (nor explicitly critiquing the jazz-as-America trope), construct distinct national narratives for jazz that are no longer dependent on the view of British jazz as a "version" of the American form. Other writers, however, have gone down this road.

Global Jazz Scholarship and the New Jazz Nationalisms

A certain strain of anti-Americanism has long been present in jazz criticism and scholarship from outside the United States, in particular from European writers. Such attitudes, however, were often manifested in forms very different from what we see today. John Gennari cites the following account of Charles Delaunay:

> All that stood between the heroic Delaunay and this "primeval ooze" . . . was his memory of first hearing Louis Armstrong, "a voice . . . now distant . . . [but] really . . . within you, a world which *was* human." Heed this voice, Delaunay implored American jazz fans. . . .
>
> What began as an inspiring, if dramatic, exhortation suddenly turned into an anti-American diatribe of the sort that seems an obligatory gesture of French cultural criticism. . . . Delaunay excoriated American culture for undermining jazz's artistic qualities by handing it over to the exploitive machinery of the entertainment business. (Gennari 2006, 112)

The particular quality of Delaunay's anti-American sentiments exhibits both similarities and differences with contemporary writings. On one hand, the criticism of American jazz audiences for allowing jazz to be corrupted by commercial influences is still a common critique of much American jazz today. On the other hand, however, Delaunay's call for a more historically based, tradition-oriented approach to jazz is different from much European jazz writing today, which casts the emphasis on tradition not as the desired result of American jazz discourse, but as the problem with it.

British writers have taken a leading role in these discourses. Graham Collier, a fixture on the British jazz scene for several decades, has been particularly vocal in his criticism of the neoclassicists, especially Wynton Marsalis, of whom he writes "When asked 'What do you think about European jazz?', [he] answered 'If it is swinging and has some blues in it, I love it,' an answer which proves how little he knows about the subject" (G. Collier n.d.). This is an important criticism, of not *knowing* about jazz, which cuts to the core of the issue, as defining jazz lays claim to knowledge of the music. Who speaks for the music, who claims ownership of its traditions and narratives, has been hotly contested in the transatlantic jazz discourse. Nowhere have such critiques been more forcefully and provocatively argued than in Stuart Nicholson's much read and much discussed polemic *Is Jazz Dead, Or Has It Moved to a New Address?* Nicholson's central thesis is that American jazz, which he takes to mean the music of Marsalis and JALC, is "dead," or at least in a state of stagnation so pronounced that America has abdicated its role as jazz's true creative center. Offering scathing critiques of neoclassicists, pop-jazz singers such as Norah Jones and Diana Krall, and institutional jazz education, Nicholson argues that "true" creative movements in jazz are now centered in Europe. Of particular importance, he argues, are jazz artists in Scandinavia, whose fusions of jazz with local musical sensibilities are not only artistically adventurous, but also more demonstrably valued, as evidenced by the levels of public subsidy for jazz. More importantly, the neoclassicist apparatus represents, in this critical view, a direct threat to the growth of jazz, "a black hole, sucking life out of a beleaguered jazz community" (Nicholson 2005, 76), drowning out difference and dissent. As Gene Lees notes, via Nicholson, "Marsalis now inspires fear, and his letters to the editor when he's offended, or even questioned, show why" (47). For Nicholson, JALC and the "Murray-Crouch-Marsalis triumvirate" represents a "risk of totalitarianism" (41) born of an "African American Exceptionalism of jazz"[9] (26). This perceived dominance over American jazz has turned international jazz musicians away from the United States as a source of inspiration, questioning whether America provides the aesthetic and historical sway it once did. British saxophonist Courtney Pine states, again via Nicholson: "There was a time when we would basically find an icon from America who's current and emulate him, but we're not happy with that. . . . So now I feel comfortable enough to present my cultural heritage" (Nicholson 2005, 176). This sense of identity in native-born jazz resonates with Atkins's discussion of Japanese writer Yui Shoichi, who argued that jazz provided the means to rediscover local traditions, and ironically, "to be free of America" (Atkins 2001, xix), and that "Artists and audiences around the world reconceptualized jazz to represent liberation from American hegemony" (xix).

Not all European voices echo Nicholson's thesis. Sholto Byrnes writes in the *Independent* in November 2003: "[One critic] thought [Gilad] Atzmon was too overtly political, and, more germanely, he found the Middle Eastern influence in his music too strong for it to be called jazz. Those of us who love jazz have a duty to emphasise its canon, and while collaborations with other traditions are healthy, ultimately the soul of jazz is in America" (Byrnes 2003). Atzmon himself writes in the left-wing journal *Counterpunch* that jazz serves as a critique against neoconservative political ideas, especially in recent times: "Jazz is a world view, an innovative form of resistance. For me, to play jazz is to fight the BBS (Bush, Blair and Sharon) world order, to aim towards liberation while knowing you may never get there, to fight the new American colonialism" (Atzmon 2004). In explicitly linking jazz performance with a sense of protest against Bush-led neoconservative political philosophies, Atzmon makes a pointed statement about jazz and contemporary geopolitics. He also refers to himself as a "bop player," and though his musical approach displays little resemblance to the contemporary neoclassical bop players, his conscious use of that term creates a rebellious identity, both musical and cultural, based in a particularly American framework. There are layers of irony here; the use of an historically American form to critique American foreign policy speaks directly to Yui Shoichi's notion of jazz as a means to "be free of America," while the adoption of a label as a "bop player" identifies squarely with an American tradition, turning the jazz tradition against its own "home" culture.

It is not that critics such as Nicholson simply do not like the music of JALC and the neoclassicists. They are questioning jazz's very core, its identity as an American art form, as *the* American art form. Nicholson's near complete avoidance of discussions of experimental American musicians such as Dave Douglas, Maria Schneider, David Ware, John Zorn, and Bill Frisell, not to mention the continued influence of figures like Anthony Braxton and Cecil Taylor, displays an inability or unwillingness to look past the public face of American jazz that the neoclassicists show to the world. American jazz is much deeper than one group of musicians, regardless of how much press and attention they garner. But this discourse is about more than just the music; it resists the legacy of deploying jazz as a weapon of the arsenal of democracy, of attempts to "Americanize" the world, to recall Madeline Albright's comments. Such efforts echo deeply held resentments against what has long been seen as American cultural imperialism and dominance in world affairs.

International critiques of American jazz cannot be easily detangled from broader critiques of neoconservatism and American exceptionalism that have gained currency over the last decade. All of this is not to say that jazz is or is not "American" or whether American jazz is better or more authentic; such judgments are inherently subjective. But as American musicians and scholars interact with an increasingly globalized jazz world, we must be aware of the changing nature of power relationships in global jazz communities. American voices no longer have a privileged place in the international jazz discourse; we are no longer greeted with a sense of deference, but more and more with defiance.

Postscript: A Tale of Two Films

The evolving nature of transnational jazz discourses can be seen in comparing two films that speak to vastly different perspectives on jazz and identity in the early twenty-first century. The first, Ken Burns's mammoth PBS series *Jazz*, which premiered in January 2001, is well known for its thrusting of jazz into an unaccustomed spotlight (at least for American television audiences), the ubiquitous Burns documentary style (already familiar from his films on the Civil War and baseball), and the passionate debates that followed concerning its perspectives on history, its omission of certain artists, and its identification of jazz that seemingly allied itself with neoclassicist musicians and critics (especially Wynton Marsalis, who served as a primary consultant and frequent "talking head" in the series). At the other end of the decade, the appearance of the film *Icons Among Us: Jazz in the Present Tense*, which appeared in April 2009 on the Documentary Channel (also in the U.S.) was seen to represent a counterweight to Burns's documentary; indeed, Ben Ratliff, reviewing the film for the *New York Times*, sees *Icons* as a "retort" to Burns, stating that even though the new film does not make direct reference to its predecessor, "it doesn't need to. There's no other elephant in the room" (Ratliff 2009, C3).

It is not too difficult to see why critics like Ratliff would come to such a conclusion about *Icons*. *Jazz* was unabashedly about jazz as "America's music," a sonic representation that reflected, in the words of Charles Hersch, "America without dissonance" (Hersch 2001, 107). The PBS website for the film still refers to the music as "the purest expression of American democracy," and Burns himself situates the film as the final part of an "American trilogy"[10] that included *The Civil War* and *Baseball*.[11] That *Jazz* reflects an overwhelmingly American view of the music is a point that, despite the sometimes brutal criticism the film received, is rarely mentioned in reviews in the American press. For most critics, it seems that the nearly exclusive focus on American perspectives is not a major problem. They seem to assume, as Burns does, an American-centered perspective, though the particularities in expressing that perspective are in dispute.[12]

Icons, by contrast, takes great pains to avoid nationalistic arguments, situating jazz as a music that reflects "everything, everywhere," which serves as the title for the series' fourth and final episode. The filmmakers focus on a number of jazz artists born outside the United States, including Courtney Pine, Essbjorn Svensson, Jamie Cullum, and Anat Cohen, to name a few. Jazz is positioned as a world music, and though the neoclassicist perspective is given voice (Marsalis himself appears in several interviews), the identity for jazz that *Icons* forges is far less harmonious, and far more "dissonant" than that advanced by Burns. It would be easy to simply see *Icons* as a response to Burns and to view its portrayal of jazz as more global vis-à-vis *Jazz*'s American exceptionalist perspective. But the reality of *Icons* is much more complex and, I would argue, reflects the inherent difficulties in trying to imagine jazz community on a global scale. The experiences of several of the artists in the film underscore this point. *Icons* does make a substantial effort both to place jazz in a global context and to feature the voices (and music) of a number of artists from outside the United States.

One artist who receives a great deal of attention in the series is the late Swedish pianist Essbjorn Svensson, whose trio is featured at the end of the third episode within a larger discussion of the bonds forged between musicians in jazz groups.[13] Svensson, who died in a diving accident in June 2008, represented for many advocates of European jazz the future and possibility of artists from outside the United States to make an impact on the global scene. Svensson noted in an interview during the film: "As a Swedish band, or European band, being signed to an American label, I think that's quite unusual. I mean when we were signed to Sony and Columbia, people were raving about it. Maybe it showed something that even here in America you start to show interest in what is happening in Europe." This idea, of a modern European band "making it" in the American jazz scene, is a crucial point, for it upsets the usual trajectory of globalization in jazz. Here, the flow of influence from the U.S. outward is reversed. To be sure, non-American influences have always shaped jazz, but rarely have jazz musicians from outside had any real success in the American scene, arguably since Django Reinhardt. Svensson's untimely death deprived us not only of a singular musical voice and talent, but an opportunity to see where such currents might lead.

The effusive treatment of European players is not universal in the film. As pianist Robert Glasper notes: "There's a whole movement of cats from Europe that play jazz, but there's a key thing missing in most of it when I hear it, not putting Europe down, but they're classically based. It's a classically trained thing and jazz isn't based on classical music, it's based on blues and church and emotion and spirit—the real shit. So you can play all the shit you want, but if you don't have none of that . . ." Glasper, it should be noted, is no neoclassicist; in other parts of the film, he is brutally frank in his assessment of the canon and prevailing perspectives on jazz's historical legacy. In one segment, he notes that the great jazz masters, so central to the canon, are "just human beings," and that modern musicians need to move beyond historicized models. This passage makes his comments about Europe particularly striking. While dismissing an historically based understanding of modern jazz performance, he nonetheless privileges approaches to the music that are, in essence, historical, drawing on specific African American roots genres.

Glasper's seemingly conflicted comments underscore something about *Icons Among Us* that comes through in many of the interviews and features: while non-American musicians are increasingly working against an hegemonic American perspective, many are still reluctant to disengage with it. Norwegian pianist and composer Bugge Wesseltoft notes: "There is a difference. I mean,

American jazz music is obviously based on African Americans' traditions. It has a black feel to it, which is different from the European. We have a much more whitish, classical touch. . . . I wish I was an African American." Whether Wesseltoft is serious or not in his wish to have been born black is not clear, but it does speak to a continued privileging of an assumed (African) American cultural authenticity, and more importantly, the palpable unease with which some white European musicians seem to approach the topic. English pianist Jamie Cullum, commenting on Wesseltoft's ability to fuse different musical influences seamlessly, states, "I don't know why he's not an international superstar." The answer to Cullum's inquiry might well be the fact that for all the de-centering of jazz as an American form, the traditionally circumscribed view of jazz still has great currency in the world.

For all of the film's iconoclasm, *Icons* itself still engages in some standard tropes of jazz discourse. There is no virtually no discussion of jazz outside the United States and Europe; Asian artists, for example, are completely ignored, and one might suggest that critical discourses on jazz's globalization (such as Nicholson) reflect a "European exceptionalism" that runs in parallel to American exceptionalism, rather than a truly global outlook. In addition, much of the film is set in and around New York; the second episode, in fact, opens with a montage of New York street scenes, before moving to an apartment where singer Gretchen Parlato is seen rehearsing with her pianist. Credits continue to roll as rooftops, train platforms, parks, and cityscapes flash across the screen. As Parlato finishes singing, a dusky shot of the Statue of Liberty appears, which fades into a nighttime scene of traffic rushing through a brightly-lit Times Square. Later in the episode, guitarist Will Bernard is seen taking a car service to a gig, and reflecting on his recent move from Berkeley to New York: "I would have to say that New York is the jazz capital of the world. There's other great places where jazz is really important, like New Orleans, but here you have so much of everything, so many musicians, so many different types of music."

This is an odd statement in a film that is trying to present a broadly inclusive view of jazz as a global music, and it underscores what I suggest is an incompleteness to the discourse of globalization in jazz. While globalization is often taken to reflect a challenge to the traditional American exceptionalist view of jazz that has long dominated perspectives on the music's practice, culture, and reception, the reality is that the jazz world, like the arenas of global economics and politics, is messy, one in which identity and knowledge about jazz are constructed and claimed, and in which authenticity and identity are formed and challenged. Communities seek to define themselves as unique entities, but must also be sensitive to jazz's histories, however flawed they may be. The authoritative voice reflected by Ken Burns or Wynton Marsalis has been challenged, but it is still a powerful force in global jazz discourses.

And so too is jazz's core narrative as an historical product of African American communities in New Orleans, where, ironically, *Icons Among Us* concludes. The final segment opens with a shot of trumpeter Efrem Towns playing an unaccompanied rendition of "Do You Know What It Means to Miss New Orleans," standing in the middle of a street still not recovered from the devastation of Hurricane Katrina; later saxophonist Donald Harrison Jr. is shown rebuilding his house, more than three years after the hurricane struck. I found the segments that invoke Katrina to be unsettling, and not simply because of the visceral images of the tragedy itself. Race is never explicitly mentioned during this sequence, but nearly all of the New Orleans musicians featured are black. And more importantly, no discussion of Katrina can escape its identification as a catastrophe that not only affected African Americans in vastly disproportionate numbers, but also as a crystalizing and disturbing moment for American society, laying bare the unresolved disparities of race and class. The contrast between European and many American musicians struggling to define themselves within the jazz tradition, set against New Orleans musicians struggling for basic needs such as housing, could not be more jarring. High-minded philosophical ideas about what jazz means seem trivial when compared with footage of saxophonist Harrison rebuilding his house.

What *does* it mean, then, to miss New Orleans? By going back to the community from which jazz is said to have sprung, to African American musicians whose predecessors have long been at the center of the jazz canon, *Icons* attempts to encapsulate the broadness of the jazz world past and present, and the film succeeds to a point. But the return to New Orleans might also be seen as undermining that very narrative, shining a bright spotlight on the exceptionality of a local narrative. The musicians of New Orleans are playing for something different, something bigger than simply aesthetic expression, no matter how lofty a goal that is. In the context of post-Katrina New Orleans, jazz is not about the global but the local, the ties that bind communities based not only on music, but also on shared space, experience, and circumstance. In a real sense, the conclusion of the film does take us full circle in the narrative of jazz, back to a time when jazz was *theirs*, not something that was so highly contested and debated within discourses of globalization and cultural production. There was no canon, no debate about authenticity or identity in relation to nationalism. It was simply what they played, the music that they danced to, and the soundtrack of a specific urban soundscape. No one had to tell them what jazz was; they knew it because they lived it every day in their own communities.

Notes

INTRODUCTION

1. I would suggest that this is more indirect—very little in either volume specifically addresses academic views on jazz.

2. In fact, the year this book was published I was entering my first year as a graduate student in a major jazz studies program at the University of North Texas, a program that has been in existence (in some form) for nearly fifty years.

3. This is all the more curious considering DeVeaux's own underlying argument that bebop players were, above all, professional musicians, and saw the world that way.

CHAPTER 1

1. See Aebersold 1971.

2. These discourses have, of course, a long and complex history that can be traced to the origins of jazz itself; the sources who engage these debates are too numerous to account for here, and I will not revisit them in this study. Most works tend to take the middle ground, pointing to both jazz's African American aesthetic and social histories, while including non-black musicians as vital contributors, though texts such as Leroi Jones's (Amiri Baraka's) *Blues People* and Albert Murray's *Stomping the Blues*, and Richard Sudhalter's *Lost Chords,* have staked out territory on opposite sides of the debates over jazz's racial identity, emphasizing the roles of black and white musicians respectively. Works like Gene Lees's *Cats of Any Color* as well as James Lincoln Collier's *Jazz: The American Theme Song* have, in the words of their authors, sought a more inclusive view, though these works have been attacked by some as attempting to diminish black artists' roles. On some level, these texts might be seen as calling for more bounded or open perspectives on the relationships between jazz communities and race, though rarely do they assess this topic specifically. An important exception is Gerard's *Jazz in Black and White*, which is discussed later.

3. This passage was quoted from a personal communication from Raeburn to Collier, as cited in the latter's book.

4. Ingrid Monson notes in *Freedom Sounds* that the discourse of integration in jazz communities in the 1960s represented for black musicians not the promise of "interracial

communion" that liberal white fans hoped for, but rather the expansion of "economic and educational opportunities for black people" (Monson 2007, 65).

5. In fact, at one point he refers to it as being "biracial."

6. Further, Winick reports that of the respondents who used drugs, 73 percent were white compared to 27 percent black, and thus black musicians had a *lower* usage rate than the sample itself. Gerard does note that blacks were "not disproportionately higher" as heroin users (86).

7. In his 2002 book *Jazz and Death*, Frederick Spencer recounts the establishment of the Musicians' Clinic in New York, an outgrowth of the 1957 Newport Jazz Festival that featured a panel, chaired by Nat Hentoff, on drug addiction among jazz musicians.

8. Attempts to obtain a copy of this document were, unfortunately, not successful.

9. Even at this late date, many still held jazz in low regard, as a genre associated with drug use and other less than savory ideas. Sociological and psychological studies of jazz from this period show a marked tendency to reflect such pathological perspectives, as evidenced by the frequency of studies like Winick's 1959 account of "The Use of Drugs by Jazz Musicians," appearing in the unfortunately titled journal *Social Problems*. As much as such studies might seem to overemphasize dysfunctional aspects of jazz musicians' lives, it should be remembered that the death of Charlie Parker, whose end was certainly hastened by years of drug abuse, had happened only four years earlier, an event whose shock waves were likely still being felt by many musicians and fans.

10. This perspective might also be viewed within a broader context of sociological studies that dealt with the "problems" of black communities, a frequent topic of research in the 1960s. One notable example of this line of research was the late Daniel Patrick Moynihan's infamous 1965 study "The Negro Family: A Case for National Action," which posited that the root cause of the challenges facing black families lay in a "tangle of pathology." The report was well intended but suspect in its conclusions, and sparked enormous backlash that led, at least indirectly, to the emergence of a whole generation of black sociologists.

11. See Becker, "The Professional Dance Musician and his Audience."

12. Stebbins makes a clear distinction between jazz-oriented and commercial-oriented performance, the former seen as having a much higher degree of prestige in the community, while the latter is, while important to providing income, viewed as inferior musically and not a major site of community formation.

13. In his later career Stebbins has devoted a good deal of attention to the sociology of occupation.

14. The Balcony, in Pittsburgh's Shadyside neighborhood, closed in 1997.

15. Represented cinematically in Frank Gilroy's 1985 film *The Gig*.

16. Allen's musical efforts were chronicled in the documentary *Wild Man Blues*, directed by Barbara Kopple, which chronicled his band's European tour. This film may give Allen the distinction of being the only amateur jazz musician to have a full-length documentary devoted to his musical efforts.

17. As I write this passage, my son is watching Cosby's *Little Bill*, with its hard bop–inspired theme song.

18. Joe Williams also had a recurring role as Claire Huxtable's father.

19. In a comical aside to Clinton's dabbling in jazz performance, MTV reporter Tabitha Soren was allegedly confused by Clinton's expressed desire to play with "The Loneliest Monk." Soren herself has denied that she ever said this, but the rumor has persisted, and undoubtedly affected public perception of both her, and *MTV News* in general.

20. This anecdote was distributed on the Jazz-L email list under the heading "Stan Getz responsible for world financial crisis."

21. As I argue in an essay entitled "Orality, Literacy and Mediating Musical Experience: Re-Thinking Oral Tradition in the Learning of Jazz Improvisation," arguments for inherent distinctions between oral and written paradigms in jazz discourse often reflect an overly generalized and highly misleading way of thinking about differences between jazz and Western art music. See Prouty 2006.

22. The NEA describes the program as "the nation's highest honor in jazz." Awarded annually since 1982, the program recognizes significant living jazz individuals whose contributions to jazz are deemed to be significant, as determined by a nomination and review process. Recipients also receive a $25,000 honorarium. While most of the program's hundred or so recipients are known mainly as performers, others who have occasionally been honored like Van Gelder include writers Dan Morgenstern and Nat Hentoff, educator David Baker, and promoter/producer George Wein.

23. See McMillan and Chavis 1986.

24. Ironically, McMillan and Chavis suggest that deviance is a means for a community to exclude non-members, while Merriam and Mack suggest that deviance serves opposite purposes, as a way for the community to define itself vis-à-vis mainstream society.

25. The fundamental importance of the practice of listening is underscored by the plethora of written works that have been devoted to cultivating needed skills that one must possess in order to effectively engage the music. General textbooks, for example, often include sections on how novice jazz students should approach the music. John Szwed's *Jazz 101* (2000) includes an entire chapter called "Listening to Jazz." Other authors devote entire texts to this topic, as evidenced by Jerry Coker's *Listening to Jazz* (1978) and Barry Kernfeld's *What to Listen for in Jazz* (1997). In these and many other books, listening is treated as a skill to be cultivated, and an active process in which one is engaged.

CHAPTER 2

1. Portions of this chapter have been adapted from Prouty 2004, Prouty 2005, and Prouty 2008. I am grateful to the respective publishers for permission to reprint this material.

2. Administrative structures take many different forms, from loosely organized departments to highly centralized, self-contained colleges. For purposes of this paper, I will refer generically to such structures as the "music school" unless otherwise indicated.

3. This is particularly true in discussion of performance, as Keith Javors notes in criticizing jazz education's loss of "indigenous" perspectives of improvisational pedagogy, as well as the field's "disparate value systems" (Javors 2001, 33). This issue is discussed in depth later in this chapter.

4. This seems to have become the case to such an extent that extended passages from Murphy's piece appear regularly in other authors' works without citation—these ideas are simply assumed to be common knowledge in the field.

5. I draw a distinction here between the incorporation of jazz into music department curricula and the performances of musicians such as Dave Brubeck and Stan Kenton on college campuses during the 1950s. Their performances were very often not supported (and sometimes opposed) by music departments. Kenton was, in fact, a major supporter of jazz education, sponsoring many workshops and seminars for young musicians.

6. The role of historically black colleges and universities is a subject of some dispute. While some have positioned such institutions as important points in the development of the field, other scholars, most notably London Branch, point out the reluctance of these schools to engage with jazz. Branch argues that HBCUs strove to emulate the Eurocentric methods and philosophies of white institutions in order to make their students better able to compete within society at large. See Branch 1975.

7. Handy, it should be noted, was not a practitioner of "oral tradition."

8. I wish to acknowledge Michael Fitzgerald and his collection of resources devoted to Lenox, which were of great benefit in this segment of the discussion. These materials may be accessed at jazzdiscography.com/Lenox/lenhome.htm.

9. This practice, I would add, continues today.

10. Although at the time of Hall's thesis bebop was still emerging, by the time the program was established in 1947 the music was widely recorded, and was well known in jazz circles outside of New York.

11. Although Hall attributes the use of the term "dance band" to cultural attitudes toward jazz at the time, it is undeniable that this term also carried a great deal more weight in terms of attracting students interested in entering the field of commercial music. Hall claims the term was merely a cover for jazz; in other contexts, this genre is defined as distinct from the more artistic styles of jazz. See Hall 1944, Cogswell 1993.

12. The increasingly complex harmonic and rhythm elements of bebop are well documented in the literature of jazz history, and will not be discussed here. Thomas Owens's 1974 dissertation "Charlie Parker: Techniques of Improvisation" and *The Birth of Bebop* by Scott DeVeaux (1999) provide particularly strong overviews of these musical features of bebop.

13. Although more contemporary styles often receive some attention within improvisation classes, earlier styles are generally completely excluded from this area of instruction in jazz. I am grateful to William Kenney for first bringing this latter concept to my attention during a question and answer session after my presentation of a paper on this topic at the 2002 meeting of the Society of American Music.

14. Russell presumably refers here to Western art music theory.

15. Earlier linear approaches, such as that of Lester Young, often adhered to a single general tonality.

16. Tanglewood, ironically, is adjacent to Lenox in Massachusetts.

17. Byrd taught at several institutions, including Howard University, Delaware State University, and more recently, Cornell. Davis and McLean, meanwhile, found permanent homes in academia: Davis at the University of Pittsburgh, McLean at the Hartt School of Music (University of Hartford). Taylor has maintained ties with a number of institutions, including a longstanding relationship with the University of Massachusetts.

18. A video of the panel, which also featured Ingrid Monson, Amiri Baraka, Guthrie Ramsey, and was moderated by Lewis Porter, can be found at rm3s.net/jalc/Default .aspx?mg=8d619912-cdbe-408d-ab4e-e4ab635403f0.

19. Collier's essay is illuminating, if anecdotal, though he does cite several musician-educators who express concern at their seeming inability to recruit black students. He cites Berklee's Larry Monroe as stating that at times jazz education is "white people teaching the blues to white people who can afford to go to college."

20. Graduate students and advanced transfers were allowed to test out of this requirement.

21. IU jazz director David Baker points out that, as long as students can play a major scale in all keys (which, presumably, almost any student at the collegiate level should be able to do), "I can teach them the rest" (Prouty 2002, 164).

22. At UNT, for example, my fourth-semester improvisation course dealt exclusively with the music of Wayne Shorter.

23. Compositions based on the standard twelve-bar blues progression.

24. Modal compositions are those in which a single static harmonic structure provides the basis for an entire section, or in some cases, the whole composition itself. Such tunes are termed modal because they are predicated upon the idea that a single related scale or mode provides the basic improvisational structure. "So What" by Miles Davis is usually regarded as the archetypal piece in this genre.

25. "Rhythm changes" are sometimes placed at the end of the beginning sequence, as a sort of repertory-based "final exam."

26. Similarly, Henry Martin, writing about the field of jazz theory, refers to "analytical" and "musician-based" approaches. See Martin 1996.

27. The use of patterns in jazz education is somewhat controversial, as many critics of the field have argued that players emerging from such instruction sound too "pattern oriented," implying that while students may be able to demonstrate that they have learned these musical units, they have not developed the skills to apply them in any meaningful way, to develop their own unique vocabulary, or to be able to depart from patterns they have learned. For some students this is certainly true, but this critical bent ignores the fact learning bits and pieces of the improvisational language has always been at the heart of learning how to improvise.

28. Some textbooks make this distinction explicit in their titles. See Lawn and Hellmer 1996.

29. One of my improvisation instructors at UNT quipped that an "A" student would be one he would hire for his group (which he sometimes put into practice).

30. Nettl's "heartland" music school is a conglomeration of several large university music programs from universities in the Midwest. Based on his reflections as a longtime teacher and ethnomusicologist associated with such institutions, his work in this area is best understood as what I would call an "ethnographic memoir" of his own experiences and observations over several decades.

31. An interesting side note is the insistence by some in American education that schools should focus upon "Western" ideals and themes, of which the Western classical canon might be one. A notable example was in the late 1980s by then Secretary of Education William Bennett, who proposed that such a philosophy should be at the core of learning in the United States. See Giroux and Simon 1989, 236–37.

32. While the improvisations of Mozart, Liszt, and other pre-to-early-Romantic figures are often studied historically, rarely do their improvisational exploits form a substantial part of instrumental pedagogy. Such individuals are still regarded primarily as composers within musical academia.

33. The idea of "increasing specification" is an important element of many curricular sequences, and is reflected in the curricula of many jazz educators, whose improvisational methods feature increasingly detailed, complex harmonic systems and frameworks (i.e., moving from modal or blues-based systems to bebop and post-bop progressions).

34. Caswell discusses at length the close relationship between the emergence of a canon in European art music (and American emulation of the canon) and the development of musical academia in the nineteenth and twentieth centuries. See Caswell 1991, 134–36.

35. Following Foucault.

36. I would stress that Small is not arguing against improvisation here, in that "anarchy," as he describes it, might not be a bad thing. For the powers that be, however, anarchy is to be avoided at all costs.

37. Baker argues this point in several publications, noting that practicing jazz musicians, especially ones who were black, were a rarity in musical academia, even among teachers of jazz. His emphasis on improvisation seems to go hand in hand with his call for more practicing jazz professionals in the academy, and speaks to the ways jazz was treated within most academic contexts to the 1960s.

38. Though not a performance idiom per se, I would suggest that the construction of an historical canon of jazz is also an exercise related to improvisation, as the vast majority of individuals within the canon are those whose contributions to jazz are seen as advancing the development of improvisational techniques (Armstrong, Parker, Coltrane, and so forth), notwithstanding composers such as Ellington, Monk, and Mingus (all of whom, it should be noted, were also innovative improvisers).

39. This followed a common practice in non-institutional learning systems.

40. The phrase "legitimate" (or "legit" for short) is one that is still in use among teachers and students to refer to studies in Western art music. The fact that this term has

survived to the present day is an indicator of the pervasiveness of this type of academic dialogue in shaping the debate around jazz education. Even teachers and students within jazz education use this term in referring to Western art music students and repertories; students often refer to applied musical study (i.e., lessons) on their major instrument as "legit" study, or pieces from the art music repertory as "legit" pieces (Prouty 2004).

41. To be sure, Nisenson and Collier come from vastly different perspectives, the former a modernist and champion of the avant-garde, the latter a traditionalist whose views were reflected in his frequent appearance in Ken Burns's famed (or infamous) documentary *Jazz*. Both, however, have been vocal critics of institutionalized jazz study, and both have also directed intense criticism at Marsalis (Marsalis wrote a blistering letter to the *New York Times* in 1993, responding to the newspaper's positive review of Collier's book). See Collier 1993 and Nisenson 2005.

42. And indeed, this emphasis on self-teaching lies at the heart of many studies of improvisation, most notably Berliner's encyclopedic account. The term "infinite" in his title refers to the seemingly inexhaustible ways in which jazz musicians individually construct and apply their own unique methods of learning and playing jazz. See Berliner.

43. There are a number of references to this in the recorded history of jazz. One notable example was tenor saxophonist Paul Quinichette, whose similarity to the playing style of Lester Young earned him the nickname Vice Prez. This was not generally meant as a compliment. See Berliner (1994, 273–76) for a more thorough discussion of these ideas.

44. To be fair, Nicholson does also cite institutional and economic pressure as a contributing factor.

45. Whether such "self-teaching" could truly ever exist is open to debate. Musicians work with other musicians, and within the context of their own communities. Nevertheless, self-teaching as a marker of identity within the traditions of jazz holds great sway within discourses on learning jazz improvisation.

46. In 1987 the U.S. Congress passed H.R. 57, which states in part that jazz "makes evident to the world an outstanding artistic model of individual expression and democratic cooperation within the creative process, thus fulfilling the highest ideals and aspirations of our republic." Former president Bill Clinton famously hosted a White House program entitled "Jazz: An Expression of Democracy" in September 1998. These are perhaps the most official expressions of an idea that has been articulated by many musicians in the literature of jazz.

CHAPTER 3

1. See works by Winthrop Sargeant (1938), Frederic Ramsey and Charles Edward Smith (1939), and Rudi Blesh (1946) as important early examples.

2. Stearns's 1942 Yale dissertation was entitled "A Study in Robert Henryson and 'The Testament of Cressid.'"

3. The development of the first major institutional jazz studies programs was still years off at this point.

4. Stearns and LaRocca engaged in a heated correspondence, as Bruce Boyd Raeburn has noted, based on what LaRocca saw as Stearns's dismissal of the ODJB, and what Stearns saw as LaRocca's outright racism in dismissing the contribution of African American artists (Raeburn 2009, 52–53).

5. Though Gennari sees Stearns and *The Story of Jazz* as critical to the development of the discipline of jazz history, he actually talks very little about the structure and content of the book itself or specific interpretations that Stearns employs.

6. As late as 1954, one could find histories of jazz that completely ignored bebop, as was the case with Rex Harris's coincidentally titled *The Story of Jazz* (1954); on the other hand, Leonard Feather asserted in *The Book of Jazz* (1957) that "jazz was not born in New Orleans" (Feather 1957, 8).

7. As Raeburn notes in the introduction to his historiographic study of New Orleans jazz, the attribution of New Orleans as jazz's birthplace was not always a universally recognized feature of the jazz narrative, but was constructed by writers through the 1940s. In placing New Orleans in the center of his early jazz narrative, Stearns echoes the sentiments of these writers.

8. I would presume that Stearns is referring to the use of chordal extensions.

9. Apart from his writings in jazz, Ostransky was best known as a composer and university professor.

10. Having said this, *Down Beat* has throughout its history made an effort to include what could be termed scholarly material. Stearns's writings might be seen as one example. In addition, the magazine frequently published transcriptions and short analytical overviews of jazz solo styles since the 1930s. These were ostensibly intended as performance aids for musicians, more akin to method books than scholarly overview; still, they provide a wealth of information on the perspectives on jazz style during this period. Curiously, a large number of *Down Beat*'s transcriptions and analytical treatises in the late 1930s dealt with the particulars of jazz accordion playing.

11. Becker's "The Professional Dance Musician and his Audience" (1951) and Cameron's "Sociological Notes on the Jam Session" (1954) are two early landmark works of jazz scholarship, both based in the study of social networks and groups within what was seen as a marginalized subculture. Other studies were less charitable, as was the case with Norman Margolis's psychoanalytic work (discussed in chapter 1), or a similarly Freudian view advanced by Dr. Miles D. Miller in his 1958 essay "Jazz and Aggression" in which jazz trombone playing is equated with "belching and passing flatus" (reprinted in Walser 1999).

12. Some have also speculated that Rollins's discomfort with Schuller's dissection of his music may have led, in part, to the saxophonist's decision to take a "sabbatical" until 1962.

13. Schuller refers here to Winthrop Sargeant's *Jazz: Hot and Hybrid* (1938) and Hodier's *Jazz: Its Evolution and Essence* (1956), both of which offer more detailed technical and analytical discussions of jazz than concurrent jazz histories.

14. An expanded version of this discussion of jazz history textbooks can be found in my article in the *Journal of Music History Pedagogy* (Prouty 2010). I am grateful to the journal editors for permission to reprint some of this material.

15. After Grout's death in 1987, Norton has continued to produce this seminal text, first under the guidance of Claude Palisca and later in association with Peter Burkholder.

16. This is somewhat ironic in light of DeVeaux's influential 1991 essay in which he rightly critiques the development of an overly canonical jazz history through college textbooks.

17. Another syllabus was appended to a 1970 reprint of *The Story of Jazz*.

18. Richard Taruskin, in his essay "The Musicologist and the Performer," claims that relationships between musicologists and performers have never been better. It should be noted, however, that he refers primarily to professional performers, not those inhabiting the educational institution as either students or teachers, where competition for resources becomes a significant issue. See Taruskin 1982.

19. Harris and Tristano in particular are regarded as exceptional artist/teachers.

20. While big bands are of course a central part of many programs, usually only a small portion of their repertoires is drawn from pre-1940s swing. Furthermore, improvisational techniques specific to such early areas are rarely addressed either in the classroom or the rehearsal hall.

21. The Hartt School is located at the University of Hartford.

CHAPTER 4

1. Sanger has since initiated a new project called Citizendium, which seeks to combine the user-friendly, open-source aspects of the wiki with the more rigorous editorial control that characterized Nupedia. In a 2008 feature on "the greatest defunct websites and dotcom disasters" (of which Nupedia is one), the massive popularity of the non-editorial approach is clear: Wikipedia is credited with 6.5 million entries, while Citizendium had 6,500.

2. This is not always the case, as Wikipedia's administration has at times been accused of "scrubbing" its edit logs; cofounder Jimbo Wales was accused of doing just that in the Seigenthaler controversy.

3. The article can be accessed at en.wikipedia.org/wiki/Jazz. For simplicity, I am omitting references to specific passages from the article, as well as edits, referring to these by dates only. All of these can be found on the aforementioned site, in the main article, history, or discussion pages as appropriate.

4. The use of personal opinion is often tagged as "POV," short for point-of-view. Accusations of editors engaging in POV-based writing or editing are some of the most frequent causes for debates and disputes among editors, as articles are supposed to present a neutral viewpoint, negotiated between authors.

5. Neutral point of view.

6. allaboutjazz.com.

7. VBulletin is a commonly used discussion board platform, utilized by numerous websites.

8. Of all posts in the AAJ forum, the twelve most replied-to are monthly "What are you listening to" discussions.

9. The original article can be viewed at allaboutjazz.com/php/article.php?id=21243.

10. The text of the letter can be found at allaboutjazz.com/php/article.php?id=26493.

11. While specific figures vary, most accept the oft-cited figure of approximately 3 percent of all record sales being comprised of jazz recordings.

12. Accessed at youtube.com/watch?v=n9bjI-dfqB8.

13. Accessed at youtube.com/watch?v=TOwEr4UaqzM.

14. An expanded version of the discussion was presented as a paper at the Leeds International Jazz Conference in March 2008.

15. Ironically, the *Monitor* itself recently became a victim of the shift in the journalism industry, abandoning its daily print version only a month after Humphries's article appeared.

16. Indeed, *Jazz Times* was saved from closure in 2008. The magazine announced in June of that year that it was suspending publication and furloughing most of its staff. In July, the publishers announced the sale of the magazine, and that it would resume publication.

17. It is worth pointing out that Mandel's article on jazz magazine circulation is published on his *own* blog, Jazz Beyond Jazz, which first appeared in July 2007. A number of journalistic outlets have initiated blogs, such as National Public Radio's A Blog Supreme, whose title is, of course, a play on that of Coltrane's 1964 album.

18. As reported in the *Wall Street Journal* on December 29, 2010, Facebook accounted for just under 9 percent of all website visits from January to November, pushing Google to the second spot on the list.

19. The URLs redirect users to other websites, in this case, a posting on Facebook about Marsalis's times in Paris.

20. The intersection of web technology and globalization is a theme that provides the foundation for Thomas Friedman's *The World Is Flat: A Brief History of the 21ˢᵗ Century*. Friedman argues that globalization is best understood as being comprised of distinct periods. Globalization 1.0 refers to the period of colonial expansion and imperialism that defined European and eastern contact to the twentieth century. This is followed by Globalization 2.0, encompassing the spread of Western (i.e., American) influence via media and multinational corporations. Globalization 3.0, a period which is now in its infancy, is characterized by a "flattening" or leveling of the global playing field, in which traditional political and economic hierarchies are replaced with more equalized relationships. Developments in web-based communication such as those discuss in this chapter form the basis for such transformations.

CHAPTER 5

1. The importance of academic credentials in jazz education is discussed in greater detail in chapter 3.

2. This document originally appeared in the January 2001 issue of the same publication. This version was intended as an update as to IAJE's progress.

3. I actually got to perform with Galper's trio as a student in Maine.

4. The phrase was used frequently in IAJE press materials.

5. Previous IAJE meetings, especially those held in New York, were notorious for being affairs on a massive scale. In one of my first conferences, a 1998 meeting in New York's Marriott Marquis hotel, the traffic inside was so heavy that elevators were said to be malfunctioning due to increased use.

6. This was a subject of debate for many years, especially as the Pulitzer committee in 1965 had considered, yet ultimately rejected, Duke Ellington (the prize jury had selected Ellington, but the Pulitzer board refused and did not give an award for the year). In 1997 the award was given to Wynton Marsalis for his composition *Blood on the Fields*, an event that was interpreted by many (especially those critics close to Marsalis) as a public vindication of jazz. Ten years later, it was awarded to another jazz musician, Ornette Coleman, for his work *Sound Grammar*.

7. See Parsonage 2005.

8. See McKay 2005.

9. Few European jazz critics have openly criticized the "African American" side of this equation as much as simply the American side. Graham Collier, for his part, seems a bit more willing to take on this sensitive topic, writing that "there is a distressing trend among some musicians and critics to think that America, and, often, specifically 'black' America, still 'owns' jazz, and that what is played elsewhere is something different and not as good."

10. This is reflected in a quote from cultural scholar and jazz critic Gerald Earley, who stated in *Baseball* that "there are only three things America will be known for 2,000 years from now when they study this civilization: the Constitution, jazz music, and baseball."

11. Burns's forays into Americana later continued with his documentaries *The War* and *The National Parks: America's Best Idea*, which premiered in 2007 and 2009 respectively.

12. It is also worth noting that very few critics of the series seem to take issue with its near exclusive focus on male artists, another canonical idea that has recently come under sustained critique.

13. The episode, titled "In the Spirit of Family," attempts to create a counternarrative to the focus on individual musicians that sometimes pervades conventional jazz narratives.

Works Cited

Adler, Eric. 2004. "Free Jazz & Free Love, or, Is Branford Marsalis a Neocon?" *The New Partisan*, October 29. newpartisan.com/home/free-jazz-free-love-or-is-branford-marsalis-a-neocon.html (accessed February 17 2009).

Aebersold, Jamey. 1973. *A New Approach to Jazz Improvisation*. New Albany, IN: Jamey Aebersold Jazz (first in a series of instructional aids, with subsequent volumes produced frequently).

Ake, David. 2002. *Jazz Cultures*. Berkeley and Los Angeles: University of California Press.

All About Jazz. n.d. "RIP Jazz Central Station." n.d. *All About Jazz*. allaboutjazz.com/birdlives/bl-57.htm (accessed December 12, 2008).

All About Jazz Publicity. 2009. "World's Top Jazz Website Teams with Jazz Video Guy." *All About Jazz*. allaboutjazz.com/php/news.php?id=39332 (accessed July 17, 2009).

Anderson, Benedict. 1983. *Imagined Communities*. London and New York: Verso.

Anderson, Iain. 2007. *This Is Our Music: Free Jazz, the Sixties and American Culture*. Philadelphia: University of Pennsylvania Press.

Anderson, Sheila. 2005. *How to Grow as a Musician: What All Musicians Must Know to Succeed*. Lakewood, NJ: Allsworth Communications.

Atkins, E. Taylor. 2001. *Blue Nippon*. Durham: Duke University Press.

———, ed. 2003. *Jazz Planet*. Jackson: University Press of Mississippi.

Atzmon, Gilad. 2004. "To Play Jazz Is to Suggest an Alternate Reality." *Counterpunch*, November 20. counterpunch.org/atzmon11202004.html (accessed February 21, 2009).

Austerlitz, Paul. 2005. *Jazz Consciousness*. Middletown, CT: Wesleyan University Press.

Baker, David. 1965. "Jazz: The Academy's Neglected Stepchild." *Down Beat* 32: 29–32.

———. 1973. "The Battle for Legitimacy: Jazz Versus Academia." *Black World* 23 (1): 20–27.

———. 1979. *Jazz Pedagogy: A Comprehensive Method for Teacher and Student*. Chicago: db Music Workshop/Maher Publications.

Barr, Walter. 1974. "The Jazz Studies Curriculum." Ph.D. diss., Arizona State University.

Baskerville, David. 1979. "Book Reviews." *Music Educator's Journal* 66 (1): 67–69.

Becker, Howard. 1951. "The Professional Dance Musician and his Audience." *American Journal of Sociology* 57 (2): 136–44.

———. 1982. *Art Worlds*. Berkeley: University of California Press.

Benjamin, Walter. 1968. "The Work of Art in the Age of Mechanical Reproduction." In *Illuminations*, trans. Harry Zohn, 217–51. New York: Schoken.

Berliner, Paul. 1994. *Thinking in Jazz: The Infinite Art of Improvisation*. Chicago: University of Chicago Press.

Blesh, Rudi. 1946. *Shining Trumpets*. New York: Knopf.

Branch, London. 1975. "Jazz Education at Predominantly Black Colleges." Ph.D. diss., Southern Illinois University.

Brookmeyer, Bob. 1959. "The Lenox School of Jazz: Faculty Views." *Jazz Review* 2 (1): 16, 18.

Brown, Marion. 1973. "Improvisation and the Aural Tradition in Afro-American Music." *Black World* 23: 15–19.

Brubeck, Darius. 2002a. "1959: The Beginning of Beyond." In *The Cambridge Companion to Jazz.*, edited by M. Cooke and D. Horn, 177–201. Cambridge: Cambridge University Press.

———. 2002b. "David Baker and the Lenox School of Jazz." *Jazz Education Journal* 35 (2): 42–55.

Byrnes, Sholto. 2003. "Talking Jazz." *Independent*, November 14. independent.co.uk/arts-entertainment/music/features/talking-jazz-735624.html (accessed February 12, 2009).

Cameron, William B. 1954. "Sociological Notes on the Jam Session." *Social Forces* 33: 177–82.

Carter, Warwick. 1977. "Jazz in the College Curriculum." *School Musician* 49: 52–53.

———. 1986. "Jazz Education: A History Still in the Making." *Jazz Educators Journal* 18: 10–13, 49–50.

Caswell, Austin B. 1991. "Canonicity in Academia: A Music Historian's View." *Journal of Aesthetic Education* 25 (3): 129–45.

Choate, R. A., et al. 1968. *Documentary Report of the Tanglewood Symposium*. Washington: Music Educators' National Conference.

Clark, Andrew. 2001. "Reetie Vouties with a Little Hot Sauce: Jazz and Language." In *Riffs and Choruses: A New Jazz Anthology*. Andrew Clark, ed. 317–20. London: Continuum International.

Cogswell, Michael. 1993. "Gene Hall in His Own Words." *Jazz Educators Journal* 25 (3): 38–40.

Coker, Jerry. 1964. *Improvising Jazz*. Englewood Cliffs, NJ: Prentice Hall.

———. 1978. *Listening to Jazz*. Englewood Cliffs, NJ: Prentice Hall.

———. 1989. *The Teaching of Jazz*. Rottenburg N., Germany: Advance Music.

Cole, George. 2007. *The Last Miles: The Music of Miles Davis 1980–1991*. Ann Arbor: University of Michigan Press.

Collier, Graham. n.d. "On Not Being American." *Jazz Continuum*. jazzcontinuum.com/jc_tnb15.html (accessed February 10, 2009).

———. 1993. "The Churchill Report on Jazz Education in America." *Jazz Continuum*. jazzcontinuum.com/ page3/page10/page10.html (accessed January 10, 2011).

Collier, James Lincoln. 1993. *Jazz: The American Theme Song*. New York and Oxford: Oxford University Press.

Coulthard, Karl. 2007. "Looking for the Band: Walter Benjamin and the Mechanical Reproduction of Jazz." *Critical Studies in Improvisation* 3 (1): criticalimprov.com/article/view/82.

Contreras, Felix. 2008. "Jazz Education Group Sounds Its Siren Song." *NPR News*, April 25. npr.org/templates/story/story.php?storyId=89953765 (accessed December 27, 2008).

Crouch, Stanley. 1990 "Play the Right Thing." *New Republic*, February 12: 30–37.

———. 2007. *Considering Genius: Writings on Jazz*. New York: Basic.

Davis, Francis. 2001. "I Hear America Scatting." *Atlantic*, January. theatlantic.com/is sues/2001/01/davis.htm (accessed June 12, 2009).

Davis, Miles, with Quincy Troupe. 1989. *Miles: The Autobiography*. New York: Simon and Schuster.

De Barros, Paul. 2008. "Post-IAJE Crash Courses." *Down Beat* 75 (August): 13–14.

De Souza, Jonathan. 2008. "Reassessing the Emergence of Indeterminate Music." *British Postgraduate Musicology*, February. bpmonline.org.uk/bpm9/desouza.html (accessed May 27, 2008).

Della Cava, Marco R. 2003. "Ugly Sentiments Sting American Tourists." *USA Today*, March 3. usatoday.com/news/world/2003-03-03-anti-american-usat_x.htm (accessed January 12, 2009).

DeVeaux, Scott. 1991. "Constructing the Jazz Tradition: Jazz Historiography." *Black American Literature Forum* 25 (3): 525–60.

———. 1998. "Review." *Journal of the American Musicological Association* 51 (2): 392–406.

———. 1999. *The Birth of Bebop: A Social and Musical History*. Berkeley: University of California Press.

DeVeaux, Scott, and Gary Giddins. *Jazz*. 2009. New York: W.W. Norton.

Dionne, E. J. 2004. *Why Americans Hate Politics*. New York: Simon and Schuster.

Dobbins, Bill. 1988. "Jazz and Academia: Street Music in the Ivory Tower." *Council for Research in Music Education Bulletin* 96 (Spring): 30–41.

Douglas, Dave. 2009. "High Speed and Broadband Ready." *NPR Jazz: A Blog Supreme*, June 16. npr.org/blogs/ablogsupreme/2009/06/dave_douglas_high_speed_and_br_1 .html (accessed June 17, 2009).

Dunscomb, Richard and Willie Hill. 2004. *Jazz Pedagogy: The Jazz Educator's Handbook and Resource Guide*. Van Nuys, CA: Warner Brothers.

Earl, Riggins. 2001. *Dark Salutations*. Philadelphia: Trinity International.

Ellis, Jason. 1998. "Booking Passage Through Jazz Central Station: A Community Study." Unpublished paper, May 4. jellis.org/research/jcs-study/jcs-paper.pdf (accessed December 12, 2008).

Feather, Leonard. 1957. *The Book of Jazz*. New York: Horizon.

Feintuch, Burt. 2001. "Longing for Community." *Western Folklore* 60 (2/3): 149–61.

Feldman, Harry. 1964. "Jazz: A Place in Music Education?" *Music Educators' Journal* 50: 60–62.

Fisher, Larry. 1981. "The Rationale for and Development of Jazz Courses for the College Music Education Curriculum." D.Ed. diss., Pennsylvania State University.

Fitzgerald, Michael, ed. 2008. "Jazz Archives in the United States." M.S. thesis, University of North Carolina.

Fitzgerald, Michael. 2003. *Earth Circles: Bahá'í Perspectives on Global Issues*. Los Angeles: Kalimet.

Floyd, Samuel, et al. 1983. "An Oral History of the Great Lakes Experience." *The Black Perspective in Music* 11: 41–60.

Foucault, Michel. 1977. *Discipline and Punish*. London: Alan Fane.

Fraser, Wilmot "Al." 1983. "Jazzology: A Study of the Tradition in Which Jazz Musicians Learn to Improvise." Ph.D. diss., University of Pennsylvania.

Friedman, Thomas. 2005. *The World Is Flat: A Brief History of the 21st Century*. New York: Farrar, Straus and Giroux.

Froese, Marc D. 2007. "The Myth of American Exceptionalism and the Tragedy of Neoconservative Foreign Policy." *Social Science Research Network*, November 9. ssrn.com/abstract=1028658 (accessed February 18, 2009).

Gabbard, Krin. 1995. "Introduction: the Canon and Its Consequences." *Jazz Among the Discourses*. Krin Gabbard, ed. 1–26. Durham, NC: Duke University Press.

Galper, Hal. n.d.a. Hal Galper's Home Page. halgalper.com (accessed August 27, 2007).

———. n.d. b. "The Oral Tradition." Halgalper.com. halgalper.com/13_arti/oraltradition.htm (accessed August 27, 2007).

Gendron, Bernard. 1995. "Moldy Figs and Modernists: Jazz at War (1942–46)." In *Jazz Among the Discourses*. Krin Gabbard, ed. 31–56. Durham, NC: Duke University Press.

Gennari, John. 2006. *Blowing Hot and Cool: Jazz and its Critics*. Chicago: University of Chicago Press.

Gerard, Charley. 1998. *Jazz in Black and White: Race, Culture, and Identity in the Jazz Community*. Westport, CT: Praeger.

Giroux, Henry, and Roger Simon. 1989. "Popular Culture and Critical Pedagogy: Everyday Life as a Basis for Curriculum Knowledge." *Critical Pedagogy, the State and Cultural Struggle*. H. Giroux and P. McLaren, eds. 236–52. Albany: State University of New York Press.

Gold, Robert. 1964. *A Jazz Lexicon*. New York: Knopf.

———. 2001 (1975). "Introduction to *Jazz Talk*." *Riffs and Choruses: A New Jazz Anthology*. Andrew Clark, ed. 321–23. London: Continuum International.

Google Corporate. n.d. "Technology Overview." Google. google.com/corporate/tech.html (accessed July 5, 2009).

Gridley, Mark. 1978. *Jazz Styles and Analysis*. Englewood Cliffs, NJ: Prentice Hall.

Gronow, Pekka. 2004. "The Record Industry: The Growth of a Mass Medium." *Popular Music: Critical Concepts in Media and Cultural Studies*. Simon Frith, ed. 108–29. London: Routledge.

Gushee, Lawrence. 1978. "Review." *Journal of the American Musicological Society* 31 (3): 535–40.

———. 1979. "Letter from Lawrence Gushee." *Journal of the American Musicological Society* 32 (3): 597–98.

Hall, Gene. 1969. "How We Hope to Foster Jazz." *Music Educators Journal* 55 (March): 44–46.

Hall, M. E. 1944. "The Development of a Curriculum for the Teaching of Dance Music at a College Level." M.A. thesis, North Texas State College.

Harris, Rex. 1954. *The Story of Jazz*. New York: Grosset and Dunlap.

Hays, Timothy Odell. 1999. "The Music Department in Higher Education: History, Connections, and Conflict, 1865–1998." Ph.D. diss., Loyola University of Chicago.

Heffley, Mike. 2005. *Northern Sun, Southern Moon: Europe's Reinvention of Jazz*. New Haven: Yale University Press.

Hersch, Charles. 2001. "America Without Dissonance: Ken Burns's *Jazz*." *Polity* 34 (1): 107–16.

Hodier, Andre. 1956. *Jazz: Its Evolution and Essence*. David Noakes, transl. New York: Grove.

Hores, Robert G. 1977. "A Comparative Study of Visual and Aural Oriented Approaches to Jazz Improvisation with Implications for Instruction." D.M.E. diss., Indiana University.

Humphries, Stephen. 2008. "Are professional music critics losing their clout?" *Christian Science Monitor*, August 29. csmonitor.com/2008/0830/p25s03-algn.html (accessed November 11, 2008).

International Association for Jazz Education. 2002. "IAJE Strategic Plan." *Jazz Education Journal* 34 (4): A62–A64.

Jackson, Jeffery. 2003. *Making Jazz French: Music and Modern Life in Interwar Paris*. Durham, NC: Duke University Press.

Jarrett, Michael. 2004. "Cutting Sides: Jazz Record Producers and Improvisation." *The Other Side of Nowhere: Jazz, Improvisation, and Communities in Dialogue*. D. Fischlin and A. Heble, eds. 319–50. Middletown, CT: Wesleyan University Press.

Javors, Keith. 2001. "An Appraisal of Collegiate Jazz Performance Programs in the Teaching of Jazz Music." D.M.E. diss., University of Illinois.

Jazz Online. n.d. "About Jazz Online." *Jazz Online*, jazzonln.com/aboutjazzonline.asp (accessed December 12, 2008).

Jenkins, Willard. 2008a. "IAJE: Gone, Gone . . . What's Next?" *Independent Ear*, May 9. openskyjazz.com/blog/?p=81 (accessed May 14, 2008).

———. 2008b. "IAJE Invades Lovely Toronto." *Independent Ear*, January 17. opensky jazz.com/blog/?m=200801 (accessed May 14, 2008).

———. 2008c. "Woe is IAJE." *Independent Ear*, April 4. openskyjazz.com/blog/?p=71 (accessed April 12, 2008).

Johnson, Benjamin Keith. 2007. "Wikipedia as Collective Action: Personal Incentives and Enabling Structures." M.A. thesis, Michigan State University.

Jones, Leroi. 1963. *Blues People: Negro Music in White America*. New York: Morrow.

Katz, Mark. 2010. *Capturing Sound: How Technology Has Changed Music*. Rev. ed. Berkeley and Los Angeles: University of California Press.

Kenney, William Howland. 2008. *Recorded Music in American Life: The Phonograph and Popular Memory, 1890–1945*. Oxford and New York: Oxford University Press.

Kernfeld, Barry. 1997. *What to Listen for in Jazz*. New Haven: Yale University Press.

Kingsbury, Henry. 1988. *Music, Talent and Performance: A Conservatory Cultural System*. Philadelphia: Temple University Press.

Klauber, Bruce. 2009. "YouTube: Jazz for Free?" *JazzTimes*, April 1. jazztimes.com/community/articles/24726-youtube-jazz-for-free (accessed June 1, 2009).

Kodat, Catherine Gunther. 2003. "Conversing with Ourselves: Canon, Freedom, Jazz." *American Quarterly* 55 (1): 1–28.

Koopman, Constantijn. 2005. "The Nature of Music and Musical Works." *Praxial Music Education: Reflections and Dialogues.* David J. Elliott, ed. 79–97. Oxford and New York: Oxford University Press.

Langfitt, David. 2007. "YouTube Guitar Lessons Pulled in Copyright Spat." *NPR News,* July 6. npr.org/templates/story/story.php?storyId=11778602 (accessed May 12, 2008).

Lawn, Richard, and Jeffrey Hellmer. 1996. *Jazz: Theory and Practice.* Los Angeles: Alfred Publishing.

Lees, Gene. 1995. *Cats of Any Color: Jazz in Black and White.* Oxford and New York: Oxford University Press.

Maggin, Donald L. 2006. *Dizzy: The Life and Times of John Birks Gillespie.* New York: Harper Collins.

Mandel, Howard. 2009. "On Magazine's Circulation Figures." *Jazz Beyond Jazz,* July 20. artsjournal.com/jazzbeyondjazz/2009/07/on_magazines_circulation_figur.html (accessed July 20, 2009).

Mangan, John Richard. 2005. "Divided Choirs: Musicologists, Music Performers, and the Course of Music Study in American Higher Education." Ph.D. diss., Columbia University.

Mardin, M. Arif. 1959. "The Lenox School of Jazz: Student Views." *Jazz Review* 2 (1): 17, 19.

Margolis, Norman. 1954. "A Theory on the Psychology of Jazz." *American Imago* 2: 263–90.

Martin, Henry. 1996. "Jazz Theory: An Overview." *Annual Review of Jazz Studies* 8: 1–17.

Martin, Henry, and Keith Waters. 2005. *Jazz: The First 100 Years.* 2nd ed. Belmont, CA: Thomson/Schirmer.

Martin, Peter. 2005. "The Jazz Community as an Art World: A Sociological Perspective." *The Source* 2: 5–13.

McCurdy, Ron. 2001. "President's Message." *Jazz Education Journal* 33 (4): 4.

McDaniel, William T., Jr. 1993. "The Status of Jazz Education in the 1990s: An Historical Commentary." *International Jazz Archives Journal* 1: 114–39.

McKay, George. 2005. *Circular Breathing: The Cultural Politics of Jazz in Britain.* Durham, NC: Duke University Press.

McMillan, D. W., and D.M. Chavis. 1986. "Sense of Community: A Definition and Theory." *Journal of Community Psychology* 14 (1): 6–23.

Megill, Donald. and Richard Demory. 1984. *Introduction to Jazz History.* Englewood Cliffs, NJ: Prentice Hall.

Mergner, Lee. 2007. "Current Trends in Jazz Education: A Roundtable Discussion with Noted Collegiate Educators." *Jazz Times,* September 27. jazztimes.com/articles/26564-current-trends-in-jazz-education (accessed January 20, 2011).

Merriam, Alan, and Raymond Mack. 1960. "The Jazz Community." *Social Forces* 38: 211–22.

Miller, Paul Eduard. 1937. "Was Importance of 1st Jazz Soloists Exaggerated by Records?" *Down Beat* 5 (September): 16.

Monson, Ingrid. 1998. "Oh Freedom: George Russell, John Coltrane and Modal Jazz." *In the Course of Performance: Studies in the World of Musical Improvisation.* Bruno Nettl and Melinda Russell, eds. 149–68. Chicago and London: University of Chicago Press.

———. 2007. *Freedom Sounds: Civil Rights Call Out to Jazz and Africa.* Oxford and New York: Oxford University Press.

Moore, Robin. 1992. "The Decline of Improvisation in Western Art Music: An Interpretation of Change." *International Review of the Aesthetics and Sociology of Music* 23 (1): 61–84.

Morgenstern, Dan, Charles Nanry, and David Cayer. 1982. "Editors' Note." *Annual Review of Jazz Studies* 1: 1.

Murphy, Daniel. 1994. "Jazz Studies in American Schools and Colleges: A Brief History." *Jazz Educators Journal* 26: 34–38.

Murphy, Judith. 1968. *Music in American Society: An Interpretive Report of the Tanglewood Symposium.* Washington: Music Educators National Conference.

Murray, Albert. 1976. *Stomping the Blues.* New York: McGraw Hill.

Music Educators' National Conference. 1971. "MENC's Associated Organizations: NAJE." *Music Educators' Journal* 57 (March): 59.

Nanry, Charles, and David Cayer. 1973. "Editors' Note." *Journal of Jazz Studies* 1 (1): 1.

National Endowment for the Arts. n.d. "Transcript of Conversation with David Baker." NEA. nea.gov/av/avCMS/Baker-podcast-transcript.html (accessed January 2, 2011).

Nettl, Bruno. 1995. *Heartland Excursion: Ethnomusicological Reflections on Schools of Music.* Chicago: University of Chicago Press.

Nicholson, Stuart. 2005. *Is Jazz Dead (Or Has It Moved to a New Address)?* New York and London: Taylor and Francis.

Nisenson, Eric. 1997. *Blue: The Murder of Jazz.* New York: Da Capo.

O'Meally, Robert, et al. 2004 "Introductory Notes." *Uptown Conversation: The New Jazz Studies.* R. O'Meally, B. Edwards, and F. Griffin, eds. 1–8. New York: Columbia University Press.

Ong, Walter. 1982. *Orality and Literacy: The Technologizing of the Word.* London and New York: Methuen.

Ortner, Sherry. 1984. "Theory in Anthropology Since the Sixties." *Comparative Studies in Society and History* 26 (January): 126–66.

Ostransky, Leroy. 1960. *The Anatomy of Jazz.* Seattle: University of Washington Press.

Owens, Thomas. 1974. "Charlie Parker: Techniques of Improvisation." Ph.D. diss., University of California, Los Angeles.

Parsonage, Catherine. 2005. *The Evolution of Jazz in Britain.* London: Ashgate.

Peretti, Burton. 1994. *The Creation of Jazz: Music, Race, and Culture in Urban America.* Urbana: University of Illinois Press.

Porter, Eric. 2002. *What Is This Thing Called Jazz?* Berkeley: University of California Press.

Porter, Lewis. 1978. "Book Reviews." *Black Perspective in Music* 6 (2): 233–37.

———. 1988. "Some Problems in Jazz Research." *Black Music Research Journal* 8 (Autumn): 195–206.

Porter, Lewis, and Michael Ullman. 1993. *Jazz from its Origins to the Present*. Englewood Cliffs, NJ: Prentice Hall.

Prestianni, Sam. 2006. "What Wynton Doesn't Hear." *San Francisco Weekly*, September 11. sfweekly.com/1996-09-11/music/what-wynton-doesn-t-hear/ (accessed February 17, 2009).

Primack, Bret. 1998. "The Revolution Is Not Being Televised." *Jazz Times*, December. jazztimes.com/articles/20805-the-revolution-is-not-being-televised (accessed June 1, 2009).

Prouty, Kenneth E. 2002. "From Storyville to State University: The Intersection of Academic and Non-Academic Learning Cultures in Post-Secondary Jazz Education." Ph.D. diss., University of Pittsburgh.

———. 2004. "Canons in Harmony, or Canons in Conflict: A Cultural Perspective on the Curriculum and Pedagogy of Jazz Improvisation." *Research Issues in Music Education* 2 (1): stthomas.edu/rimeonline/vol2/prouty.htm.

———. 2005. "The History of Jazz Education: A Critical Reassessment." *Journal of Historical Research in Music Education* 26 (2): 79–100.

———. 2006. "Orality, Literacy and Mediating Musical Experience: Re-Thinking Oral Tradition in the Learning of Jazz Improvisation." *Popular Music and Society* 29 (3): 317–34.

———. 2008. "The 'Finite' Art of Improvisation: Pedagogy and Power in Jazz Education." *Critical Studies in Improvisation* 4 (1) criticalimprov.com/article/view/346.

———. 2010. "Towards Jazz's 'Official' History: The Debates and Discourses of Jazz History Textbooks." *Journal of Music History Pedagogy* 1 (1): 19–43.

Raeburn, Bruce Boyd. 2009. *New Orleans Style and the Writing of American Jazz History*. Ann Arbor: University of Michigan Press.

Ramsey, Frederic, and Charles Edward Smith. 1939. *Jazzmen*. New York: Harcourt Brace.

Rasula, Jed. 1995. "The Memory of Media: The Seductive Menace of Records in Jazz History." *Jazz Among the Discourses*, ed. Krin Gabbard, 134–62. Durham, NC: Duke University Press.

Ratliff, Ben. 2009. "Another Documentary, Another Riff on the History and Mystery of Jazz." *New York Times*, April 20: E3.

Reece, Doug. 1998. "Jazz Central Station." *Billboard* 4 July: 22.

Ribot, Mark. 2007. "The Care and Feeding of a Musical Margin." *All About Jazz*, June 5. allaboutjazz.com/php/article.php?id=25889 (accessed September 12, 2007).

Russell, George. 1959. *The Lydian Chromatic Concept of Tonal Organization*. New York: Concept.

Sargeant, Winthrop. 1938. *Jazz Hot and Hybrid*. New York: Arrow Editions.

Schiff, Stacy. 2006. "Know It All: Can Wikipedia Conquer Expertise?" *New Yorker*, July 31. newyorker.com/archive/2006/07/31/060731fa_fact (accessed December 10, 2008).

Schuller, Gunther. 1958. "Sonny Rollins and the Challenge of Thematic Improvisation." *Jazz Review* 1 (1): 6–11, 21.

———. 1959. "Review of *Jazz Advance* and *At Newport*." *Jazz Review* 2 (1): 30–31.

———. 1968. *Early Jazz*. Oxford and New York: Oxford University Press.

Schneider, Mark A. 1987. "Culture-as-Text in the Work of Clifford Geertz." *Theory and Society* 16 (6): 809–39.

Scott, Allen. 1973. *Jazz Educated, Man!* Washington: American International.

Sidran, Ben. 1995. *Talking Jazz: An Oral History.* New York: Da Capo.

Small, Christopher. 1977. *Music, Society, Education.* New York: Schirmer.

———. 1987. *Music of the Common Tongue: Survival and Celebration in African American Music.* Hannover and London: University Press of New England.

———. 1998. *Musicking: The Meanings of Performing and Listening.* Middletown, CT: Wesleyan University Press.

Smalley, Roger. 1970. "Some Aspects of the Changing Relationship between Composer and Performer in Contemporary Music." *Proceedings of the Royal Musical Association* 96: 73–5.

Snyder, Randy. 1999. "College Jazz Education During the 1960s: Its Development and Acceptance." D.M.A. diss., University of Houston.

Spellman, A. B. 1966. *Four Lives in the Bebop Business.* New York: Pantheon.

Stearns, Marshall. 1956. *The Story of Jazz.* Oxford and New York: Oxford University Press.

Stebbins, Robert. 1968. "A Theory of the Jazz Community." *Sociological Quarterly* 9 (3): 318–31.

Stringham, Edwin J. 1926. "'Jazz'—An Educational Problem." *Musical Quarterly* 12 (2): 190–95.

Suber, Charles. 1976. "Jazz Education." *The Encyclopedia of Jazz in the Seventies,* Leonard Feather and Ira Gitler, eds. 366–81. New York: Horizon.

Sudhalter, Richard. 2001. *Lost Chords: White Musicians and Their Contributions to Jazz.* Oxford and New York: Oxford University Press.

Szwed, John. 2000. *Jazz 101: A Complete Guide to Listening and Loving Jazz.* New York: Hyperion.

Tanner, Paul. 1971. "Jazz Goes to College." *Music Educator's Journal* 5 (7): 57, 105–9, 111–13.

Tanner, Paul, and Maurice Gerow. 1964. *A Study in Jazz.* Dubuque, IA: W.C. Browne.

Taruskin, Richard. 1982. "The Musicologist and the Performer." *Musicology in the 1980s: Methods, Goals, Opportunities,* D. K. Holoman and C. Palisca, eds. 101–17. New York: Da Capo.

Taylor, Timothy. 2001. *Strange Sounds: Music, Technology and Culture.* London and New York: Routledge.

Teachout, Terry. 1995. "The Color of Jazz." *Commentary* 100 (3): 50–53.

———. 1999a. "Masterpieces of Jazz: A Critical Guide." *Commentary* 108 (4): 46–51.

———. 1999b. "Jazz Masterpieces: Part 2." *Commentary* 108 (5): 59–64.

———. 1999c. "Jazz Masterpieces: A Finale." *Commentary* 109 (1): 55–61.

Tirro, Frank. 1977. *Jazz: A History.* New York: W.W. Norton.

———. 1979. "To the Editor of the *Journal.*" *Journal of the American Musicological Society* 32.3 (3): 594–97.

Townsend, Peter. 2000. *Jazz in American Culture.* Edinburgh: Edinburgh University Press.

Troupe, Quincy. 2000. *Miles and Me.* Berkeley: University of California Press.

Truax, Barry. 2003. "Homoeroticism and Electroacoustic Music: Absence and Personal Voice." *Organised Sound* 8.1: 117–24.

Tucker, Mark. 1998. "Review." *Journal of the American Musicological Society* 51 (1): 131–48.

Tucker, Sherrie. 2000. *Swing Shift: "All-Girl" Bands of the 1940s.* Durham, NC: Duke University Press.

———. 2004. "Bordering on Community: Improvising Women, Improvising Women-in-Jazz." *The Other Side of Nowhere: Jazz, Improvisation, and Communities in Dialogue.* D. Fischlin and A. Heble, eds. 244–67. Middletown, CT: Wesleyan University Press.

Turkenburg, Walter. 2008. "From the Editor: Alone, But Not Lonely at the Top." *IASJ Newsletter*, October. iasj.com/articles-reports/documents/NewslettA4Oct2008website .pdf (accessed June 13, 2009).

Veal, Michael. 2002. "Miles Davis's Unfinished Electric Revolution." *Raritan* 22 (1): 153–63.

Walser, Robert, ed. 1999. *Keeping Time: Readings in Jazz History.* New York and Oxford: Oxford University Press.

Watrous, Peter. 1990. "The Danes Prize American Jazz. Why Don't the Americans?" *New York Times*, June 24: 2/24.

Waxer, Lise. 2002. *The City of Musical Memory: Salsa, Record Grooves, and Popular Culture in Cali, Colombia.* Middletown, CT: Wesleyan University Press.

Waxman, Ken. 2003. "Art Blakey: Jazz Messenger [review]." *Jazzword*, March 24. jazz-word.com/reviews/103339 (accessed February 17, 2009).

Weinstein, Norman. 2008. "Woody Allen Takes Manhattan." *Christian Science Monitor*, February 20: B7.

Wenger, Etienne. n.d. "Communities of Practice." *Ewenger.com.* ewenger.com/theory/ (accessed March 1, 2009).

Wikipedia contributors. n.d. "Essjay controversy." *wikipedia.com.* en.wikipedia.org/wiki/ Essjay_controversy (accessed December 1, 2008).

Wikipedia Foundation. n.d. "Wikipedia: Consensus." *Wikipedia.* en.wikipedia.org/wiki/ Wikipedia:Consensus (accessed July 1, 2009).

Williams, Raymond. 1976. *Keywords: A Vocabulary of Culture and Society.* London: Fontana Communications Series.

Wilson, James Q. 2009. "American Exceptionalism." *The Pursuit of Liberty: Can the Ideas That Made America Great Provide a Model for the World?* James Peirson, ed. 1–16. New York: Encounter.

Winick, Charles. 1959. "The Use of Drugs by Jazz Musicians." *Social Problems* 7: 240–53.

Wink, Joan. 1997. *Critical Pedagogy: Notes from the Real World.* New York: Longman.

Wogan, Peter. 2001. "Imagined Communities Reconsidered: Is Print-Capitalism What We Think It Is?" *Anthropological Theory* 1 (4): 403–18.

Yudkin, Jeremy. 2006. *The Lenox School of Jazz: A Vital Chapter in the History of American Music and Race Relations.* South Egremont, MA: Farshaw.

Index